HOLT McDOUGAL

The Americas

Christopher L. Salter

HISTORY™

HOLT McDOUGAL

 HOUGHTON MIFFLIN HARCOURT

Author

Dr. Christopher L. Salter

Dr. Christopher L. "Kit" Salter is Professor Emeritus of geography and former Chair of the Department of Geography at the University of Missouri. He did his undergraduate work at Oberlin College and received both his M.A. and Ph.D. degrees in geography from the University of California at Berkeley.

Dr. Salter is one of the country's leading figures in geography education. In the 1980s he helped found the national Geographic Alliance network to promote geography education in all 50 states. In the 1990s Dr. Salter was Co-Chair of the National Geography Standards Project, a group of distinguished geographers who created *Geography for Life* in 1994, the document outlining national standards in geography. In 1990 Dr. Salter received the National Geographic Society's first-ever Distinguished Geography Educator Award. In 1992 he received the George Miller Award for distinguished service in geography education from the National Council for Geographic Education. In 2006 Dr. Salter was awarded Lifetime Achievement Honors by the Association of American Geographers for his transformation of geography education.

Over the years, Dr. Salter has written or edited more than 150 articles and books on cultural geography, China, field work, and geography education. His primary interests lie in the study of the human and physical forces that create the cultural landscape, both nationally and globally.

ISBN-13   978-0-547-48482-2

2 3 4 5 6 7 8 9 10   0918   19 18 17 16 15 14 13 12 11

4500335852   ^ B C D E F G

Reviewers

Academic Reviewers

Elizabeth Chako, Ph. D.
Department of Geography
The George Washington
 University

Altha J. Cravey, Ph. D.
Department of Geography
University of North Carolina

Eugene Cruz-Uribe, Ph.D.
Department of History
Northern Arizona University

Toyin Falola, Ph.D.
Department of History
University of Texas

Sandy Freitag, Ph.D.
Director, Monterey Bay History
 and Cultures Project
Division of Social Sciences
University of California,
 Santa Cruz

Oliver Froehling, Ph.D.
Department of Geography
University of Kentucky

Reuel Hanks, Ph.D.
Department of Geography
Oklahoma State University

Phil Klein, Ph.D.
Department of Geography
University of Northern Colorado

B. Ikubolajeh Logan, Ph. D.
Department of Geography
Pennsylvania State University

Marc Van De Mieroop, Ph.D.
Department of History
Columbia University
New York, New York

Christopher Merrett, Ph.D.
Department of History
Western Illinois University

Thomas R. Paradise, Ph.D.
Department of Geosciences
University of Arkansas

Jesse P. H. Poon, Ph.D.
Department of Geography
University at Buffalo–SUNY

Robert Schoch, Ph.D.
CGS Division of Natural Science
Boston University

Derek Shanahan, Ph.D.
Department of Geography
Millersville University
Millersville, Pennsylvania

David Shoenbrun, Ph.D.
Department of History
Northwestern University
Evanston, Illinois

Sean Terry, Ph.D.
Department of Interdisciplinary
 Studies, Geography and
 Environmental Studies
Drury University
Springfield, Missouri

Educational Reviewers

Dennis Neel Durbin
Dyersburg High School
Dyersburg, Tennessee

Carla Freel
Hoover Middle School
Merced, California

Tina Nelson
Deer Park Middle School
Randallstown, Maryland

Don Polston
Lebanon Middle School
Lebanon, Indiana

Robert Valdez
Pioneer Middle School
Tustin, California

Teacher Review Panel

Heather Green
LaVergne Middle School
LaVergne, Tennessee

John Griffin
Wilbur Middle School
Wichita, Kansas

Rosemary Hall
Derby Middle School
Birmingham, Michigan

Rose King
Yeatman-Liddell School
St. Louis, Missouri

Mary Liebl
Wichita Public Schools USD 259
Wichita, Kansas

Jennifer Smith
Lake Wood Middle School
Overland Park, Kansas

Melinda Stephani
Wake County Schools
Raleigh, North Carolina

Contents

The Americas 1

CHAPTER 1 Early History of the Americas, 500 BC–AD 1537 12

References

Available @

↗ hmhsocialstudies.com

- Facts About the World
- Regions of the World Handbook
- Standardized Test-Taking Strategies
- Economics Handbook

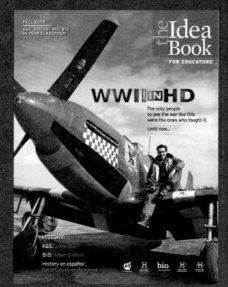

The Idea Book for Educators

Classroom resources that bring the past to life

Live webcasts

HISTORY Take a Veteran to School Day

In addition to premium video-based resources, **HISTORY** has extensive offerings for teachers, parents, and students to use in the classroom and in their in-home educational activities, including:

▶ *The Idea Book for Educators* is a biannual teacher's magazine, featuring guides and info on the latest happenings in history education to help keep teachers on the cutting edge.

▶ **HISTORY Classroom (www.history.com/classroom)** is an interactive website that serves as a portal for history educators nationwide. Streaming videos on topics ranging from the Roman aqueducts to the civil rights movement connect with classroom curricula.

▶ **HISTORY email newsletters** feature updates and supplements to our award-winning programming relevant to the classroom with links to teaching guides and video clips on a variety of topics, special offers, and more.

▶ **Live webcasts** are featured each year as schools tune in via streaming video.

▶ **HISTORY Take a Veteran to School Day** connects veterans with young people in our schools and communities nationwide.

In addition to **HOUGHTON MIFFLIN HARCOURT**, our partners include the *Library of Congress*, the *Smithsonian Institution, National History Day, The Gilder Lehrman Institute of American History,* the *Organization of American Historians*, and many more. HISTORY video is also featured in museums throughout America and in over 70 other historic sites worldwide.

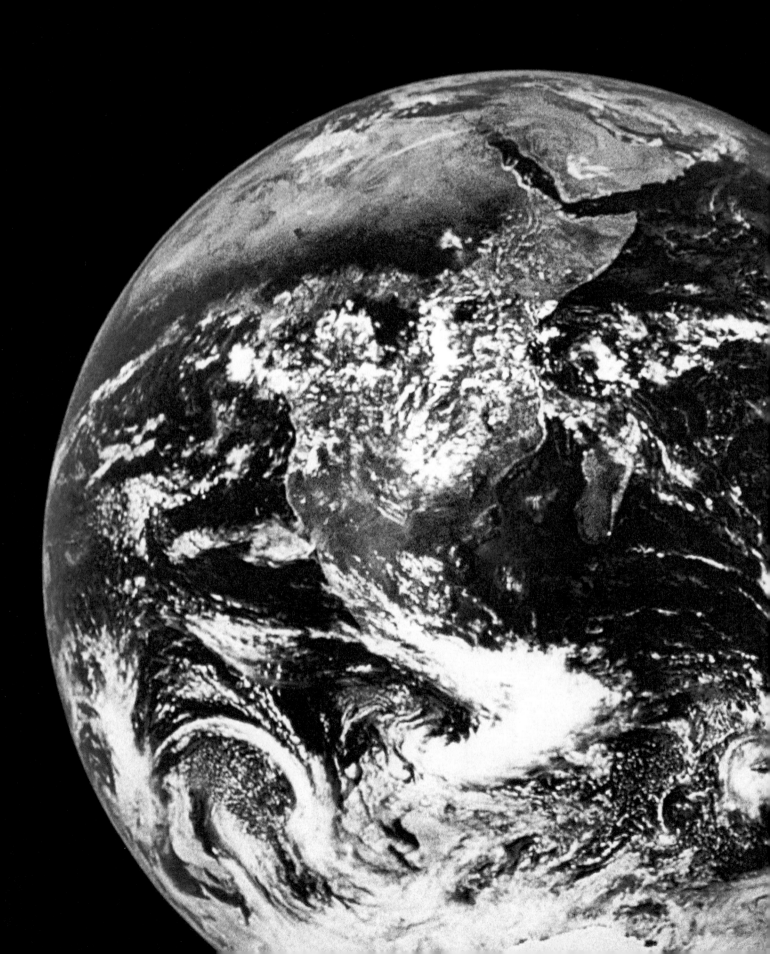

Geography and Map Skills Handbook

Contents

Throughout this textbook, you will be studying the world's people, places, and landscapes. One of the main tools you will use is the map—the primary tool of geographers. To help you begin your studies, this Geography and Map Skills Handbook explains some of the basic features of maps. For example, it explains how maps are made, how to read them, and how they can show the round surface of Earth on a flat piece of paper. This handbook will also introduce you to some of the types of maps you will study later in this book. In addition, you will learn about the different kinds of features on Earth and about how geographers use themes and elements to study the world.

↗ hmhsocialstudies.com INTERACTIVE MAPS

Geography Skills With map zone geography skills, you can go online to find interactive versions of the key maps in this book. Explore these interactive maps to learn and practice important map skills and bring geography to life.

You can access all of the interactive maps in this book through the Interactive Student Edition at

↗ hmhsocialstudies.com

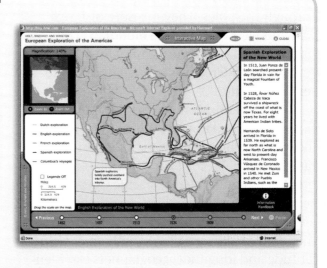

Mapping the Earth
Using Latitude and Longitude

A **globe** is a scale model of the Earth. It is useful for showing the entire Earth or studying large areas of Earth's surface.

To study the world, geographers use a pattern of imaginary lines that circles the globe in east-west and north-south directions. It is called a **grid**. The intersection of these imaginary lines helps us find places on Earth.

The east-west lines in the grid are lines of **latitude**, which you can see on the diagram. Lines of latitude are called **parallels** because they are always parallel to each other. These imaginary lines measure distance north and south of the **equator**. The equator is an imaginary line that circles the globe halfway between the North and South Poles. Parallels measure distance from the equator in **degrees**. The symbol for degrees is °. Degrees are further divided into **minutes**. The symbol for minutes is ´. There are 60 minutes in a degree. Parallels north of the equator are labeled with an N. Those south of the equator are labeled with an S.

The north-south imaginary lines are lines of **longitude**. Lines of longitude are called **meridians**. These imaginary lines pass through the poles. They measure distance east and west of the **prime meridian**. The prime meridian is an imaginary line that runs through Greenwich, England. It represents 0° longitude.

Lines of latitude range from 0°, for locations on the equator, to 90°N or 90°S, for locations at the poles. Lines of longitude range from 0° on the prime meridian to 180° on a meridian in the mid-Pacific Ocean. Meridians west of the prime meridian to 180° are labeled with a W. Those east of the prime meridian to 180° are labeled with an E. Using latitude and longitude, geographers can identify the exact location of any place on Earth.

Lines of Latitude

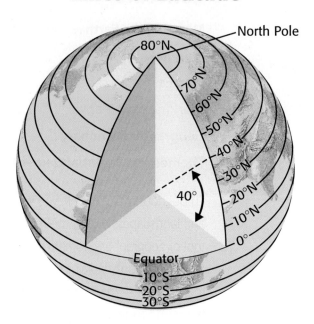

Lines of Longitude

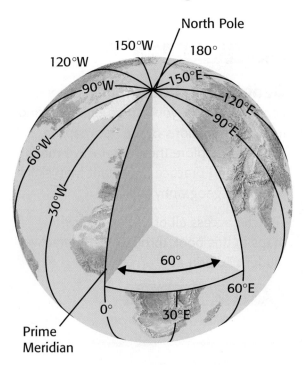

The equator divides the globe into two halves, called **hemispheres**. The half north of the equator is the Northern Hemisphere. The southern half is the Southern Hemisphere. The prime meridian and the 180° meridian divide the world into the Eastern Hemisphere and the Western Hemisphere. Look at the diagrams on this page. They show each of these four hemispheres.

Earth's land surface is divided into seven large landmasses, called **continents**. These continents are also shown on the diagrams on this page. Landmasses smaller than continents and completely surrounded by water are called **islands**.

Geographers organize Earth's water surface into major regions too. The largest is the world ocean. Geographers divide the world ocean into the Pacific Ocean, the Atlantic Ocean, the Indian Ocean, and the Arctic Ocean. Lakes and seas are smaller bodies of water.

Northern Hemisphere

Southern Hemisphere

Western Hemisphere

Eastern Hemisphere

Mapmaking
Understanding Map Projections

A **map** is a flat diagram of all or part of Earth's surface. Mapmakers have created different ways of showing our round planet on flat maps. These different ways are called **map projections**. Because Earth is round, there is no way to show it accurately on a flat map. All flat maps are distorted in some way. Mapmakers must choose the type of map projection that is best for their purposes. Many map projections are one of three kinds: cylindrical, conic, or flat-plane.

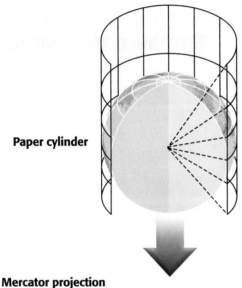

Paper cylinder

Cylindrical Projections

Cylindrical projections are based on a cylinder wrapped around the globe. The cylinder touches the globe only at the equator. The meridians are pulled apart and are parallel to each other instead of meeting at the poles. This causes landmasses near the poles to appear larger than they really are. The map below is a Mercator projection, one type of cylindrical projection. The Mercator projection is useful for navigators because it shows true direction and shape. However, it distorts the size of land areas near the poles.

Mercator projection

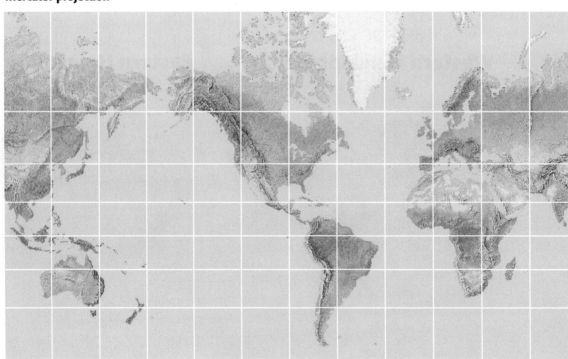

Conic Projections

Conic projections are based on a cone placed over the globe. A conic projection is most accurate along the lines of latitude where it touches the globe. It retains almost true shape and size. Conic projections are most useful for showing areas that have long east-west dimensions, such as the United States.

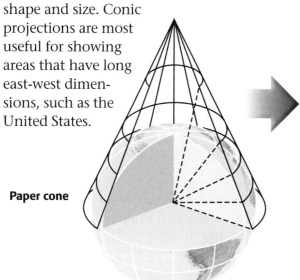

Paper cone

Conic projection

Flat-plane Projections

Flat-plane projections are based on a plane touching the globe at one point, such as at the North Pole or South Pole. A flat-plane projection is useful for showing true direction for airplane pilots and ship navigators. It also shows true area. However, it distorts the true shapes of landmasses.

Flat plane

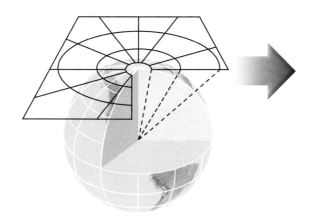

Flat-plane projection

Map Essentials
How to Read a Map

Maps are like messages sent out in code. To help us translate the code, mapmakers provide certain features. These features help us understand the message they are presenting about a particular part of the world. Of these features, almost all maps have a title, a compass rose, a scale, and a legend. The map below has these four features, plus a fifth—a locator map.

❶ Title

A map's **title** shows what the subject of the map is. The map title is usually the first thing you should look at when studying a map, because it tells you what the map is trying to show.

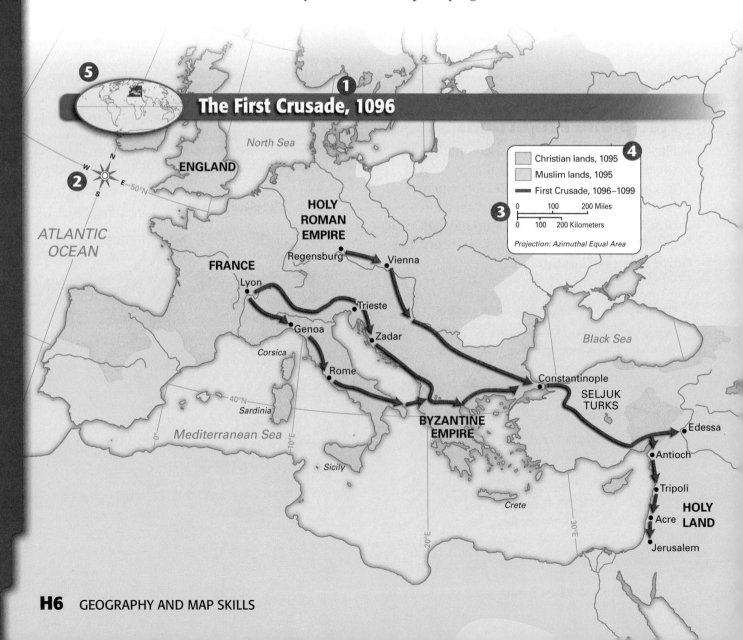

The First Crusade, 1096

Christian lands, 1095
Muslim lands, 1095
First Crusade, 1096–1099

0   100   200 Miles
0   100   200 Kilometers

Projection: Azimuthal Equal Area

North Sea
ENGLAND
ATLANTIC OCEAN
FRANCE
HOLY ROMAN EMPIRE
Regensburg
Vienna
Lyon
Trieste
Genoa
Zadar
Corsica
Rome
Sardinia
Sicily
Crete
Mediterranean Sea
BYZANTINE EMPIRE
Black Sea
Constantinople
SELJUK TURKS
Edessa
Antioch
Tripoli
Acre
HOLY LAND
Jerusalem
40°N
50°N
N
W   E
S

❷ Compass Rose

A directional indicator shows which way north, south, east, and west lie on the map. Some mapmakers use a "north arrow," which points toward the North Pole. Remember, "north" is not always at the top of a map. The way a map is drawn and the location of directions on that map depend on the perspective of the mapmaker. Most maps in this textbook indicate direction by using a compass rose. A **compass rose** has arrows that point to all four principal directions.

❸ Scale

Mapmakers use scales to represent the distances between points on a map. Scales may appear on maps in several different forms. The maps in this textbook provide a **bar scale**. Scales give distances in miles and kilometers.

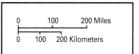

To find the distance between two points on the map, place a piece of paper so that the edge connects the two points. Mark the location of each point on the paper with a line or dot. Then, compare the distance between the two dots with the map's bar scale. The number on the top of the scale gives the distance in miles. The number on the bottom gives the distance in kilometers. Because the distances are given in large intervals, you may have to approximate the actual distance on the scale.

❹ Legend

The **legend**, or key, explains what the symbols on the map represent. Point symbols are used to specify the location of things, such as cities, that do not take up much space on the map. Some legends show colors that represent certain features like empires or other regions. Other maps might have legends with symbols or colors that represent features such as roads. Legends can also show economic resources, land use, population density, and climate.

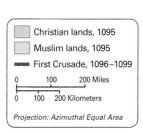

❺ Locator Map

A **locator map** shows where in the world the area on the map is located. The area shown on the main map is shown in red on the locator map. The locator map also shows surrounding areas so the map reader can see how the information on the map relates to neighboring lands.

Working with Maps
Using Different Kinds of Maps

As you study the world's regions and countries, you will use a variety of maps. Political maps and physical maps are two of the most common types of maps you will study. In addition, you will use special-purpose maps. These maps might show climate, population, resources, ancient empires, or other topics.

Political Maps

Political maps show the major political features of a region. These features include country borders, capital cities, and other places. Political maps use different colors to represent countries, and capital cities are often shown with a special star symbol.

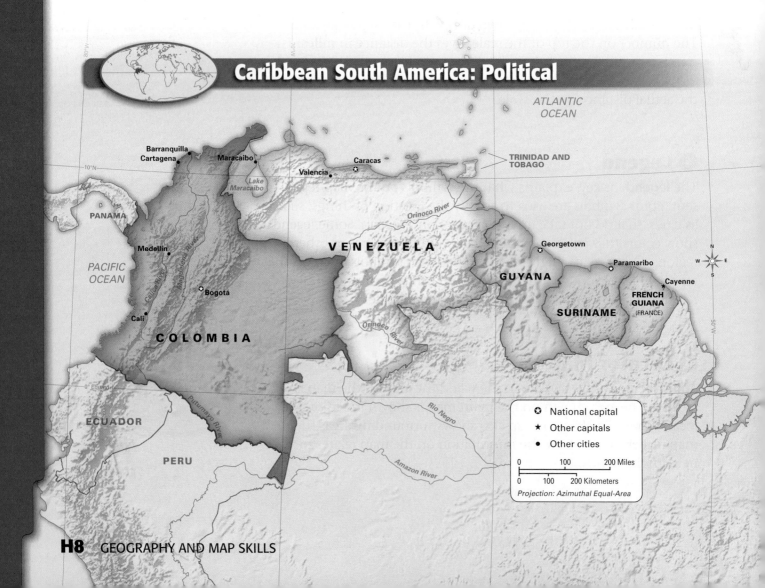

Caribbean South America: Political

ATLANTIC OCEAN

Barranquilla
Cartagena
Maracaibo
Caracas
Valencia
Lake Maracaibo
TRINIDAD AND TOBAGO

Orinoco River

PANAMA

VENEZUELA

Georgetown

Medellín

Paramaribo

PACIFIC OCEAN

GUYANA

Cayenne

Bogotá

FRENCH GUIANA (FRANCE)

Cali

SURINAME

COLOMBIA

Orinoco River

Rio Negro

0° Equator

ECUADOR

Putumayo River

PERU

Amazon River

- ✪ National capital
- ★ Other capitals
- ● Other cities

0   100   200 Miles
0   100   200 Kilometers
Projection: Azimuthal Equal-Area

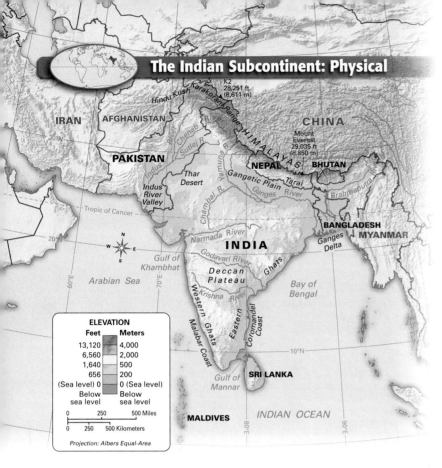

The Indian Subcontinent: Physical

Physical Maps

Physical maps show the major physical features of a region. These features may include mountain ranges, rivers, oceans, islands, deserts, and plains. Often, these maps use different colors to represent different elevations of land. As a result, the map reader can easily see which areas are high elevations, like mountains, and which areas are lower.

Special-Purpose Maps

Special-purpose maps focus on one special topic, such as climate, resources, or population. These maps present information on the topic that is particularly important in the region. Depending on the type of special-purpose map, the information may be shown with different colors, arrows, dots, or other symbols.

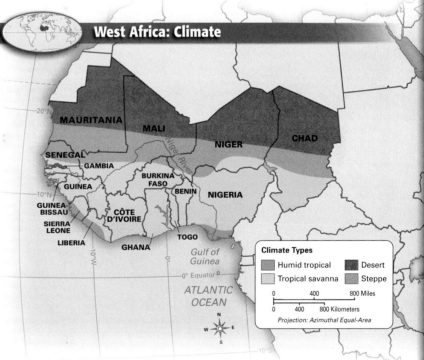

West Africa: Climate

Using Maps in Geography The different kinds of maps in this textbook will help you study and understand geography. By working with these maps, you will see what the physical geography of places is like, where people live, and how the world has changed over time.

Geographic Dictionary

OCEAN
a large body of water

CORAL REEF
an ocean ridge made up of
skeletal remains of tiny sea animals

GULF
a large part of
the ocean that
extends into land

PENINSULA
an area of land that sticks
out into a lake or ocean

ISTHMUS
a narrow piece of land
connecting two larger
land areas

BAY
part of a large
body of water
that is smaller
than a gulf

ISLAND
an area of land
surrounded entirely
by water

DELTA
an area where a
river deposits soil
into the ocean

STRAIT
a narrow body of
water connecting two
larger bodies of water

SINKHOLE
a circular depression
formed when the roof
of a cave collapses

WETLAND
an area of land
covered by
shallow water

RIVER
a natural flow of
water that runs
through the land

LAKE
an inland body
of water

FOREST
an area of densely
wooded land

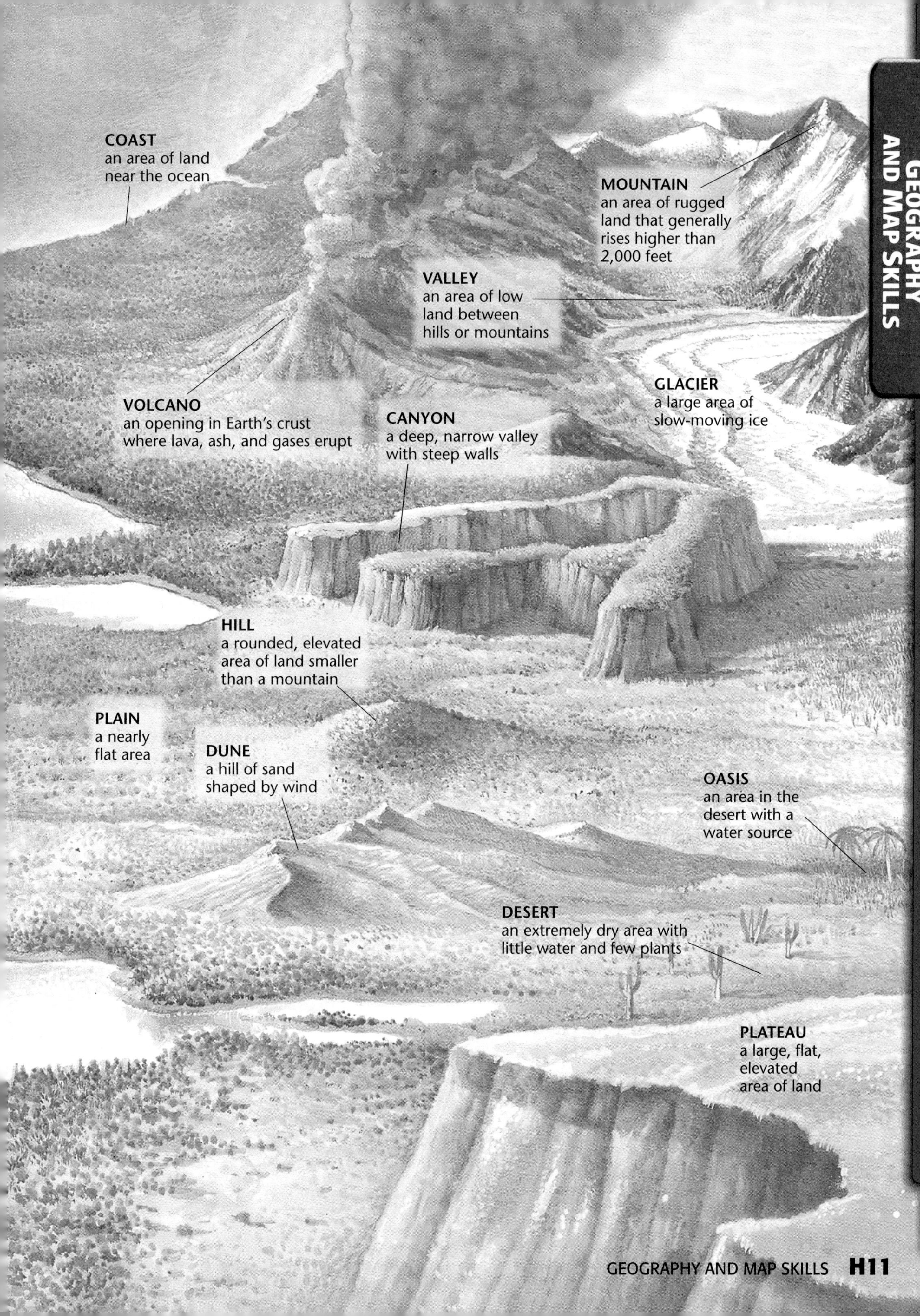

COAST
an area of land
near the ocean

MOUNTAIN
an area of rugged
land that generally
rises higher than
2,000 feet

VALLEY
an area of low
land between
hills or mountains

GLACIER
a large area of
slow-moving ice

VOLCANO
an opening in Earth's crust
where lava, ash, and gases erupt

CANYON
a deep, narrow valley
with steep walls

HILL
a rounded, elevated
area of land smaller
than a mountain

PLAIN
a nearly
flat area

DUNE
a hill of sand
shaped by wind

OASIS
an area in the
desert with a
water source

DESERT
an extremely dry area with
little water and few plants

PLATEAU
a large, flat,
elevated
area of land

GEOGRAPHY
AND MAP SKILLS

Themes and Essential Elements of Geography

by Dr. Christopher L. Salter

To study the world, geographers have identified 5 key themes, 6 essential elements, and 18 geography standards.

"How should we teach and learn about geography?" Professional geographers have worked hard over the years to answer this important question.

In 1984 a group of geographers identified the 5 Themes of Geography. These themes did a wonderful job of laying the groundwork for good classroom geography. Teachers used the 5 Themes in class, and geographers taught workshops on how to apply them in the world.

By the early 1990s, however, some geographers felt the 5 Themes were too broad. They created the 18 Geography Standards and the 6 Essential Elements. The 18 Geography Standards include more detailed information about what geography is, and the 6 Essential Elements are like a bridge between the 5 Themes and 18 Standards.

Look at the chart to the right. It shows how each of the 5 Themes connects to the Essential Elements and Standards. For example, the theme of Location is related to The World in Spatial Terms and the first three Standards. Study the chart carefully to see how the other themes, elements, and Standards are related.

The last Essential Element and the last two Standards cover The Uses of Geography. These key parts of geography were not covered by the 5 Themes. They will help you see how geography has influenced the past, present, and future.

5 Themes of Geography

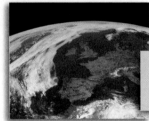
Location The theme of location describes where something is.

Place Place describes the features that make a site unique.

Regions Regions are areas that share common characteristics.

Movement This theme looks at how and why people and things move.

Human-Environment Interaction People interact with their environment in many ways.

6 Essential Elements

18 Geography Standards

I. **The World in Spatial Terms**

1. How to use maps and other tools
2. How to use mental maps to organize information
3. How to analyze the spatial organization of people, places, and environments

II. **Places and Regions**

4. The physical and human characteristics of places
5. How people create regions to interpret Earth
6. How culture and experience influence people's perceptions of places and regions

III. **Physical Systems**

7. The physical processes that shape Earth's surface
8. The distribution of ecosystems on Earth

IV. **Human Systems**

9. The characteristics, distribution, and migration of human populations
10. The complexity of Earth's cultural mosaics
11. The patterns and networks of economic interdependence on Earth
12. The patterns of human settlement
13. The forces of cooperation and conflict

V. **Environment and Society**

14. How human actions modify the physical environment
15. How physical systems affect human systems
16. The distribution and meaning of resources

VI. **The Uses of Geography**

17. How to apply geography to interpret the past
18. How to apply geography to interpret the present and plan for the future

Become an Active Reader

Did you ever think you would begin reading your social studies book by reading about *reading*? Actually, it makes better sense than you might think. You would probably make sure you knew some soccer skills and strategies before playing in a game. Similarly, you need to know something about reading skills and strategies before reading your social studies book. In other words, you need to make sure you know whatever you need to know in order to read this book successfully.

Tip #1

Read Everything on the Page!

You can't follow the directions on the cake-mix box if you don't know where the directions are! Cake-mix boxes always have directions on them telling you how many eggs to add or how long to bake the cake. But, if you can't find that information, it doesn't matter that it is there.

Likewise, this book is filled with information that will help you understand what you are reading. If you don't study that information, however, it might as well not be there. Let's take a look at some of the places where you'll find important information in this book.

The Chapter Opener
The chapter opener gives you a brief overview of what you will learn in the chapter. You can use this information to prepare to read the chapter.

The Section Openers
Before you begin to read each section, preview the information under What You Will Learn. There you'll find the main ideas of the section and key terms that are important in it. Knowing what you are looking for before you start reading can improve your understanding.

Boldfaced Words
Those words are important and are defined somewhere on the page where they appear—either right there in the sentence or over in the side margin.

Maps, Charts, and Artwork
These things are not there just to take up space or look good! Study them and read the information beside them. It will help you understand the information in the chapter.

Questions at the End of Sections
At the end of each section, you will find questions that will help you decide whether you need to go back and re-read any parts before moving on. If you can't answer a question, that is your cue to go back and re-read.

Questions at the End of the Chapter
Answer the questions at the end of each chapter, even if your teacher doesn't ask you to. These questions are there to help you figure out what you need to review.

Tip #2

Use the Reading Skills and Strategies in Your Textbook

Good readers use a number of skills and strategies to make sure they understand what they are reading. In this textbook you will find help with important reading skills and strategies such as "Predicting," "Making Inferences," and "Using Context Clues."

We teach the reading skills and strategies in several ways. Use these activities and lessons and you will become a better reader.

- First, on the opening page of every chapter we identify and explain the reading skill or strategy you will focus on as you work through the chapter. In fact, these activities are called "Focus on Reading."

- Second, as you can see in the example at right, we tell you where to go for more help. The back of the book has a reading handbook with a full-page practice lesson to match the reading skill or strategy in every chapter.

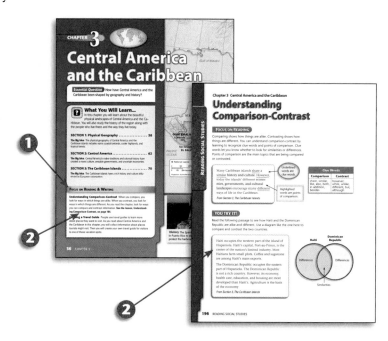

- Third, we give you short practice activities and examples as you read the chapter. These activities and examples show up in the margin of your book. Again, look for the words, "Focus on Reading."

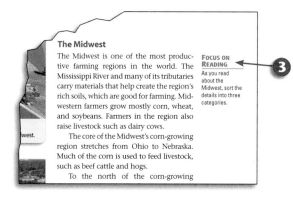

FOCUS ON READING AND WRITING

12. Using Context Clues Look through the chapter and pick out two difficult words that you had to figure out by using context clues. Then, note the context clues you used to help you figure out the definitions of the difficult words.

13. Creating a Web Site You can create a real Web site or a paper version of a Web site. First, look back through your notes and choose key ideas about each country to include. In designing your site, first include a home page that briefly describes the region. Indicate links for pages about each of the countries in the region. Each of your country pages should include one short paragraph and one image. Remember to keep the pages simple—too much text might overwhelm your readers and send them off to another site!

- Finally, we provide another practice activity in the Chapter Review at the end of every chapter. That activity gives you one more chance to make sure you know how to use the reading skill or strategy.

Tip #3

Pay Attention to Vocabulary

It is no fun to read something when you don't know what the words mean, but you can't learn new words if you only use or read the words you already know. In this book, we know we have probably used some words you don't know. But, we have followed a pattern as we have used more difficult words.

- First, at the beginning of each section you will find a list of key terms that you will need to know. Be on the lookout for those words as you read through the section. You will find that we have defined those words right there in the paragraph where they are used. Look for a word that is in boldface with its definition highlighted in yellow.

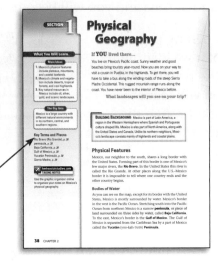

- Second, when we use a word that is important in all classes, not just social studies, we define it in the margin under the heading Academic Vocabulary. You will run into these academic words in other textbooks, so you should learn what they mean while reading this book.

Tip #4

Read Like a Skilled Reader

You won't be able to climb to the top of Mount Everest if you do not train! If you want to make it to the top of Mount Everest then you must start training to climb that huge mountain.

Training is also necessary to become a good reader. You will never get better at reading your social studies book—or any book for that matter—unless you spend some time thinking about how to be a better reader.

Skilled readers do the following:

1. They preview what they are supposed to read before they actually begin reading. When previewing, they look for vocabulary words, titles of sections, information in the margin, or maps or charts they should study.

2. They get ready to take some notes while reading by dividing their notebook paper into two parts. They title one side "Notes from the Chapter" and the other side "Questions or Comments I Have."

3. As they read, they complete their notes.

4. They read like **active readers**. The Active Reading list below shows you what that means.

5. Finally, they use clues in the text to help them figure out where the text is going. The best clues are called signal words. These are words that help you identify chronological order, causes and effects, or comparisons and contrasts.

Chronological Order Signal Words: *first, second, third, before, after, later, next, following that, earlier, subsequently, finally*

Cause and Effect Signal Words: *because of, due to, as a result of, the reason for, therefore, consequently, so, basis for*

Comparison/Contrast Signal Words: *likewise, also, as well as, similarly, on the other hand*

Active Reading

There are three ways to read a book: You can be a turn-the-pages-no-matter-what type of reader. These readers just keep on turning pages whether or not they understand what they are reading. Or, you can be a stop-watch-and-listen kind of reader. These readers know that if they wait long enough, someone will tell them what they need to know. Or, you can be an active reader. These readers know that it is up to them to figure out what the text means. Active readers do the following as they read:

Predict what will happen next based on what has already happened. When your predictions don't match what happens in the text, re-read the confusing parts.

Question what is happening as you read. Constantly ask yourself why things have happened, what things mean, and what caused certain events. Jot down notes about the questions you can't answer.

Summarize what you are reading frequently. Do not try to summarize the entire chapter! Read a bit and then summarize it. Then read on.

Connect what is happening in the section you're reading to what you have already read.

Clarify your understanding. Be sure that you understand what you are reading by stopping occasionally to ask yourself whether you are confused by anything. Sometimes you might need to re-read to clarify. Other times you might need to read further and collect more information before you can understand. Still other times you might need to ask the teacher to help you with what is confusing you.

Visualize what is happening in the text. In other words, try to see the events or places in your mind. It might help you to draw maps, make charts, or jot down notes about what you are reading as you try to visualize the action in the text.

Social Studies Words

As you read this textbook, you will be more successful if you learn the meanings of the words on this page. You will come across these words many times in your social studies classes, like geography and history. Read through these words now to become familiar with them before you begin your studies.

Social Studies Words

WORDS ABOUT TIME

AD	refers to dates after the birth of Jesus
BC	refers to dates before Jesus's birth
BCE	refers to dates before Jesus's birth, stands for "before the common era"
CE	refers to dates after Jesus's birth, stands for "common era"
century	a period of 100 years
decade	a period of 10 years
era	a period of time
millennium	a period of 1,000 years

WORDS ABOUT THE WORLD

climate	the weather conditions in a certain area over a long period of time
geography	the study of the world's people, places, and landscapes
physical features	features on Earth's surface, such as mountains and rivers
region	an area with one or more features that make it different from surrounding areas
resources	materials found on Earth that people need and value

WORDS ABOUT PEOPLE

anthropology	the study of people and cultures
archaeology	the study of the past based on what people left behind
citizen	a person who lives under the control of a government
civilization	the way of life of people in a particular place or time
culture	the knowledge, beliefs, customs, and values of a group of people
custom	a repeated practice or tradition
economics	the study of the production and use of goods and services
economy	any system in which people make and exchange goods and services
government	the body of officials and groups that run an area
history	the study of the past
politics	the process of running a government
religion	a system of beliefs in one or more gods or spirits
society	a group of people who share common traditions
trade	the exchange of goods or services

Academic Words

What are academic words? They are important words used in all of your classes, not just social studies. You will see these words in other textbooks, so you should learn what they mean while reading this book. Review this list now. You will use these words again in the chapters of this book.

Academic Words

affect	to change or influence		**policy**	rule, course of action
aspects	parts		**process**	a series of steps by which a task is accomplished
cause	to make something happen		**rebel**	to fight against authority
development	the process of growing or improving		**traditional**	customary, time-honored
distinct	separate		**vary**	to be different
establish	to set up or create			
influence	change or have an effect on			

Academic Words features provide definitions for important terms that will help you understand social studies content.

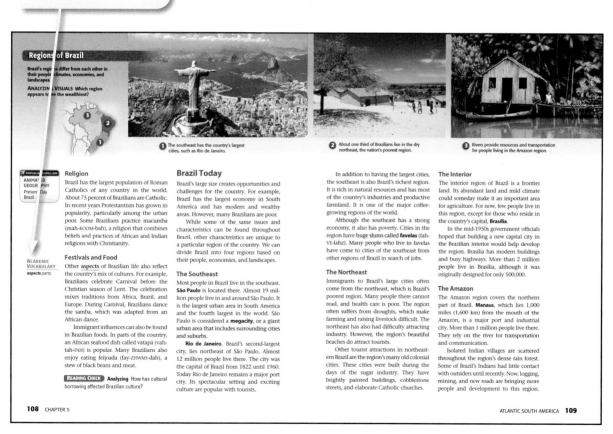

Regions of Brazil

Brazil's regions differ from each other in their people, climates, economies, and landscapes.

ANALYZING VISUALS Which region appears to be the wealthiest?

1 The southeast has the country's largest cities, such as Rio de Janeiro.

2 About one third of Brazilians live in the dry northeast, the nation's poorest region.

3 Rivers provide resources and transportation for people living in the Amazon region.

Religion

hmhsocialstudies.com
ANIMATED GEOGRAPHY
Present-Day Brazil

Brazil has the largest population of Roman Catholics of any country in the world. About 75 percent of Brazilians are Catholic. In recent years Protestantism has grown in popularity, particularly among the urban poor. Some Brazilians practice macumba (mah-KOOM-bah), a religion that combines beliefs and practices of African and Indian religions with Christianity.

Festivals and Food

ACADEMIC VOCABULARY
aspects parts

Other **aspects** of Brazilian life also reflect the country's mix of cultures. For example, Brazilians celebrate Carnival before the Christian season of Lent. The celebration mixes traditions from Africa, Brazil, and Europe. During Carnival, Brazilians dance the samba, which was adapted from an African dance.

Immigrant influences can also be found in Brazilian foods. In parts of the country, an African seafood dish called vatapá (vah-tah-PAH) is popular. Many Brazilians also enjoy eating feijoada (fay-ZHWAH-dah), a stew of black beans and meat.

READING CHECK **Analyzing** How has cultural borrowing affected Brazilian culture?

Brazil Today

Brazil's large size creates opportunities and challenges for the country. For example, Brazil has the largest economy in South America and has modern and wealthy areas. However, many Brazilians are poor.

While some of the same issues and characteristics can be found throughout Brazil, other characteristics are unique to a particular region of the country. We can divide Brazil into four regions based on their people, economies, and landscapes.

The Southeast

Most people in Brazil live in the southeast. **São Paulo** is located there. Almost 19 million people live in and around São Paulo. It is the largest urban area in South America and the fourth largest in the world. São Paulo is considered a **megacity**, or a giant urban area that includes surrounding cities and suburbs.

Rio de Janeiro, Brazil's second-largest city, lies northeast of São Paulo. Almost 12 million people live there. The city was the capital of Brazil from 1822 until 1960. Today Rio de Janeiro remains a major port city. Its spectacular setting and exciting culture are popular with tourists.

In addition to having the largest cities, the southeast is also Brazil's richest region. It is rich in natural resources and has most of the country's industries and productive farmland. It is one of the major coffee-growing regions of the world.

Although the southeast has a strong economy, it also has poverty. Cities in the region have huge slums called **favelas** (fah-VE-lahz). Many people who live in favelas have come to cities of the southeast from other regions of Brazil in search of jobs.

The Northeast

Immigrants to Brazil's large cities often come from the northeast, which is Brazil's poorest region. Many people there cannot read, and health care is poor. The region often suffers from droughts, which make farming and raising livestock difficult. The northeast has also had difficulty attracting industry. However, the region's beautiful beaches do attract tourists.

Other tourist attractions in northeastern Brazil are the region's many old colonial cities. These cities were built during the days of the sugar industry. They have brightly painted buildings, cobblestone streets, and elaborate Catholic churches.

The Interior

The interior region of Brazil is a frontier land. Its abundant land and mild climate could someday make it an important area for agriculture. For now, few people live in this region, except for those who reside in the country's capital, **Brasília**.

In the mid-1950s government officials hoped that building a new capital city in the Brazilian interior would help develop the region. Brasília has modern buildings and busy highways. More than 2 million people live in Brasília, although it was originally designed for only 500,000.

The Amazon

The Amazon region covers the northern part of Brazil. **Manaus**, which lies 1,000 miles (1,600 km) from the mouth of the Amazon, is a major port and industrial city. More than 1 million people live there. They rely on the river for transportation and communication.

Isolated Indian villages are scattered throughout the region's dense rain forest. Some of Brazil's Indians had little contact with outsiders until recently. Now, logging, mining, and new roads are bringing more people and development to this region.

Making This Book Work for You

Studying geography will be easy for you with this textbook. Take a few minutes now to become familiar with the easy-to-use structure and special features of your book. See how it will make geography come alive for you!

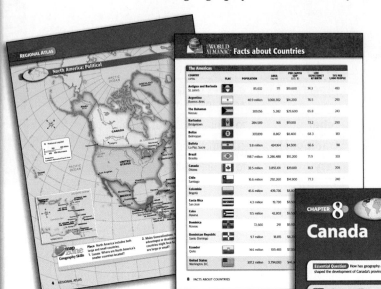

Your book begins with a satellite image, a regional atlas, and a table with facts about each country. Use these pages to get an overview of the region you will study.

Chapter

Each chapter includes an introduction, a Social Studies Skills activity, Chapter Review pages, and a Standardized Test Practice page.

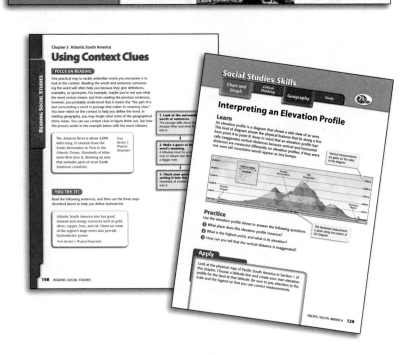

Reading Social Studies Chapter reading lessons give you skills and practice to help you read the textbook. More help with each lesson can be found in the back of the book. Margin notes and questions in the chapter make sure you understand the reading skill.

Social Studies Skills The Social Studies Skills lessons give you an opportunity to learn, practice, and apply an important skill. Chapter Review questions then follow up on what you learned.

Section

The section opener pages include Main Ideas, an overarching Big Idea, and Key Terms and Places. In addition, each section includes these special features.

If YOU Lived There . . . Each section begins with a situation for you to respond to, placing you in a place that relates to the content you will be studying in the section.

Building Background Building Background connects what will be covered in each section with what you already know.

Short Sections of Content The information in each section is organized into small chunks of text that you can easily understand.

Taking Notes Suggested graphic organizers help you read and take notes on the important ideas in the section.

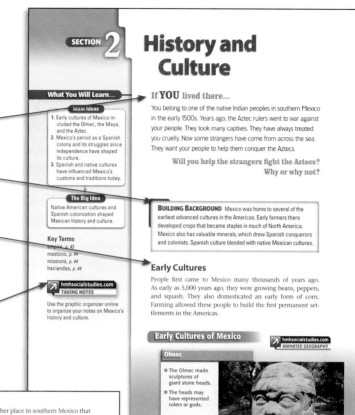

SECTION 2

History and Culture

What You Will Learn...

Main Ideas

1. Early cultures of Mexico included the Olmec, the Maya, and the Aztec.
2. Mexico's period as a Spanish colony and its struggles since independence have shaped its culture.
3. Spanish and native cultures have influenced Mexico's customs and traditions today.

The Big Idea

Native American cultures and Spanish colonization shaped Mexican history and culture.

Key Terms

empire, p. 43
mestizos, p. 44
missions, p. 44
haciendas, p. 44

hmhsocialstudies.com
TAKING NOTES

Use the graphic organizer online to organize your notes on Mexico's history and culture.

If YOU lived there...

You belong to one of the native Indian peoples in southern Mexico in the early 1500s. Years ago, the Aztec rulers went to war against your people. They took many captives. They have always treated you cruelly. Now some strangers have come from across the sea. They want your people to help them conquer the Aztecs.

Will you help the strangers fight the Aztecs? Why or why not?

BUILDING BACKGROUND Mexico was home to several of the earliest advanced cultures in the Americas. Early farmers there developed crops that became staples in much of North America. Mexico also has valuable minerals, which drew Spanish conquerors and colonists. Spanish culture blended with native Mexican cultures.

Early Cultures

People first came to Mexico many thousands of years ago. As early as 5,000 years ago, they were growing beans, peppers, and squash. They also domesticated an early form of corn. Farming allowed these people to build the first permanent settlements in the Americas.

Early Cultures of Mexico

hmhsocialstudies.com
ANIMATED GEOGRAPHY

Olmec

- The Olmec made sculptures of giant stone heads.
- The heads may have represented rulers or gods.

ACADEMIC VOCABULARY
affect to change or influence

Northern Mexico's closeness to the border has **affected** the region's culture as well as its economy. American television, music, and other forms of entertainment are popular there. Many Mexicans cross the border to shop, work, or live in the United States. While many people cross the border legally, the U.S. government tries to prevent Mexicans and others from crossing the border illegally.

Southern Mexico

Southern Mexico is the least populated and industrialized region of the country. Many people in this region speak Indian languages and practice traditional ways of life. Subsistence farming and slash-and-burn agriculture are common.

FOCUS ON READING
What do you think makes southern Mexico vital to the country's economy?

However, southern Mexico is vital to the country's economy. Sugarcane and coffee, two major export crops, grow well in the region's warm, humid climate. Also, oil production along the Gulf coast has increased in recent years. The oil business has brought more industry and population growth to this coastal area of southern Mexico.

Another place in southern Mexico that has grown in recent years is the Yucatán Peninsula. Maya ruins, beautiful sunny beaches, and clear blue water have made tourism a major industry in this area. Many cities that were just tiny fishing villages only 20 years ago are now booming with new construction for the tourist industry.

Mexico will continue to change in the future. Changes are likely to bring more development. However, maintaining the country's unique regional cultures may be a challenge as those changes take place.

READING CHECK Comparing and Contrasting
What similarities and differences exist between greater Mexico City and southern Mexico?

SUMMARY AND PREVIEW Mexico has a democratic government and a growing economy. It also has distinct regions with different cultures, economies, and environments. In the next chapter you will learn about the countries to the south of Mexico.

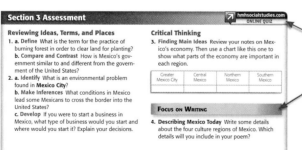

Section 3 Assessment

hmhsocialstudies.com
ONLINE QUIZ

Reviewing Ideas, Terms, and Places

1. **a. Define** What is the term for the practice of burning forest in order to clear land for planting?
   b. Compare and Contrast How is Mexico's government similar to and different from the government of the United States?
2. **a. Identify** What is an environmental problem found in **Mexico City**?
   b. Make Inferences What conditions in Mexico lead some Mexicans to cross the border into the United States?
   c. Develop If you were to start a business in Mexico, what type of business would you start and where would you start it? Explain your decisions.

Critical Thinking

3. **Finding Main Ideas** Review your notes on Mexico's economy. Then use a chart like this one to show what parts of the economy are important in each region.

Greater Mexico City	Central Mexico	Northern Mexico	Southern Mexico

FOCUS ON WRITING

4. **Describing Mexico Today** Write some details about the four culture regions of Mexico. Which details will you include in your poem?

Reading Check Questions end each section of content so you can check to make sure you understand what you just studied.

Summary and Preview The Summary and Preview connects what you studied in the section to what you will study in the next section.

Section Assessment Finally, the section assessment boxes make sure that you understand the main ideas of the section. We also provide assessment practice online!

Scavenger Hunt

Are you ready to explore the world of geography? *Holt McDougal: The Americas* is your ticket to this exciting world. Before you begin your journey, complete this scavenger hunt to get to know your book and discover what's inside.

   On a separate sheet of paper, fill in the blanks to complete each sentence below. In each answer, one letter will be in a yellow box. When you have answered every question, copy these letters in order to reveal the answer to the question at the bottom of the page.

1 According to the Table of Contents, the title of Chapter 4 is ☐☐☐☐☐☐☐☐ South America. What else can you find in the Table of Contents?

2 Section 1 of Chapter 7 is called ☐☐☐☐☐☐☐ Geography. What are the other sections of this chapter?

3 The Connecting to Technology feature on page 43 is called ☐☐☐☐☐☐☐☐☐.

4 The first Key Term on page 130 is ☐☐☐☐☐☐☐.

5 In the English and Spanish Glossary, the third word in the definition of megacity is ☐☐☐☐☐.

6 The title of the Geography and History feature in Chapter 3 is The ☐☐☐☐☐☐ ☐☐☐☐☐.

7 The Close-up feature on pages 184–185 is called Quebec's ☐☐☐☐☐☐ Carnival. What other Close-up features can you find in the book?

8 The Social Studies Skills lesson on page 32 is called ☐☐☐☐☐☐☐☐☐ Information.

Fact!

Venezuela is home to the largest rodent in the world. What is this animal called? ☐☐☐☐☐☐☐☐☐

The Americas

The Great Lakes

Five huge lakes in North America known as the Great Lakes make up the largest group of fresh water lakes on Earth.

The Andes

Stretching along South America's western coast, the Andes are the longest mountain range in the world.

The Americas

The Amazon

In the heart of South America, the Amazon rain forest is home to millions of plant and animal species.

Explore the Satellite Image
Forests, mountains, and plains stretch from north to south across the Americas. How do you think the features you can see on this satellite image influence life in the Americas?

The Satellite's Path

>44'56.08<

>>>>>>>>>665.00'87<

567.476.348   +799   +803   +996   +355

456.094.

The Americas: Physical

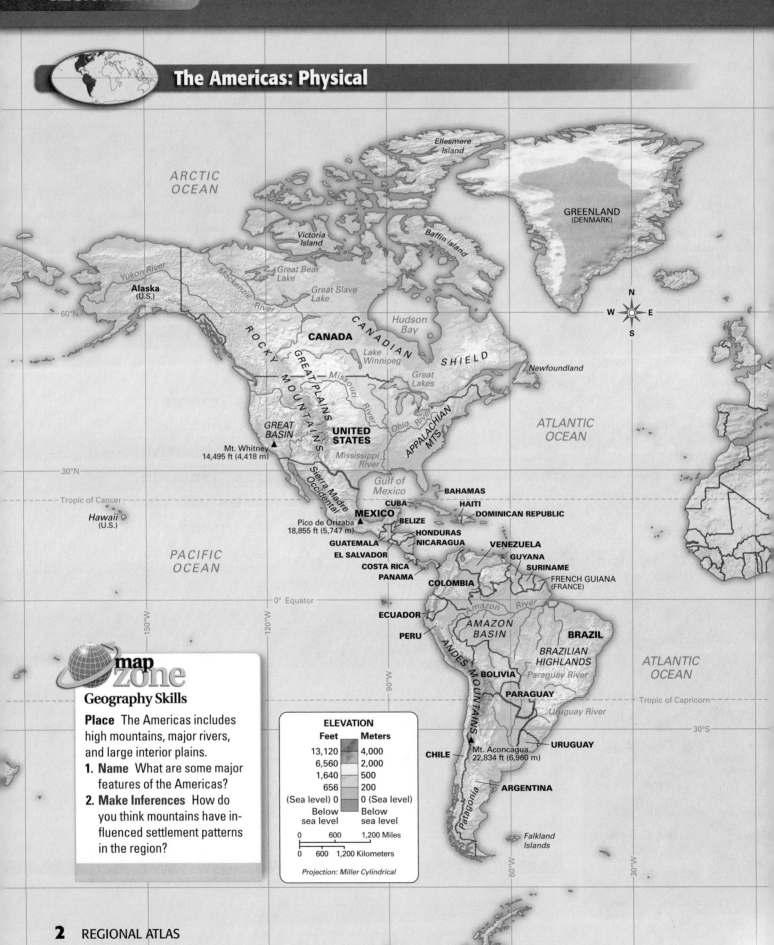

ARCTIC OCEAN

Ellesmere Island

GREENLAND (DENMARK)

Victoria Island

Baffin Island

Yukon River

Great Bear Lake

Alaska (U.S.)

Mackenzie River

Great Slave Lake

Hudson Bay

CANADIAN

60°N

CANADA

R O C K Y   M O U N T A I N S

G R E A T   P L A I N S

Lake Winnipeg

Missouri

S H I E L D

Newfoundland

Great Lakes

Ohio River

ATLANTIC OCEAN

GREAT BASIN

UNITED STATES

APPALACHIAN MTS.

Mt. Whitney 14,495 ft (4,418 m)

Mississippi River

30°N

Sierra Madre Occidental

Gulf of Mexico

Tropic of Cancer

BAHAMAS

Hawaii (U.S.)

CUBA

HAITI

MEXICO

DOMINICAN REPUBLIC

Pico de Orizaba 18,855 ft (5,747 m)

BELIZE

HONDURAS

GUATEMALA

NICARAGUA

VENEZUELA

PACIFIC OCEAN

EL SALVADOR

GUYANA

COSTA RICA

SURINAME

PANAMA

FRENCH GUIANA (FRANCE)

COLOMBIA

0° Equator

Amazon River

ECUADOR

AMAZON BASIN

PERU

BRAZIL

A N D E S   M O U N T A I N S

BRAZILIAN HIGHLANDS

ATLANTIC OCEAN

BOLIVIA

Paraguay River

PARAGUAY

Tropic of Capricorn

Uruguay River

30°S

Mt. Aconcagua 22,834 ft (6,960 m)

CHILE

URUGUAY

ARGENTINA

Patagonia

Falkland Islands

150°W

120°W

90°W

60°W

30°W

map zone

Geography Skills

Place The Americas includes high mountains, major rivers, and large interior plains.

1. **Name** What are some major features of the Americas?

2. **Make Inferences** How do you think mountains have influenced settlement patterns in the region?

ELEVATION

Feet		Meters
13,120		4,000
6,560		2,000
1,640		500
656		200
(Sea level) 0		0 (Sea level)
Below sea level		Below sea level

0   600   1,200 Miles

0   600   1,200 Kilometers

Projection: Miller Cylindrical

The Americas

Geographical Extremes: The Americas

THE WORLD ALMANAC® — Facts about the World

Longest River	Amazon River, Brazil/Peru: 4,000 miles (6,435 km)
Highest Point	Mt. Aconcagua, Argentina: 22,834 feet (6,960 m)
Lowest Point	Death Valley, United States: 282 feet (86 m) below sea level
Highest Recorded Temperature	Death Valley, United States: 134°F (56.6°C)
Lowest Recorded Temperature	Snag, Canada: −81.4°F (−63°C)
Wettest Place	Lloro, Colombia: 523.6 inches (1,329.9 cm) average precipitation per year
Driest Place	Arica, Chile: .03 inches (.08 cm) average precipitation per year
Highest Waterfall	Angel Falls, Venezuela: 3,212 feet (979 m)
Most Tornadoes	United States: More than 1,000 per year

Death Valley, United States

hmhsocialstudies.com

Size Comparison: The United States and the Americas

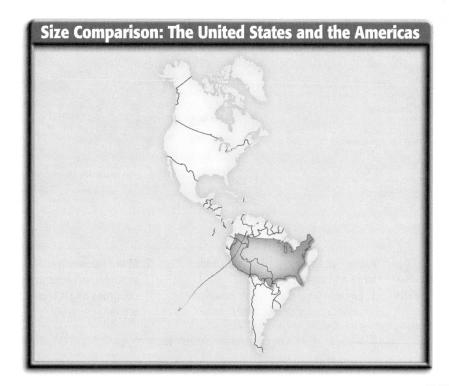

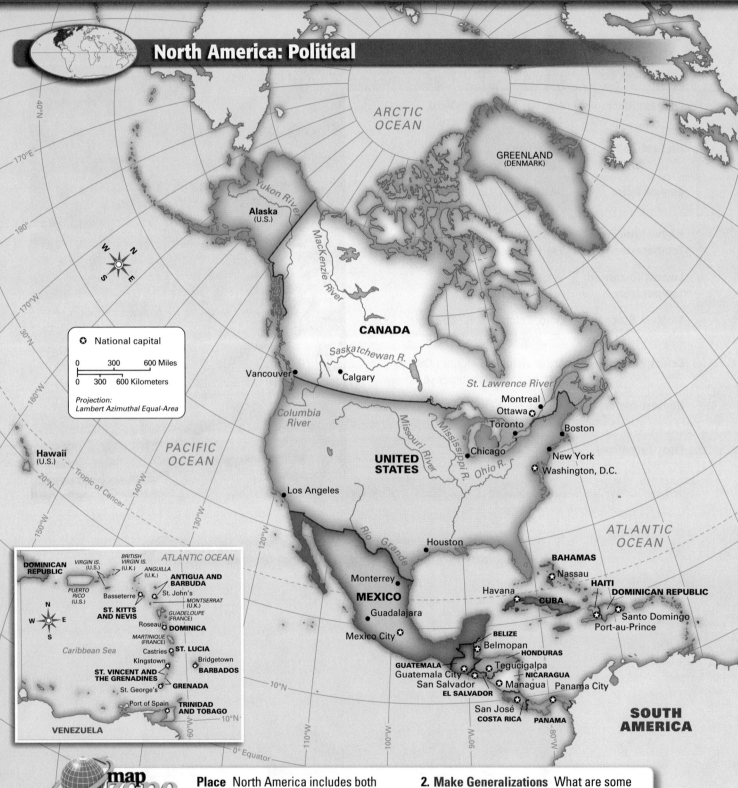

North America: Political

ARCTIC OCEAN

GREENLAND
(DENMARK)

Yukon River

Alaska
(U.S.)

Mackenzie River

CANADA

Saskatchewan R.

St. Lawrence River

⊙ National capital

| 0 | 300 | 600 Miles |

| 0 | 300 | 600 Kilometers |

Projection:
Lambert Azimuthal Equal-Area

Vancouver

Calgary

Montreal
Ottawa ⊙
Toronto
Boston

Columbia River

Missouri River

Mississippi R.

Ohio R.

Chicago
New York
Washington, D.C. ⊙

PACIFIC OCEAN

Hawaii
(U.S.)

Tropic of Cancer

UNITED STATES

Los Angeles

ATLANTIC OCEAN

Rio Grande

Houston

BAHAMAS

Nassau

HAITI

Monterrey

MEXICO

Havana ⊙

DOMINICAN REPUBLIC

CUBA

Guadalajara

Santo Domingo ⊙
Port-au-Prince ⊙

Mexico City ⊙

BELIZE

Belmopan ⊙

HONDURAS

GUATEMALA

Tegucigalpa ⊙

NICARAGUA

Guatemala City ⊙

San Salvador ⊙
EL SALVADOR

Managua ⊙

Panama City ⊙

San José ⊙
COSTA RICA

PANAMA

SOUTH AMERICA

Caribbean inset map:

ATLANTIC OCEAN

DOMINICAN REPUBLIC

VIRGIN IS.
(U.S.)

BRITISH VIRGIN IS.
(U.K.)

ANGUILLA
(U.K.)

ANTIGUA AND BARBUDA

PUERTO RICO
(U.S.)

Basseterre ⊙

St. John's ⊙

MONTSERRAT
(U.K.)

ST. KITTS AND NEVIS

GUADELOUPE
(FRANCE)

Roseau ⊙

DOMINICA

MARTINIQUE
(FRANCE)

Caribbean Sea

Castries ⊙

ST. LUCIA

Kingstown ⊙

Bridgetown ⊙

ST. VINCENT AND THE GRENADINES

BARBADOS

St. George's ⊙

GRENADA

Port of Spain ⊙

TRINIDAD AND TOBAGO

VENEZUELA

Equator

map zone
Geography Skills

Place North America includes both large and small countries.

1. Locate Where are North America's smaller countries located?

2. Make Generalizations What are some advantages or disadvantages that countries might face because they are large or small?

The Americas

South America: Political

Cartagena

Caracas

VENEZUELA

Georgetown
Paramaribo

GUYANA

French Guiana
(FRANCE)

Bogotá

SURINAME

COLOMBIA

0° Equator

Quito

ECUADOR

Guayaquil

Galápagos Islands

Manaus

Amazon River

10°N

PACIFIC OCEAN

PERU

BRAZIL

Lima

10°S

Salvador

La Paz

BOLIVIA

Brasília

Sucre

Parana River

ATLANTIC OCEAN

20°S

Tropic of Capricorn

Rio de Janeiro

PARAGUAY

São Paulo

CHILE

Asunción

⊕ National capital

0   300   600 Miles

0   300   600 Kilometers

Projection: Lambert Azimuthal Equal-Area

Córdoba

URUGUAY

30°S

Santiago

Buenos Aires

Montevideo

ARGENTINA

40°S

Falkland Islands

South Georgia Island

50°S

map zone

Geography Skills

Place South America includes 12 countries and one overseas department of France.

1. **Name** Which country is by far the largest in South America?

2. **Compare** Compare this map to the physical map of the Americas. What physical feature separates Chile and Argentina?

N W E S

The Americas: Population

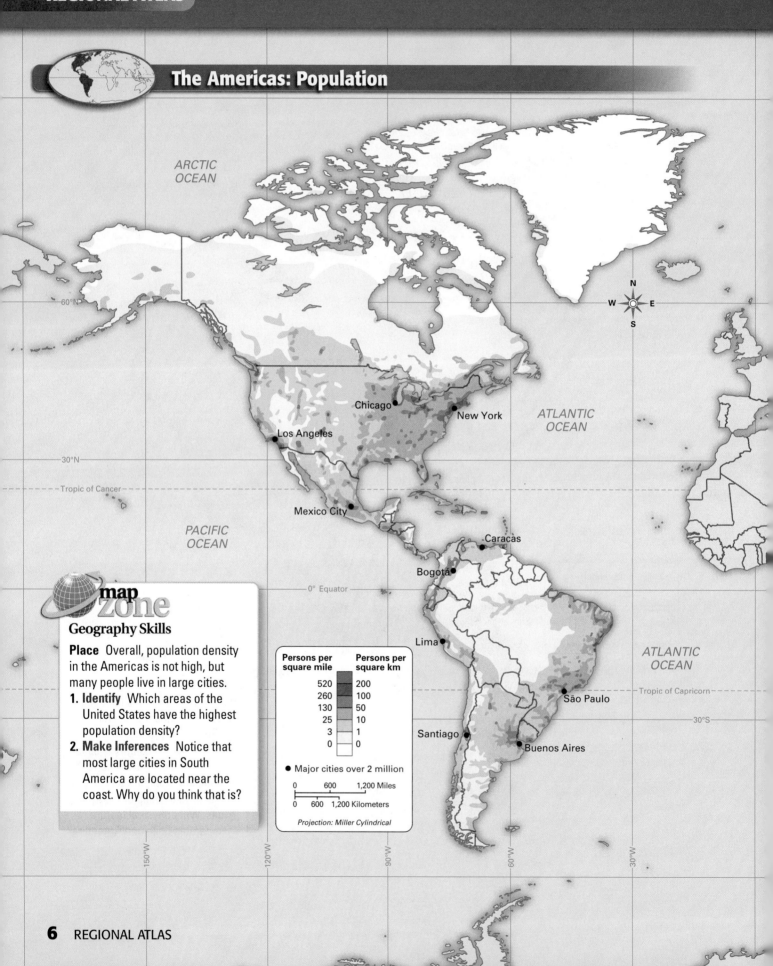

ARCTIC OCEAN

60°N

Chicago

New York

ATLANTIC OCEAN

N
W   E
S

Los Angeles

30°N

Tropic of Cancer

Mexico City

PACIFIC OCEAN

Caracas

Bogotá

0° Equator

map zone

Geography Skills

Place Overall, population density in the Americas is not high, but many people live in large cities.

1. Identify Which areas of the United States have the highest population density?

2. Make Inferences Notice that most large cities in South America are located near the coast. Why do you think that is?

Persons per square mile	Persons per square km
520	200
260	100
130	50
25	10
3	1
0	0

● Major cities over 2 million

Lima

ATLANTIC OCEAN

Tropic of Capricorn

São Paulo

30°S

Santiago

Buenos Aires

0   600   1,200 Miles
0   600   1,200 Kilometers

Projection: Miller Cylindrical

150°W   120°W   90°W   60°W   30°W

The Americas

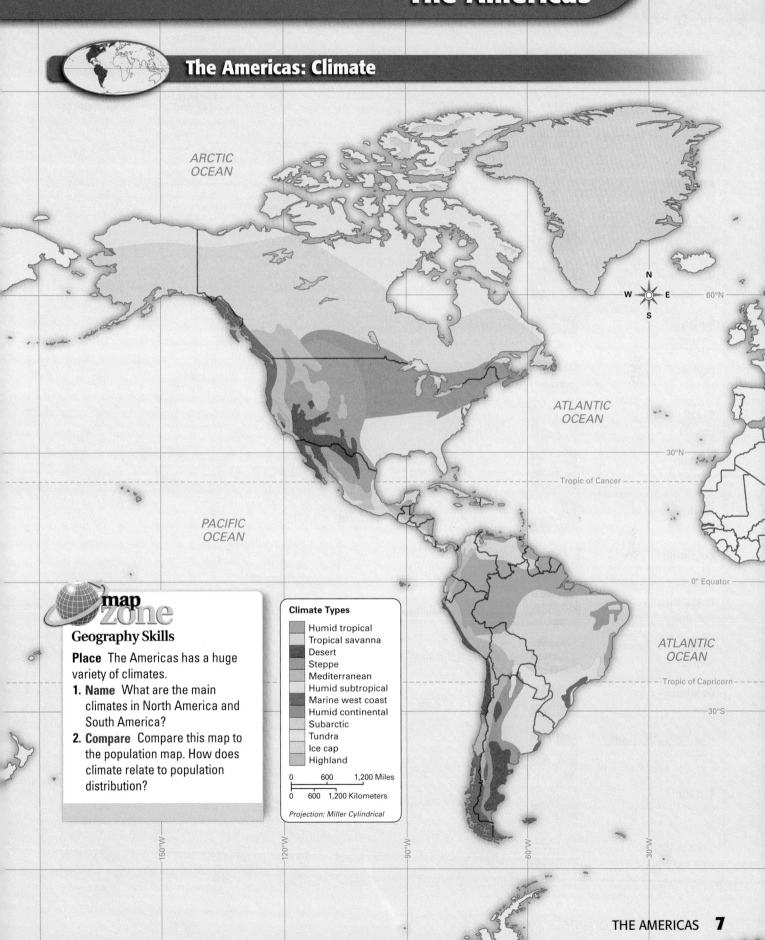

ARCTIC OCEAN

ATLANTIC OCEAN

N
W — E
S

60°N

30°N

Tropic of Cancer

PACIFIC OCEAN

ATLANTIC OCEAN

0° Equator

Tropic of Capricorn

30°S

map zone

Geography Skills

Place The Americas has a huge variety of climates.

1. **Name** What are the main climates in North America and South America?

2. **Compare** Compare this map to the population map. How does climate relate to population distribution?

Climate Types

- Humid tropical
- Tropical savanna
- Desert
- Steppe
- Mediterranean
- Humid subtropical
- Marine west coast
- Humid continental
- Subarctic
- Tundra
- Ice cap
- Highland

0   600   1,200 Miles

0   600   1,200 Kilometers

Projection: Miller Cylindrical

150°W   120°W   90°W   60°W   30°W

The Americas

COUNTRY CAPITAL	FLAG	POPULATION	AREA (sq mi)	PER CAPITA GDP (U.S. $)	LIFE EXPECTANCY AT BIRTH	TVS PER 1,000 PEOPLE
Antigua and Barbuda St. John's		85,632	171	$19,600	74.3	493
Argentina Buenos Aires		40.9 million	1,068,302	$14,200	76.5	293
The Bahamas Nassau		309,156	5,382	$29,600	65.8	243
Barbados Bridgetown		284,589	166	$19,100	73.2	290
Belize Belmopan		307,899	8,867	$8,400	68.3	183
Bolivia La Paz, Sucre		9.8 million	424,164	$4,500	66.6	118
Brazil Brasília		198.7 million	3,286,488	$10,200	71.9	333
Canada Ottawa		33.5 million	3,855,101	$39,100	81.3	709
Chile Santiago		16.6 million	292,260	$14,900	77.3	240
Colombia Bogotá		45.6 million	439,736	$8,800	72.6	279
Costa Rica San José		4.3 million	19,730	$11,500	77.5	229
Cuba Havana		11.5 million	42,803	$9,500	77.3	248
Dominica Roseau		72,660	291	$9,900	75.4	232
Dominican Republic Santo Domingo		9.7 million	18,815	$8,200	73.4	96
Ecuador Quito		14.6 million	109,483	$7,500	76.9	213
United States Washington, D.C.		307.2 million	3,794,083	$46,900	78.2	844

COUNTRY Capital	FLAG	POPULATION	AREA (sq mi)	PER CAPITA GDP (U.S. $)	LIFE EXPECTANCY AT BIRTH	TVS PER 1,000 PEOPLE
El Salvador San Salvador		7.2 million	8,124	$6,200	72.2	191
Grenada Saint George's		90,739	133	$12,900	65.6	376
Guatemala Guatemala City		13.3 million	42,043	$5,300	70.1	61
Guyana Georgetown		772,298	83,000	$3,800	66.5	70
Haiti Port-au-Prince		9 million	10,714	$1,300	57.6	5
Honduras Tegucigalpa		7.8 million	43,278	$4,100	69.4	95
Jamaica Kingston		2.8 million	4,244	$7,500	73.7	191
Mexico Mexico City		111.2 million	761,606	$14,200	75.9	272
Nicaragua Managua		5.9 million	49,998	$2,900	71.3	69
Panama Panama City		3.4 million	30,193	$11,700	77	192
Paraguay Asunción		7 million	157,047	$4,200	75.7	205
Peru Lima		29.5 million	496,226	$8,500	70.5	147
Saint Kitts and Nevis Basseterre		40,131	101	$19,500	73.1	256
Saint Lucia Castries		160,267	238	$11,100	76.3	368
Saint Vincent and the Grenadines; Kingstown		104,574	150	$10,200	74.4	230
United States Washington, D.C.		307.2 million	3,794,083	$46,900	78.2	844

COUNTRY Capital	FLAG	POPULATION	AREA (sq mi)	PER CAPITA GDP (U.S. $)	LIFE EXPECTANCY AT BIRTH	TVS PER 1,000 PEOPLE
Suriname Paramaribo		481,267	63,039	$8,900	73.6	241
Trinidad and Tobago Port-of-Spain		1.2 million	1,980	$23,600	67.1	337
Uruguay Montevideo		3.5 million	68,039	$12,400	76.2	531
Venezuela Caracas		26.8 million	352,144	$13,500	73.6	185
United States Washington, D.C.		307.2 million	3,794,083	$46,900	78.2	844

ANALYSIS SKILL ANALYZING TABLES

1. Compare the information for the United States, Canada, Brazil, and Mexico. How do these four countries compare?
2. Which country has the lowest per capita GDP?

Largest Cities and Urban Populations

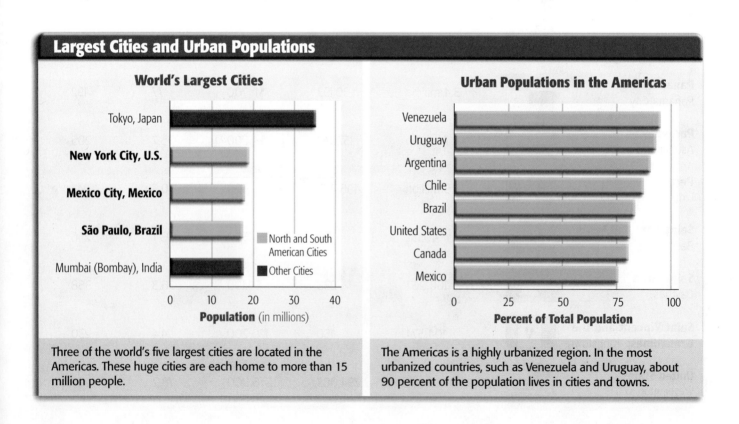

World's Largest Cities

Tokyo, Japan
New York City, U.S.
Mexico City, Mexico
São Paulo, Brazil
Mumbai (Bombay), India

■ North and South American Cities
■ Other Cities

0   10   20   30   40
Population (in millions)

Urban Populations in the Americas

Venezuela
Uruguay
Argentina
Chile
Brazil
United States
Canada
Mexico

0   25   50   75   100
Percent of Total Population

Three of the world's five largest cities are located in the Americas. These huge cities are each home to more than 15 million people.

The Americas is a highly urbanized region. In the most urbanized countries, such as Venezuela and Uruguay, about 90 percent of the population lives in cities and towns.

Major Food Exports of the Americas

Coffee Exports

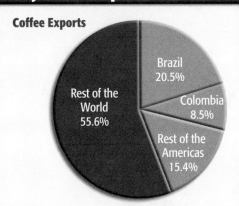

- Brazil 20.5%
- Colombia 8.5%
- Rest of the Americas 15.4%
- Rest of the World 55.6%

Wheat Exports

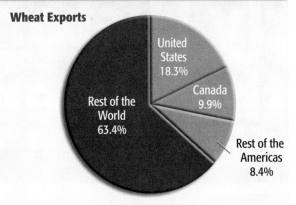

- United States 18.3%
- Canada 9.9%
- Rest of the Americas 8.4%
- Rest of the World 63.4%

Corn Exports

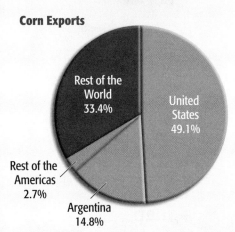

- United States 49.1%
- Rest of the World 33.4%
- Rest of the Americas 2.7%
- Argentina 14.8%

Banana Exports

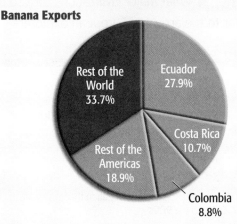

- Ecuador 27.9%
- Costa Rica 10.7%
- Colombia 8.8%
- Rest of the Americas 18.9%
- Rest of the World 33.7%

The Americas is a major exporter of some crops, like coffee, wheat, corn, and bananas. While the United States leads in wheat and corn exports, other crops like coffee and bananas are exported from Central and South America.

ANALYSIS SKILL **ANALYZING GRAPHS**

1. What percentage of the world's corn exports come from the Americas?
2. Which countries in the Americas export the most coffee?

Workers harvest coffee beans in Costa Rica.

Early History of the Americas

500 BC–AD 1537

Essential Question What major civilizations thrived in the Americas prior to the arrival of European explorers?

What You Will Learn...

In this chapter you will learn about the location, growth, and decline of the Maya, Aztec, and Inca civilizations in the Americas.

FOCUS ON READING AND WRITING

Setting a Purpose Setting a purpose for your reading can help give you a focus. Before you read, look at pictures and headings to find out what the text is about. Then decide what your purpose in reading the text is. Keep your purpose in mind as you read. **See the lesson, Setting a Purpose, on page 194.**

Writing a Newspaper Article You are a writer for a European newspaper who is traveling with some explorers to the Americas. As you read this chapter, you will decide what you want to share with readers in a newspaper article—the land, the people, or the events that occurred after the explorers arrived.

PACIFIC OCEAN

map zone **Geography Skills**

Regions Three great civilizations existed in North and South America before 1537.
1. **Identify** Which civilization was located in South America?
2. **Make Inferences** What do you think happened when the Spanish arrived in the Americas?

The Maya The Maya traded jade between their cities in Mesoamerica.

The Americas, 500 BC–AD 1537

ATLANTIC OCEAN

Maya temple

Tenochtitlán

Palenque

Aztec warrior

HISTORY Machu Picchu

hmhsocialstudies.com VIDEO

Spanish explorers' ship

Inca with llama

Cuzco

- Ancient city

0   300   600 Miles
0   300   600 Kilometers

Projection:
Lambert Azimuthal Equal-Area

Tropic of Capricorn

The Aztecs The Aztecs were known for warfare as well as for their arts.

The Incas The Incas built well-crafted stone cities high in the Andes.

The Maya

What You Will Learn...

Main Ideas

1. Geography helped shape the lives of the early Maya.
2. During the Classic Age, the Maya built great cities linked by trade.
3. Maya culture included a strict social structure, a religion with many gods, and achievements in science and the arts.
4. The decline of Maya civilization began in the 900s.

The Big Idea

The Maya developed an advanced civilization that thrived in Mesoamerica from about 250 until the 900s.

Key Terms and Places

maize, *p. 14*
Palenque, *p. 15*
observatories, *p. 18*

hmhsocialstudies.com
TAKING NOTES

Use the graphic organizer online to organize your notes on the Maya.

If YOU lived there...

You are a Maya farmer, growing corn in fields outside a city. Often you enter the city to join in religious ceremonies. You watch the king and his priests standing at the top of a tall pyramid. They wear capes of brightly colored feathers and gold ornaments that glitter in the sun. Far below them, thousands of worshippers crowd into the plaza with you to honor the gods.

How do these ceremonies make you feel?

BUILDING BACKGROUND Religion was very important to the Maya, one of the early peoples in the Americas. The Maya believed the gods controlled everything in the world around them.

Geography and the Early Maya

The region known as Mesoamerica stretches from the central part of Mexico south to include the northern part of Central America. It was in this region that a people called the Maya (MY-uh) developed a remarkable civilization.

Around 1000 BC the Maya began settling in the lowlands of what is now northern Guatemala. Thick tropical forests covered most of the land, but the people cleared areas to farm. They grew a variety of crops, including beans, squash, avocados, and **maize**, or corn. The forests provided valuable resources, too. Forest animals such as deer, rabbits, and monkeys were sources of food. In addition, trees and other forest plants made good building materials. For example, some Maya used wooden poles and vines, along with mud, to build their houses.

The early Maya lived in small, isolated villages. Eventually, though, these villages started trading with one another and with other groups in Mesoamerica. As trade increased, the villages grew. By about AD 200, the Maya had begun to build large cities in Mesoamerica.

READING CHECK Finding Main Ideas How did the early Maya make use of their physical environment?

The Classic Age

The Maya civilization reached its height between about AD 250 and 900. This time in Maya history is known as the Classic Age. During this time, Maya territory grew to include more than 40 large cities. Each had its own government and its own king. No single ruler united the many cities into one empire.

Instead, the Maya cities were linked through trade. People exchanged goods for products that were not available locally. Look at the trade routes on the map to see the goods that were available in different areas of Maya civilization. For example,

the warm lowlands were good for growing cotton and cacao (kuh-KOW), the source of chocolate. But lowland crops did not grow well in the cool highlands. Instead, the highlands had valuable stones, such as jade and obsidian. People carried these and other products along trade routes.

Through trade, the Maya got supplies for construction. Maya cities had grand buildings, such as palaces decorated with carvings and paintings. The Maya also built stone pyramids topped with temples. Some temples honored local kings. For example, in the city of **Palenque** (pah-LENG-kay), the king Pacal (puh-KAHL) had a temple built to record his achievements.

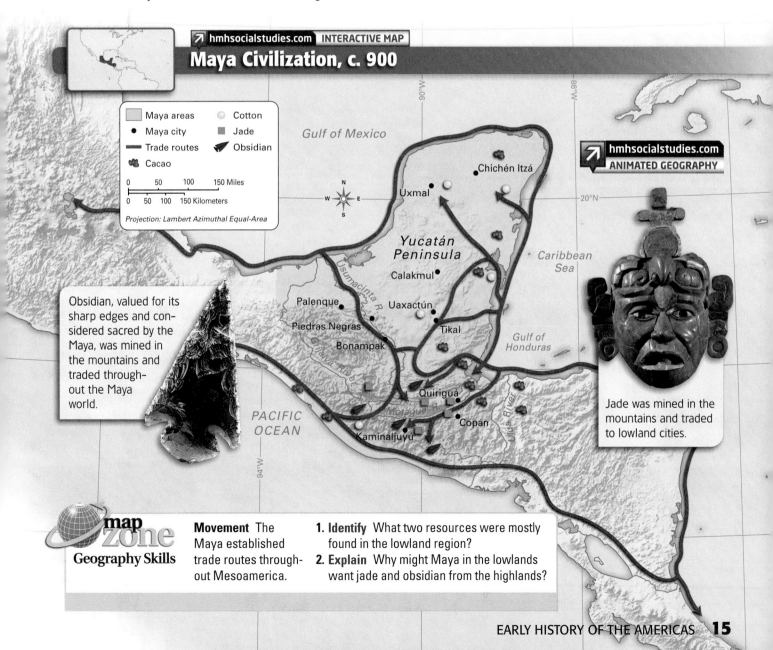

↗ hmhsocialstudies.com INTERACTIVE MAP

Maya Civilization, c. 900

Maya areas
● Maya city
━ Trade routes
🌰 Cacao
◯ Cotton
◼ Jade
◣ Obsidian

0 50 100 150 Miles
0 50 100 150 Kilometers

Projection: Lambert Azimuthal Equal-Area

Gulf of Mexico

90°W

88°W

Chichén Itzá

Uxmal

Yucatán Peninsula

Calakmul

20°N

Caribbean Sea

↗ hmhsocialstudies.com ANIMATED GEOGRAPHY

Palenque

Usumacinta R.

Uaxactún

Piedras Negras

Tikal

Gulf of Honduras

Bonampak

Balsa River

Quiriguá

Motagua

Copán

Ulúa River

PACIFIC OCEAN

Kaminaljuyú

94°W

Obsidian, valued for its sharp edges and considered sacred by the Maya, was mined in the mountains and traded throughout the Maya world.

Jade was mined in the mountains and traded to lowland cities.

map zone

Geography Skills

Movement The Maya established trade routes throughout Mesoamerica.

1. **Identify** What two resources were mostly found in the lowland region?
2. **Explain** Why might Maya in the lowlands want jade and obsidian from the highlands?

In addition to palaces and temples, the Maya built canals and paved large plazas, or open squares, for public gatherings. Farmers used stone walls to shape hillsides into flat terraces so they could grow crops on them. Almost every Maya city also had a stone court for playing a special ball game. Using only their heads, shoulders, or hips, players tried to bounce a heavy rubber ball through stone rings attached high on the court walls. The winners of these games received jewels and clothing. The losers were often killed.

READING CHECK Analyzing Why is Maya civilization not considered an empire?

Maya Culture

In Maya society, people's daily lives were heavily influenced by two main forces. One was the social structure, and the other was religion.

Social Structure

The king held the highest position in Maya society. The Maya believed their kings were related to the gods, so Maya kings had religious as well as political authority. Priests, rich merchants, and noble warriors were also part of the upper class. Together with the king, these people held all the power in Maya society.

Close-up

Palenque

The ancient Maya city of Palenque was a major power on the border between the Maya highlands and lowlands. Its great temples and plazas were typical of the Classic Age of Maya civilization.

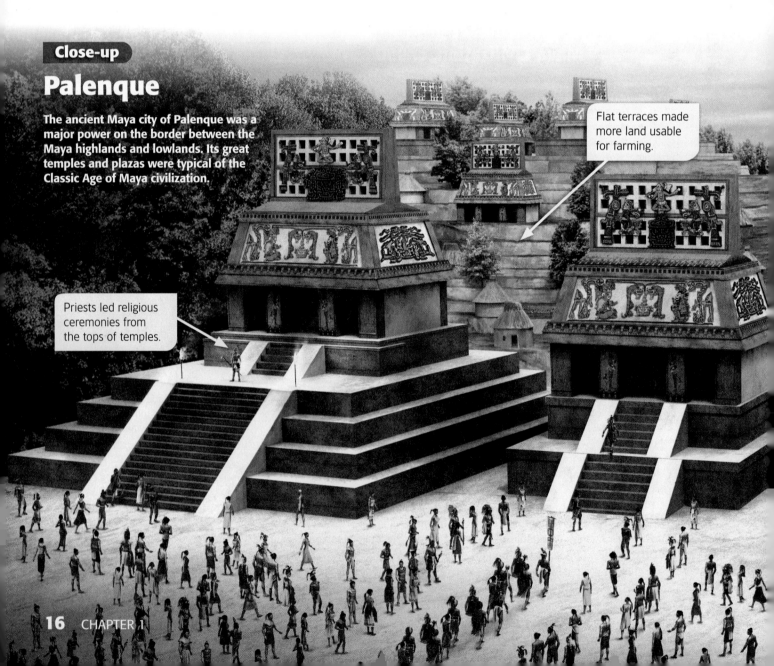

Flat terraces made more land usable for farming.

Priests led religious ceremonies from the tops of temples.

Most Maya, though, belonged to the lower class. This group was made up of farming families who lived outside the cities. The women cared for the children, cooked, made yarn, and wove cloth. The men farmed, hunted, and crafted tools.

Lower-class Maya had to "pay" their rulers by giving the rulers part of their crops and goods such as cloth and salt. They also had to help construct temples and other public buildings. If their city went to war, Maya men had to serve in the army, and if captured in battle, they often became slaves. Slaves carried goods along trade routes or worked for upper-class Maya as servants or farmers.

Religion

The Maya worshipped many gods, such as a creator, a sun god, a moon goddess, and a maize god. Each god was believed to control a different aspect of daily life.

According to Maya beliefs, the gods could be helpful or harmful, so people tried to please the gods to get their help. The Maya believed their gods needed blood to prevent disasters or the end of the world. Every person offered blood to the gods by piercing their tongue or skin. On special occasions, the Maya made human sacrifices. They usually used prisoners captured in battle, offering their hearts to stone carvings of the gods.

Maya temples were shaped like mountains, which the Maya considered sacred because they allowed people to approach the gods.

Maya buildings were covered with stucco and painted in bright colors.

BIOGRAPHY

Pacal
(603–683)

Pacal became king of the Maya city of Palenque when he was just 12 years old. As king, Pacal led many important community events, such as religious dances and public meetings. When he died, he was buried at the bottom of the Temple of the Inscriptions shown to the near left.

ANALYSIS SKILL **ANALYZING VISUALS**

In what ways might Palenque's setting have helped the city? In what ways might it have hurt the city?

Maya Astronomy and Writing

October 28, AD 709

She is letting blood.

Lady Xoc

The Maya studied the stars from their observatory (left) at Chichén Itzá. The stone carving (above) shows a religious ceremony.

ANALYZING VISUALS What is happening in this religious ceremony?

Achievements

FOCUS ON READING

What will be your purpose in reading about Maya achievements?

The Maya's religious beliefs led them to make impressive advances in science. They built large **observatories**, or buildings from which people could study the sky, so their priests could watch the stars and plan the best times for religious festivals. With the knowledge they gained about astronomy, the Maya developed two calendars. One, with 365 days, guided farming activities, such as planting and harvesting. This calendar was more accurate than the one used in Europe at that time. The Maya also had a separate 260-day calendar that they used for keeping track of religious events.

The Maya were able to measure time accurately partly because they were skilled mathematicians. They created a number system that helped them make complex calculations, and they were among the first people with a symbol for zero. The Maya used their number system to record key dates in their history.

The Maya also developed a writing system. Anthropologists, or scholars who study people and cultures, have figured out that symbols used in Maya writing represented both objects and sounds. The Maya carved these symbols into large stone tablets to record their history. They also wrote in bark-paper books and passed down stories and poems orally.

The Maya created amazing art and architecture as well. Their jade and gold jewelry was exceptional. Also, their huge temple-pyramids were masterfully built. The Maya had neither metal tools for cutting nor wheeled vehicles for carrying heavy supplies. Instead, workers used obsidian tools to cut limestone into blocks. Then workers rolled the giant blocks over logs and lifted them with ropes. The Maya decorated their buildings with paintings.

READING CHECK **Categorizing** What groups made up the different classes in Maya society?

Decline of Maya Civilization

Maya civilization began to collapse in the AD 900s. People stopped building temples and other structures. They left the cities and moved back to the countryside. What caused this collapse? Historians are not sure, but they think that a combination of factors was probably responsible.

One factor could have been the burden on the common people. Maya kings forced their subjects to farm for them or work on building projects. Perhaps people didn't want to work for the kings. They might have decided to **rebel** against their rulers' demands and abandon their cities.

Increased warfare between cities could also have caused the decline. Maya cities had always fought for power. But if battles became more widespread or destructive, they would have disrupted trade and cost many lives. People might have fled from the cities for their safety.

A related theory is that perhaps the Maya could not produce enough food to feed everyone. Growing the same crops year after year would have weakened the soil. In addition, as the population grew, the demand for food would have increased. To meet this demand, cities might have begun competing fiercely for new land. But the resulting battles would have hurt more crops, damaged more farmland, and caused even greater food shortages.

Climate change could have played a role, too. Scientists know that Mesoamerica suffered from droughts during the period when the Maya were leaving their cities. Droughts would have made it hard to grow enough food to feed people in the cities.

Whatever the reasons, the collapse of Maya civilization happened gradually. The Maya scattered after 900, but they did not disappear entirely. In fact, the Maya civilization later revived in the Yucatán Peninsula. By the time Spanish conquerors reached the Americas in the 1500s, though, Maya power had faded.

READING CHECK **Summarizing** What factors may have caused the end of Maya civilization?

SUMMARY AND PREVIEW The Maya built a civilization that peaked between about 250 and 900 but later collapsed for reasons still unknown. In Section 2 you will learn about another people who lived in Mesoamerica, the Aztecs.

HISTORY

VIDEO
The Disappearance

hmhsocialstudies.com

ACADEMIC VOCABULARY
rebel to fight against authority

Section 1 Assessment

hmhsocialstudies.com
ONLINE QUIZ

Reviewing Ideas, Terms, and Places

1. **a. Recall** What resources did the Maya get from the forest?
   b. Elaborate How do you think Maya villages grew into large cities?
2. **a. Describe** What features did Maya cities include?
   b. Make Inferences How did trade strengthen the Maya civilization?
3. **a. Identify** Who belonged to the upper class in Maya society?
   b. Explain Why did the Maya build **observatories**?
   c. Rank What do you think was the most impressive cultural achievement of the Maya? Why?
4. **a. Describe** What happened to the Maya after 900?
   b. Evaluate What would you consider to be the key factor in the collapse of Maya civilization? Explain.

Critical Thinking

5. **Evaluating** Draw a diagram like the one to the right. Use your notes to rank Maya achievements, with the most important at the top.

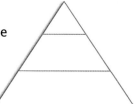

Focus on Writing

6. **Gathering Information about the Maya** Part of your article will probably be devoted to the Maya. Use the map and pictures in this section to help you decide what to write about. How would you describe the land and the Maya cities? What could you add about the history and culture of the Maya? Take notes on your ideas.

The Aztecs

What You Will Learn...

Main Ideas

1. The Aztecs built a rich and powerful empire in central Mexico.
2. Social structure, religion, and warfare shaped life in the empire.
3. Hernán Cortés conquered the Aztec Empire in 1521.

The Big Idea

The strong Aztec Empire, founded in central Mexico in 1325, lasted until the Spanish conquest in 1521.

Key Terms and Places

Tenochtitlán, *p. 20*
causeways, *p. 20*
conquistadors, *p. 24*

hmhsocialstudies.com
TAKING NOTES

Use the graphic organizer online to organize your notes on the Aztecs.

If YOU lived there...

You live in a village in southeastern Mexico that is ruled by the powerful Aztec Empire. Each year your village must send the emperor many baskets of corn. You have to dig gold for him, too. One day some pale, bearded strangers arrive by sea. They want to overthrow the emperor, and they ask for your help.

Should you help the strangers? Why or why not?

BUILDING BACKGROUND The Aztecs ruled a large empire in Mesoamerica. Each village they conquered had to contribute heavily to the Aztec economy. This system helped create a mighty state, but one that did not inspire loyalty.

The Aztecs Build an Empire

The first Aztecs were farmers who migrated from the north to central Mexico. Finding the good farmland already occupied, they settled on a swampy island in the middle of Lake Texcoco (tays-KOH-koh). There, in 1325, they began building their capital and conquering nearby towns.

War was a key factor in the Aztecs' rise to power. The Aztecs fought fiercely and demanded tribute payments from the people they conquered. The cotton, gold, and food that poured in as a result became vital to their economy. The Aztecs also controlled a huge trade network. Merchants carried goods to and from all parts of the empire. Many merchants doubled as spies, keeping the rulers informed about what was happening in their lands.

War, tribute, and trade made the Aztec Empire strong and rich. By the early 1400s the Aztecs ruled the most powerful state in Mesoamerica. Nowhere was the empire's greatness more visible than in its capital, **Tenochtitlán** (tay-nawch-teet-LAHN).

To build this amazing island city, the Aztecs first had to overcome many geographic challenges. One problem was the difficulty getting to and from the city. The Aztecs addressed this challenge by building three wide **causeways**—raised roads across water or wet ground—to connect the island to the lakeshore.

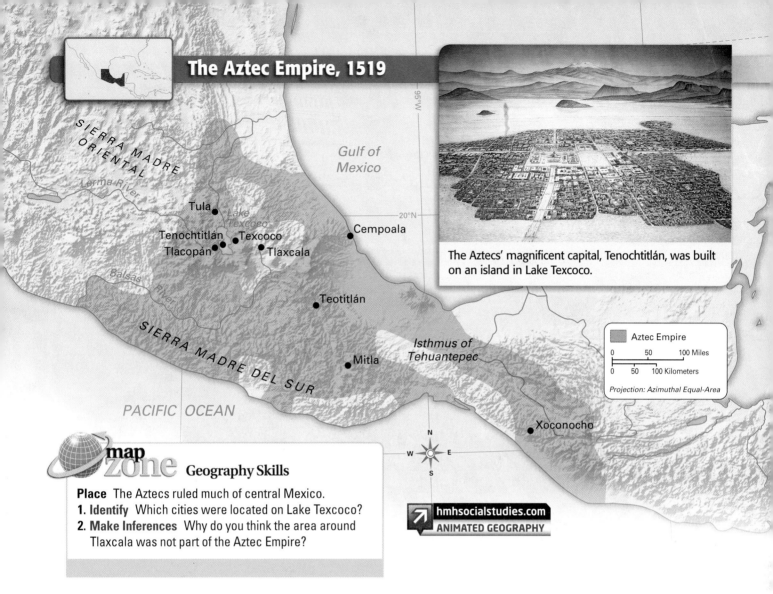

The Aztec Empire, 1519

SIERRA MADRE ORIENTAL

Lerma River

Gulf of Mexico

Tula

Lake Texcoco

Tenochtitlán Texcoco
Tlacopán   Tlaxcala

Balsas River

Cempoala

20°N

Teotitlán

SIERRA MADRE DEL SUR

Isthmus of Tehuantepec

Mitla

PACIFIC OCEAN

Xoconocho

95°W

N W E S

The Aztecs' magnificent capital, Tenochtitlán, was built on an island in Lake Texcoco.

Aztec Empire

0   50   100 Miles
0   50   100 Kilometers

Projection: Azimuthal Equal-Area

map zone Geography Skills

Place The Aztecs ruled much of central Mexico.
1. **Identify** Which cities were located on Lake Texcoco?
2. **Make Inferences** Why do you think the area around Tlaxcala was not part of the Aztec Empire?

hmhsocialstudies.com
ANIMATED GEOGRAPHY

They also built canals that crisscrossed the city. The causeways and canals made travel and trade much easier.

Tenochtitlán's island location also limited the amount of land available for farming. To solve this problem, the Aztecs created floating gardens called *chinampas* (chee-NAHM-pahs). They piled soil on top of large rafts, which they anchored to trees that stood in the water.

The Aztecs made Tenochtitlán a truly magnificent city. Home to some 200,000 people at its height, it had huge temples, a busy market, and a grand palace.

READING CHECK **Finding Main Ideas** How did the Aztecs rise to power?

Life in the Empire

The Aztecs' way of life was as distinctive as their capital city. They had a complex social structure, a demanding religion, and a rich culture.

Aztec Society

The Aztec emperor, like the Maya king, was the most important person in society. From his great palace, he attended to law, trade, tribute, and warfare. Trusted nobles helped him as tax collectors, judges, and other government officials. These noble positions were passed down from fathers to sons, and young nobles went to school to learn their responsibilities.

Mexico's capital, Mexico City, is located where Tenochtitlán once stood.

Close-up

Tenochtitlán

The Aztecs turned a swampy, uninhabited island into one of the largest and grandest cities in the world. The first Europeans to visit Tenochtitlán were amazed. At the time, the Aztec capital was about five times bigger than London.

The Great Temple stood at the heart of the city. On top of the temple were two shrines—a blue shrine for the rain god and a red shrine for the sun god.

Gold, silver, cloaks, and precious stones were among the many items sold at the market.

A network of canals linked different parts of the city.

Aztec farmers grew crops on floating gardens called *chinampas*.

ANALYSIS SKILL **ANALYZING VISUALS**

What is the most important building in this picture? How can you tell?

22

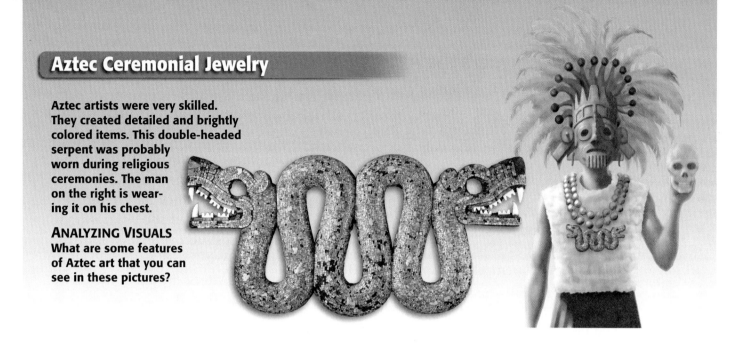

Aztec Ceremonial Jewelry

Aztec artists were very skilled. They created detailed and brightly colored items. This double-headed serpent was probably worn during religious ceremonies. The man on the right is wearing it on his chest.

ANALYZING VISUALS What are some features of Aztec art that you can see in these pictures?

Just below the emperor and his nobles was a class of warriors and priests. Aztec warriors were highly respected and had many privileges, but priests were more influential. They led religious ceremonies and, as keepers of the calendars, decided when to plant and harvest.

The next level of Aztec society included merchants and artisans. Below them, in the lower class, were farmers and laborers, who made up the majority of the population. Many didn't own their land, and they paid so much in tribute that they often found it tough to survive. Only slaves, at the very bottom of society, struggled more.

Religion and Warfare

Like the Maya, the Aztecs worshipped many gods whom they believed controlled both nature and human activities. To please the gods, Aztec priests regularly made human sacrifices. Most victims were battle captives or slaves. In bloody ritual ceremonies, priests would slash open their victims' chests to "feed" human hearts and blood to the gods. The Aztecs sacrificed as many as 10,000 people a year. To supply enough victims, Aztec warriors often fought battles with neighboring peoples.

Cultural Achievements

As warlike as the Aztecs were, they also appreciated art and beauty. Architects and sculptors created fine stone pyramids and statues. Artisans used gold, gems, and bright feathers to make jewelry and masks. Women embroidered colorful designs on the cloth they wove.

The Aztecs valued learning as well. They studied astronomy and devised a calendar much like the Maya one. They kept detailed written records of historical and cultural events. They also had a strong oral tradition. Stories about ancestors and the gods were passed from one generation to the next. The Aztecs also enjoyed fine speeches and riddles such as these:

" What is a little blue-green jar filled with popcorn? Someone is sure to guess our riddle: it is the sky.
What is a mountainside that has a spring of water in it? Our nose. "
–Bernardino de Sahagún, from Florentine Codex

Knowing the answers to riddles showed that one had paid attention in school.

READING CHECK **Identifying Cause and Effect** How did Aztec religious practices influence warfare?

Cortés Conquers the Aztecs

FOCUS ON READING

If your purpose is to learn about the end of the Aztecs, how will reading about the Spanish help you?

In the late 1400s the Spanish arrived in the Americas, seeking adventure, riches, and converts to Catholicism. One group of **conquistadors** (kahn-KEES-tuh-dohrz), or Spanish conquerors, reached Mexico in 1519. Led by Hernán Cortés (er-NAHN kawr-TEZ), their motives were to find gold, claim land, and convert the native peoples to Christianity.

The Aztec emperor, Moctezuma II (MAWK-tay-SOO-mah), cautiously welcomed the strangers. He believed Cortés to be the god Quetzalcoatl (ket-suhl-kuh-WAH-tuhl), whom the Aztecs believed had left Mexico long ago. According to legend, the god had promised to return in 1519.

Moctezuma gave the Spanish gold and other gifts, but Cortés wanted more. He took the emperor prisoner, enraging the Aztecs, who attacked the Spanish. They managed to drive out the conquistadors, but Moctezuma was killed in the fighting.

Within a year, Cortés and his men came back. This time they had help from other peoples in the region who resented the Aztecs' harsh rule. In addition, the Spanish had better weapons, including armor, cannons, and swords. Furthermore, the Aztecs were terrified of the enemy's big horses—animals they had never seen before. The Spanish had also unknowingly brought diseases such as smallpox to the Americas. Diseases weakened or killed thousands of Aztecs. In 1521 the Aztec Empire came to an end.

READING CHECK **Summarizing** What factors helped the Spanish defeat the Aztecs?

SUMMARY AND PREVIEW The Aztec Empire, made strong by warfare and tribute, fell to the Spanish in 1521. In the next section you will learn about another empire in the Americas, that of the Incas.

Section 2 Assessment

hmhsocialstudies.com
ONLINE QUIZ

Reviewing Ideas, Terms, and Places

1. a. Recall Where and when did Aztec civilization develop?
b. Explain How did the Aztecs in **Tenochtitlán** adapt to their island location?
c. Elaborate How might Tenochtitlán's location have been both a benefit and a hindrance to the Aztecs?

2. a. Recall What did the Aztecs feed their gods?
b. Rate Consider the roles of the emperor, warriors, priests, and others in Aztec society. Who do you think had the hardest role? Explain.

3. a. Identify Who was Moctezuma II?
b. Make Generalizations Why did allies help Cortés defeat the Aztecs?
c. Predict The Aztecs vastly outnumbered the **conquistadors**. If the Aztecs had first viewed Cortés as a threat rather than a god, how might history have changed?

Critical Thinking

4. Evaluating Draw a diagram like the one shown. Use your notes to identify three factors that contributed to the Aztecs' power. Put the factor you consider most important first and put the least important last. Explain your choices.

1.	2.	3.

FOCUS ON WRITING

5. Describing the Aztec Empire Tenochtitlán would certainly be described in your article. Make notes about how you would describe it. Be sure to explain the causeways, chinampas, and other features. What activities went on in the city? Your article should also describe the events that occurred when the Spanish discovered the Aztec capital. Make notes on the fall of the Aztec Empire.

The Incas

If YOU lived there...

You live in the Andes Mountains, where you raise llamas. You weave their wool into warm cloth. Last year, soldiers from the powerful Inca Empire took over your village. They brought in new leaders, who say you must all learn a new language and send much of your woven cloth to the Inca ruler. They also promise that the government will provide for you in times of trouble.

How do you feel about living in the Inca Empire?

> **BUILDING BACKGROUND** The Incas built their huge empire by taking over village after village in South America. They brought many changes to the people they conquered before they were themselves conquered by the Spanish.

The Incas Create an Empire

While the Aztecs were ruling Mexico, the Inca Empire arose in South America. The Incas began as a small tribe in the Andes. Their capital was **Cuzco** (KOO-skoh) in what is now Peru.

In the mid-1400s a ruler named Pachacuti (pah-chah-KOO-tee) began to expand Inca territory. Later leaders followed his example, and by the early 1500s the Inca Empire was huge. It stretched from what is now Ecuador south to central Chile. It included coastal deserts, snowy mountains, fertile valleys, and thick forests. About 12 million people lived in the empire. To rule effectively, the Incas formed a strong central government.

What You Will Learn...

Main Ideas

1. The Incas created an empire with a strong central government in South America.
2. Life in the Inca Empire was influenced by social structure, religion, and the Incas' cultural achievements.
3. Francisco Pizarro conquered the Incas and took control of the region in 1537.

The Big Idea

The Incas controlled a huge empire in South America, but it was conquered by the Spanish.

Key Terms and Places

Cuzco, *p. 25*
Quechua, *p. 26*
masonry, *p. 27*

hmhsocialstudies.com
TAKING NOTES

Use the graphic organizer online to organize your notes on the Inca Empire.

The Incas lived in a region of high plains and mountains.

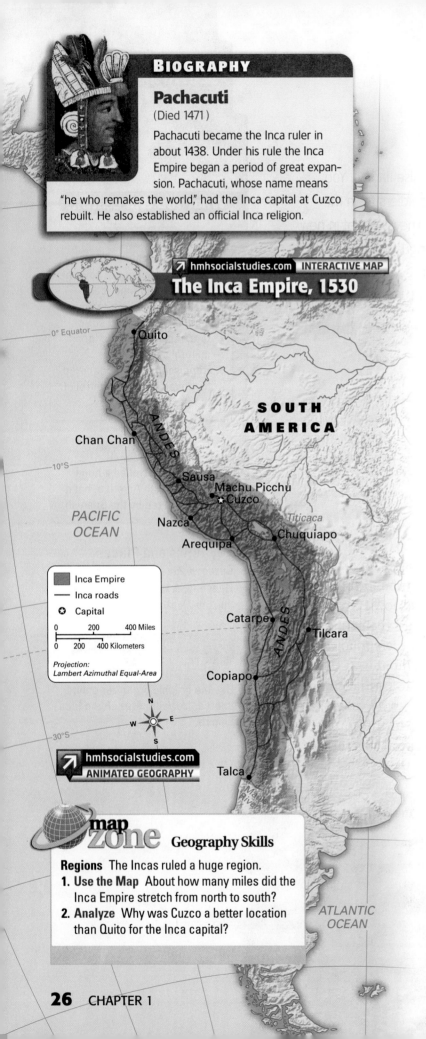

Pachacuti
(Died 1471)

Pachacuti became the Inca ruler in about 1438. Under his rule the Inca Empire began a period of great expansion. Pachacuti, whose name means "he who remakes the world," had the Inca capital at Cuzco rebuilt. He also established an official Inca religion.

↗ hmhsocialstudies.com **INTERACTIVE MAP**

The Inca Empire, 1530

0° Equator

Quito

SOUTH
AMERICA

ANDES

Chan Chan

10°S

Sausa
Machu Picchu
Cuzco

PACIFIC
OCEAN

Nazca

Titicaca

Chuquiapo

Arequipa

■ Inca Empire
— Inca roads
✪ Capital

0   200   400 Miles
0   200   400 Kilometers

Projection:
Lambert Azimuthal Equal-Area

Catarpe
ANDES
Tilcara

30°S

Copiapo

↗ hmhsocialstudies.com
ANIMATED GEOGRAPHY

Talca

Maule River

ATLANTIC
OCEAN

map zone Geography Skills

Regions The Incas ruled a huge region.
1. **Use the Map** About how many miles did the Inca Empire stretch from north to south?
2. **Analyze** Why was Cuzco a better location than Quito for the Inca capital?

Central Rule

Pachacuti did not want the people he conquered to have too much power. He began a policy of removing local leaders and replacing them with new officials whom he trusted. He also made the children of conquered leaders travel to Cuzco to learn about Inca government and religion. When the children were grown, they were sent back to govern their villages, where they taught their people about the Incas' history, traditions, and way of life.

As another way of unifying the empire, the Incas used an official Inca language, **Quechua** (KE-chuh-wuh). Although people spoke many other languages, all official business had to be done in Quechua. Even today, many people in Peru and the other former Inca lands still speak Quechua.

A Well-Organized Economy

The Inca government strictly controlled the economy and told each household what work to do. Most Incas had to spend time working for the government as well as themselves. Farmers tended government land in addition to their own. Villagers made cloth and other goods for the army. Some Incas served as soldiers, worked in mines, or built roads and bridges. In this way the people paid taxes in the form of labor rather than money. This labor tax system was called the *mita* (MEE-tah).

Another feature of the Inca economy was that there were no merchants or markets. Instead, government officials would distribute goods collected through the *mita*. Leftover goods were stored in the capital for emergencies. If a natural disaster struck, or if people simply could not care for themselves, the government provided supplies to help them.

READING CHECK **Summarizing** How did the Incas control their empire?

Life in the Inca Empire

Because the rulers controlled Inca society so closely, the common people had little personal freedom. At the same time, the government protected the general welfare of all in the empire. But that did not mean everyone was treated equally.

Social Divisions

Inca society had two main social classes. The emperor, government officials, and priests made up the upper class. Members of this class lived in stone houses in Cuzco and wore the best clothes. They did not have to pay the labor tax, and they enjoyed many other privileges. The Inca rulers, for example, could relax in luxury at Machu Picchu (MAH-choo PEEK-choo). This royal retreat lay nestled high in the Andes.

The people of the lower class in Inca society included farmers, artisans, and servants. There were no slaves, however, because the Incas did not practice slavery. Most Incas were farmers. In the warmer valleys they grew crops such as maize and peanuts. In the cooler mountains they carved terraces into the hillsides and grew potatoes. High in the Andes, people raised llamas—South American animals related to camels—for wool and meat.

Lower-class Incas dressed in plain clothes and lived simply. By law, they could not own more goods than just what they needed to survive. Most of what they made went to the *mita* and the upper class.

Religion

The Inca social structure was partly related to religion. For example, the Incas thought that their rulers were related to the sun god and never really died. As a result, priests brought mummies of former kings to many ceremonies. People gave these royal mummies food and gifts.

Most Incas were farmers. The Incas in this drawing from the mid-1500s are harvesting potatoes.

THE GRANGER COLLECTION, NEW YORK

Inca ceremonies included sacrifices. But unlike the Maya and the Aztecs, the Incas rarely sacrificed humans. They sacrificed llamas, cloth, or food instead.

In addition to practicing the official religion, people outside Cuzco worshipped other gods at local sacred places. The Incas believed certain mountaintops, rocks, and springs had magical powers. Many Incas performed sacrifices at these places as well as at the temple in Cuzco.

Achievements

Inca temples were grand buildings. The Incas were master builders, known for their expert **masonry**, or stonework. They cut stone blocks so precisely that they did not need cement to hold them together. The Incas also built a major network of roads.

The Incas produced works of art as well. Artisans made pottery as well as gold and silver jewelry. They even created a life-sized cornfield of gold and silver, crafting each cob, leaf, and stalk individually. Inca weavers also made some of the finest textiles in the Americas.

FOCUS ON READING

What will be your purpose in reading about Inca achievements?

Inca Arts

Inca arts included beautiful textiles and gold and silver objects.

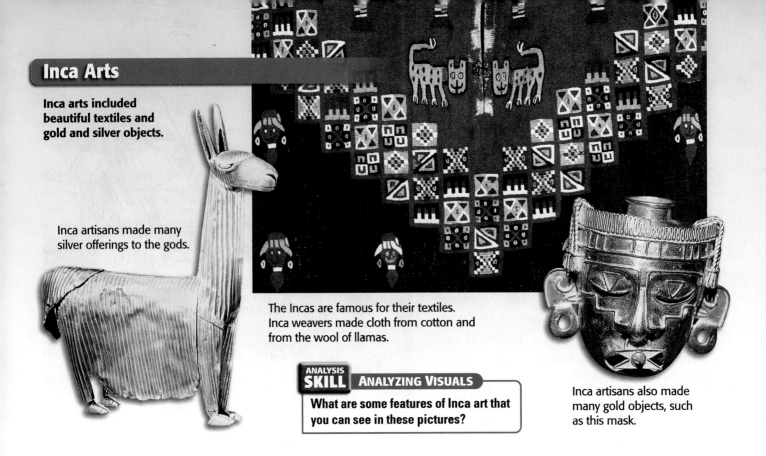

Inca artisans made many silver offerings to the gods.

The Incas are famous for their textiles. Inca weavers made cloth from cotton and from the wool of llamas.

ANALYSIS SKILL **ANALYZING VISUALS**

What are some features of Inca art that you can see in these pictures?

Inca artisans also made many gold objects, such as this mask.

While such artifacts tell us much about the Incas, nothing was written about their empire until the Spanish arrived. Indeed, the Incas had no writing system. Instead, they kept records with knotted cords called *quipus* (KEE-pooz). Knots in the cords stood for numbers. Different colors represented information about crops, land, and other important topics.

The Incas also passed down their stories and history orally. People sang songs and told stories about daily life and military victories. Official "memorizers" learned long poems about Inca legends and history. When the conquistadors arrived, the Inca records were written in Spanish and Quechua. We know about the Incas from these records and from the stories that survive in the songs and religious practices of the people in the region today.

READING CHECK **Contrasting** How did daily life differ for upper- and lower-class Incas?

Pizarro Conquers the Incas

The arrival of conquistadors changed more than how the Incas recorded history. In the late 1520s a civil war began in the Inca Empire after the death of the ruler. Two of the ruler's sons, Atahualpa (ah-tah-WAHL-pah) and Huáscar (WAHS-kahr), fought to claim the throne. Atahualpa won the war in 1532, but fierce fighting had weakened the Inca army.

On his way to be crowned as king, Atahualpa got news that a band of about 180 Spanish soldiers had arrived in the Inca Empire. They were conquistadors led by Francisco Pizarro. When Atahualpa came to meet the group, the Spanish attacked. They were greatly outnumbered, but they caught the unarmed Incas by surprise. They quickly captured Atahualpa and killed thousands of Inca soldiers.

To win his freedom, Atahualpa asked his people to fill a room with gold and silver for Pizarro. Incas brought jewelry, states, and other valuable items from all parts of the empire. Melted down, the gold and silver may have totaled 24 tons. The precious metals would have been worth millions of dollars today. Despite this huge payment, the Spanish killed Atahualpa. They knew that if they let the Inca ruler live, he might rally his people and defeat the smaller Spanish forces.

Some Incas did fight back after the emperor's death. In 1537, though, Pizarro defeated the last of the Incas. Spain took control over the entire Inca Empire and ruled the region for the next 300 years.

READING CHECK **Identifying Cause and Effect** What events ended the Inca Empire?

SUMMARY AND PREVIEW The Incas built a huge empire in South America. But even with a strong central government, they could not withstand the Spanish conquest in 1537. In the next chapters you will learn about how the Americas have changed since the great civilizations of the Maya, Aztecs, and Incas and what these places are like today.

BIOGRAPHY

Atahualpa
(1502–1533)

Atahualpa was the last Inca emperor. He was a popular ruler, but he didn't rule for long. At his first meeting with Pizarro, he was offered a religious book to convince him to accept Christianity. Atahualpa held the book to his ear and listened. When the book didn't speak, Atahualpa threw it on the ground. The Spanish considered this an insult and a reason to attack.

Identifying Bias How do you think the Spanish viewed non-Christians?

BIOGRAPHY

Francisco Pizarro
(1475–1541)

Francisco Pizarro organized expeditions to explore the west coast of South America. His first two trips were mostly uneventful. But on his third trip, Pizarro met the Incas. With only about 180 men, he conquered the Inca Empire, which had been weakened by disease and civil war. In 1535 Pizarro founded Lima, the capital of modern Peru.

Predicting If Pizarro had not found the Inca Empire, what do you think might have happened?

Section 3 Assessment

hmhsocialstudies.com
ONLINE QUIZ

Reviewing Ideas, Terms, and Places

1. **a. Identify** Where was the Inca Empire located? What kinds of terrain did it include?
   b. Evaluate Do you think the *mita* system was a good government policy? Why or why not?
2. **a. Describe** What was a unique feature of Inca **masonry**?
   b. Make Inferences How might the Inca road system have helped strengthen the empire?
3. **a. Recall** When did the Spanish defeat the last of the Incas?
   b. Analyze Why do you think Pizarro was able to defeat the much larger forces of the Incas? Name at least two possible reasons.

Critical Thinking

4. **Analyzing** Draw a diagram like the one below. Using your notes, write a sentence in each box about how that topic influenced the next topic.

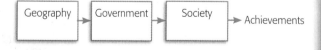

FOCUS ON WRITING

5. **Adding Information about the Inca Empire** Your article would also describe the Inca Empire. Include some comments about how the Incas' building activities related to their environment. Also, note what happened when the Spanish arrived.

North America's Native Cultures

Native Americans once lived all over North America. Their lifestyles varied depending on their local landscapes. Many Native Americans still carry on the traditions of their ancestors.

Far West Native Americans in the Far West relied on the sea for food.

Desert West In the Desert West, Native Americans dealt with their dry, rocky environment by building their homes into the sides of cliffs.

Bering Sea

Inuit
Inuit
Ingalik
Aleut
Saschutkenne
Beaver
Haida
Nootka
Columbia
Plains Cree
Blackfoot
Chinook
ROCKY MOUNTAINS
Walla Walla
Nez Percé
Crow
Northern Paiute
Cheyenne
Modoc
Northern Shoshone
PACIFIC OCEAN
Miwok
Western Shoshone
Ute
Chumash
Hopi (Pueblo)
Apache
Navajo
Mohave
Zuni
Apache
Yaqui
Tarahumara

MESOAMERICA

Arctic and Subarctic In the cold north, Native Americans adapted to life in permanent snow and ice.

Eastern Woodlands The forests of the east provided Native Americans there with good building material.

Great Plains Native Americans moved around the Great Plains in search of good hunting grounds.

Inuit

Inuit

Hudson Bay

Naskapi

Beothuk

Swampy Cree

Montagnais

Micmac

NORTH AMERICA

Algonquian

Pequot Mohegan

Great Lakes

Iroquois

Narraganset

Mohawk

Teton Sioux

Omaha

Powhatan

Shawnee

ATLANTIC OCEAN

Cherokee

Osage

Chickasaw

Kiowa

Comanche
Wichita

Choctaw

Caddo

Seminole

Gulf of Mexico

Caribbean Sea

Arctic and Subarctic
Eastern Woodlands
Great Plains
Desert West
Far West

0   150   300 Miles
0   150   300 Kilometers

Projection: Azimuthal Equal-Area

ANALYSIS SKILL **ANALYZING VISUALS**

1. **Regions** In what region did the Osage live?
2. **Human-Environment Interaction** What resources did Native Americans in the Far West use?

EARLY HISTORY OF THE AMERICAS **31**

Social Studies Skills

Analyzing Information

Learn

An important skill to learn is analyzing information presented in the text you read. One way to do this is to identify main ideas and supporting details. Everything in the paragraph should support the main idea.

After you identify the main idea, watch out for anything that is not related to it or necessary for its understanding. Don't let that extra information distract you from the most important material.

Practice

Look at the paragraph on this page about communication in the Maya civilization. Some unrelated and unnecessary information has been added so that you can learn to identify it. Use the paragraph to answer the questions here.

❶ Which sentence expresses the main idea? What details support it?

❷ What information is unnecessary or unrelated to the main idea?

The Maya

Communication The Maya developed an advanced form of writing that used many symbols. Our writing system uses 26 letters. They recorded information on large stone monuments. Some early civilizations drew pictures on cave walls. The Maya also made books of paper made from the bark of fig trees. Fig trees need a lot of light.

Religion The Maya believed in many gods and goddesses. More than 160 gods and goddesses are named in a single Maya manuscript. Among the gods they worshipped were a corn god, a rain god, a sun god, and a moon goddess. The early Greeks also worshipped many gods and goddesses.

Apply

Use the passage on this page about Maya religion to answer the following questions.

1. What is the main idea of the paragraph?
2. What details support the main idea?
3. What information is unnecessary or unrelated?

Chapter Review

Geography's Impact
video series
Review the video to answer the closing question:
How do archaeologists know the Maya built their pyramids without the aid of metal tools?

Visual Summary

Use the visual summary below to help you review the main ideas of the chapter.

QUICK FACTS

The Maya
The Maya traded valuable goods like jade along trade routes that linked their great cities.

The Aztecs
The Aztec capital, Tenochtitlán, was a huge, bustling city. People came to its marketplace from all over the empire.

The Incas
The Incas are known for their organized empire, impressive stone-work, and crafts in gold and silver.

Reviewing Vocabulary, Terms, and Places

For each statement below, write T if it is true and F if it is false. If the statement is false, replace the underlined term with one that would make the sentence a true statement.

1. The main crops of the Maya included <u>maize</u> and beans.

2. The <u>Quechua</u> came to the Americas to find land, gold, and converts to Catholicism.

3. <u>Palenque</u>, located on a swampy island, was the capital of the Aztec Empire.

4. Maya priests studied the sun, moon, and stars from stone <u>observatories</u>.

5. The official language of the Inca Empire was <u>Cuzco</u>.

6. The Aztecs built raised roads called <u>masonry</u> to cross from Tenochtitlán to the mainland.

7. <u>Tenochtitlán</u> was the Inca capital.

8. Many people in Mesoamerica died at the hands of the <u>conquistadors</u>.

Comprehension and Critical Thinking

SECTION 1 *(Pages 14–19)*

9. **a. Recall** Where did the Maya live, and when was their Classic Age?

   b. Analyze What was the connection between Maya religion and astronomy? How do you think this connection influenced Maya achievements?

   c. Elaborate Why did Maya cities trade with each other? Why did they fight?

SECTION 2 *(Pages 20–24)*

10. **a. Describe** What was Tenochtitlán like? Where was it located?

    b. Make Inferences Why do you think warriors had many privileges and were such respected members of Aztec society?

SECTION 2 (continued)

c. Evaluate What factor do you think played the biggest role in the Aztecs' defeat? Defend your answer.

SECTION 3 (Pages 25–29)

11. a. Identify Name two Inca leaders and explain their roles in Inca history.

b. Draw Conclusions What geographic and cultural problems did the Incas overcome to rule their empire?

c. Elaborate Do you think most people in the Inca Empire appreciated or resented the *mita* system? Explain your answer.

Using the Internet

12. Activity: Making Diagrams In this chapter you learned about the rise and fall of the Maya, Aztecs, and Incas. Through your online text-book, track the rise and fall of empires in the Americas. Then create a diagram that shows the factors that cause empires to form and the factors that cause empires to fall apart.

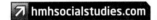

Social Studies Skills

Analyzing Information *In the passage below, the first sentence expresses the main idea. One of the following sentences is nonessential to the main idea. Identify the nonessential sentence.*

13. Cacao beans had great value to the Maya. Cacao trees are evergreens. They were the source of chocolate, known as a favorite food of rulers and the gods. The Maya also used cacao beans as money.

Map Activity

14. Early History of the Americas On a separate sheet of paper, match the letters on the map with their correct labels.

Palenque   Tenochtitlán

Cuzco

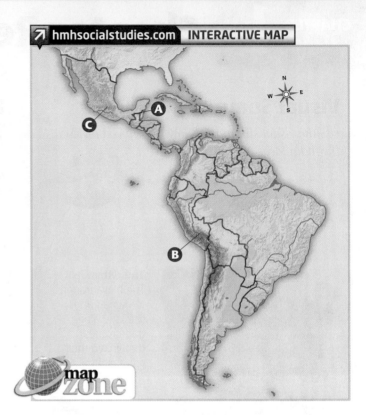

FOCUS ON READING AND WRITING

15. Setting a Purpose Look back over the information about the Maya in Section 1. For each blue heading, write down the purpose of reading that text. Then describe how reading the text below each heading achieves your purpose.

16. Writing Your Article Now that you have collected information about the Americas, you are ready to write a newspaper article. Your purpose is to inform readers in Europe about these fascinating civilizations. Write a headline or title and a two- or three-sentence introduction to the civilizations. Then write a short paragraph about one aspect of each civilization. Choose the most interesting topic to discuss. For example, you might discuss their religion, their social structure, or their scientific achievements.

Standardized Test Prep

DIRECTIONS: Read questions 1 through 6 and write the letter of the best response. Then read question 7 and write your own well-constructed response.

1 Maya, Aztec, and Inca societies were similar in many ways. Which of the following practices was common to all three civilizations?

  A developing calendars

  B keeping written historical records

  C building stone temples

  D practicing slavery

2 Farming was important to the Maya, the Aztecs, and the Incas. Which of the following statements about farming is false?

  A The Maya grew crops on *chinampas*.

  B Farmers in all three civilizations grew maize, but only the Incas raised llamas.

  C Maya farmers might not have been able to produce enough food to feed the entire population.

  D Maya and Aztec priests decided the best times to plant and harvest.

3 Which of the following factors helped the Spanish to conquer the Aztecs and the Incas?

  A a greater number of soldiers

  B superior weapons

  C surprise attacks

  D good knowledge of the land

4 Which of the following was a possible reason for the decline of Maya civilization?

  A increased warfare and lack of good farmland

  B the arrival of Spanish conquistadors and spread of disease

  C the development and misuse of guns

  D floods that destroyed crops and cities

Early Civilizations of the Americas

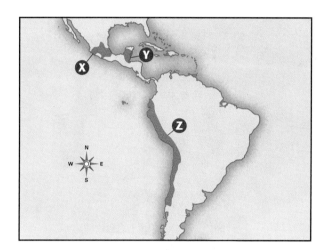

5 The Aztec and Inca empires are indicated on the map above by

  A X for the Inca and Y for the Aztec.

  B Y for the Aztec and Z for the Inca.

  C Y for the Inca and Z for the Aztec.

  D X for the Aztec and Z for the Inca.

6 Which statement *best* describes the social structure in Maya, Aztec, and Inca civilizations?

  A The ruler held the highest position in society, and merchants held the lowest.

  B The Aztecs had a simpler class structure than the Maya or the Incas.

  C Social divisions were very important to the Maya and the Aztecs, but power and wealth were equally distributed in the Inca Empire.

  D Social class helped shape daily life, with the upper class enjoying special privileges made possible by the labor of the common people.

7 **Extended Response** Use the map above and your knowledge of the Maya and Aztecs to write a brief essay comparing and contrasting the two civilizations. Be sure to discuss the physical geography, achievements, and decline of both civilizations.

THE Maya

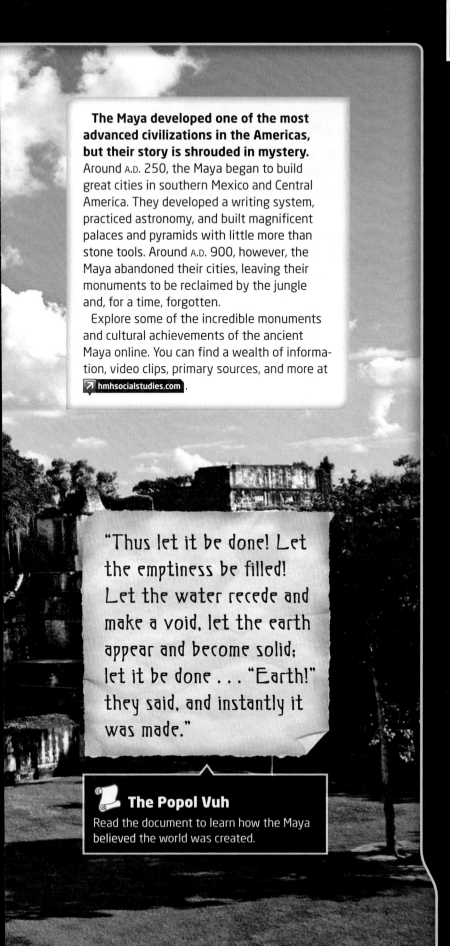

The Maya developed one of the most advanced civilizations in the Americas, but their story is shrouded in mystery. Around A.D. 250, the Maya began to build great cities in southern Mexico and Central America. They developed a writing system, practiced astronomy, and built magnificent palaces and pyramids with little more than stone tools. Around A.D. 900, however, the Maya abandoned their cities, leaving their monuments to be reclaimed by the jungle and, for a time, forgotten.

Explore some of the incredible monuments and cultural achievements of the ancient Maya online. You can find a wealth of information, video clips, primary sources, and more at ↗ hmhsocialstudies.com .

"Thus let it be done! Let the emptiness be filled! Let the water recede and make a void, let the earth appear and become solid; let it be done ... "Earth!" they said, and instantly it was made."

📜 **The Popol Vuh**
Read the document to learn how the Maya believed the world was created.

🎥 **Destroying the Maya's Past**
Watch the video to learn how the actions of one Spanish missionary nearly destroyed the written record of the Maya world.

🎥 **Finding the City of Palenque**
Watch the video to learn about the great Maya city of Palenque and the European discovery of the site in the eighteenth century.

🎥 **Pakal's Tomb**
Watch the video to explore how the discovery of the tomb of a great king helped archaeologists piece together the Maya past.

Mexico

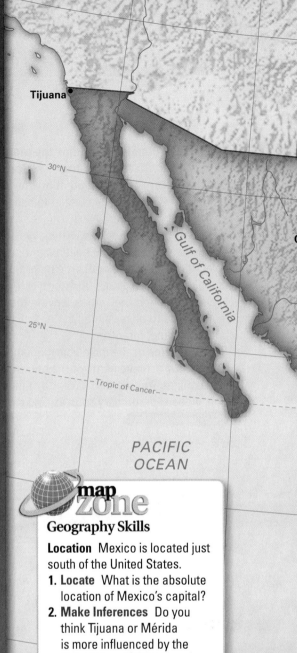

Essential Question What are the major physical, cultural, and economic features of Mexico?

? **What You Will Learn...**

In this chapter you will learn about Mexico's physical geography. You will also study the influence of early cultures and Spanish colonial history on Mexico's culture. Today, Mexico is experiencing many changes in its government and economy.

FOCUS ON READING AND WRITING

Predicting Predicting is trying to guess what will happen next. As you read a chapter, stop along the way and consider what you have read. Does the text provide any clues about what will happen next? If it does, see if you can make a prediction about the text. **See the lesson, Predicting, on page 195.**

Writing an "I Am" Poem Countries have stories to tell, just like people do. As you read this chapter, gather details about Mexico—how it looks, what its history was like, and what it is like today. Then write an "I Am" poem from the point of view of Mexico telling what you have learned.

map zone

Geography Skills

Location Mexico is located just south of the United States.
1. **Locate** What is the absolute location of Mexico's capital?
2. **Make Inferences** Do you think Tijuana or Mérida is more influenced by the United States? Why?

Culture Brightly costumed dancers perform a traditional dance in Cancún.

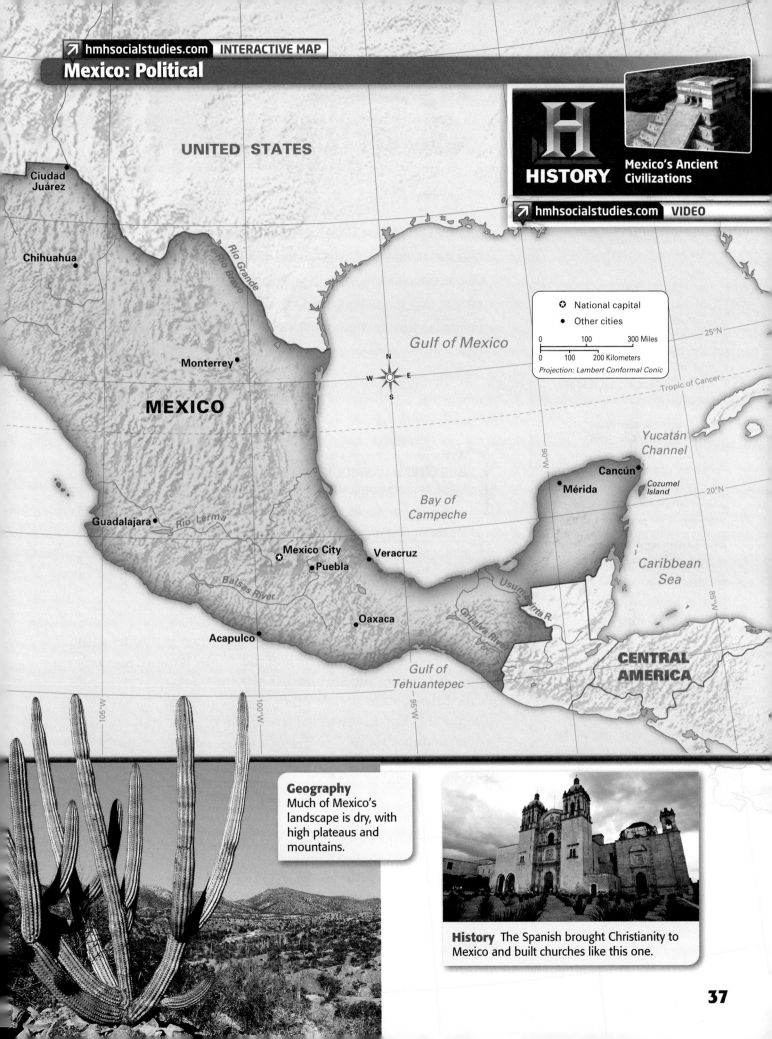

HISTORY Mexico's Ancient Civilizations

hmhsocialstudies.com VIDEO

UNITED STATES

Ciudad Juárez

Chihuahua

Rio Bravo

Rio Grande

Monterrey

MEXICO

Gulf of Mexico

National capital
Other cities

0   100   300 Miles
0 100 200 Kilometers
Projection: Lambert Conformal Conic

25°N

Tropic of Cancer

Yucatán Channel

Cancún

Mérida

Cozumel Island

20°N

Bay of Campeche

Guadalajara

Rio Lerma

Mexico City
Puebla

Veracruz

Caribbean Sea

85°W

Balsas River

Usumacinta R.

Grijalva River

Oaxaca

Acapulco

CENTRAL AMERICA

Gulf of Tehuantepec

105°W

100°W

95°W

90°W

Geography
Much of Mexico's landscape is dry, with high plateaus and mountains.

History The Spanish brought Christianity to Mexico and built churches like this one.

37

Physical Geography

What You Will Learn...

Main Ideas

1. Mexico's physical features include plateaus, mountains, and coastal lowlands.
2. Mexico's climate and vegetation include deserts, tropical forests, and cool highlands.
3. Key natural resources in Mexico include oil, silver, gold, and scenic landscapes.

The Big Idea

Mexico is a large country with different natural environments in its northern, central, and southern regions.

Key Terms and Places

Río Bravo (Rio Grande), *p. 38*
peninsula, *p. 38*
Baja California, *p. 38*
Gulf of Mexico, *p. 38*
Yucatán Peninsula, *p. 38*
Sierra Madre, *p. 39*

hmhsocialstudies.com
TAKING NOTES

Use the graphic organizer online to organize your notes on Mexico's physical geography.

If **YOU** lived there...

You live on Mexico's Pacific coast. Sunny weather and good beaches bring tourists year-round. Now you are on your way to visit a cousin in Puebla, in the highlands. To get there, you will have to take a bus along the winding roads of the steep Sierra Madre Occidental. This rugged mountain range runs along the coast. You have never been to the interior of Mexico before.

What landscapes will you see on your trip?

BUILDING BACKGROUND Mexico is part of Latin America, a region in the Western Hemisphere where Spanish and Portuguese culture shaped life. Mexico is also part of North America, along with the United States and Canada. Unlike its northern neighbors, Mexico's landscape consists mainly of highlands and coastal plains.

Physical Features

Mexico, our neighbor to the south, shares a long border with the United States. Forming part of this border is one of Mexico's few major rivers, the **Río Bravo**. In the United States this river is called the Rio Grande. At other places along the U.S.–Mexico border it is impossible to tell where one country ends and the other country begins.

Bodies of Water

As you can see on the map, except for its border with the United States, Mexico is mostly surrounded by water. Mexico's border in the west is the Pacific Ocean. Stretching south into the Pacific Ocean from northern Mexico is a narrow **peninsula**, or piece of land surrounded on three sides by water, called **Baja California**. To the east, Mexico's border is the **Gulf of Mexico**. The Gulf of Mexico is separated from the Caribbean Sea by a part of Mexico called the **Yucatán** (yoo-kah-TAHN) **Peninsula**.

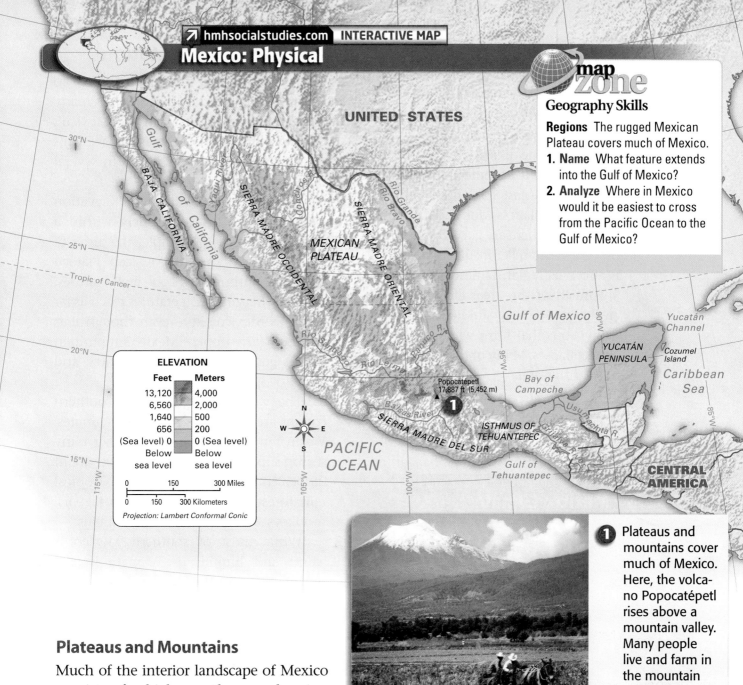

UNITED STATES

Gulf of California

BAJA CALIFORNIA

SIERRA MADRE OCCIDENTAL

Colorado R.

Yaqui River

Rio Grande

Rio Bravo

SIERRA MADRE ORIENTAL

MEXICAN PLATEAU

Rio Santiago

Rio Lerma

Pánuco R.

Balsas River

Popocatépetl
17,887 ft (5,452 m) ▲ **1**

SIERRA MADRE DEL SUR

ISTHMUS OF TEHUANTEPEC

Gulf of Tehuantepec

PACIFIC OCEAN

Gulf of Mexico

Bay of Campeche

Usumacinta R.

Grijalva River

YUCATÁN PENINSULA

Yucatán Channel

Cozumel Island

Caribbean Sea

CENTRAL AMERICA

30°N
25°N
Tropic of Cancer
20°N
15°N
115°W
105°W
100°W
95°W
90°W
85°W

ELEVATION

Feet	Meters
13,120	4,000
6,560	2,000
1,640	500
656	200
(Sea level) 0	0 (Sea level)
Below sea level	Below sea level

0   150   300 Miles
0   150   300 Kilometers

Projection: Lambert Conformal Conic

N W E S

map zone

Geography Skills

Regions The rugged Mexican Plateau covers much of Mexico.
1. **Name** What feature extends into the Gulf of Mexico?
2. **Analyze** Where in Mexico would it be easiest to cross from the Pacific Ocean to the Gulf of Mexico?

1 Plateaus and mountains cover much of Mexico. Here, the volcano Popocatépetl rises above a mountain valley. Many people live and farm in the mountain valleys.

Plateaus and Mountains

Much of the interior landscape of Mexico consists of a high, mostly rugged region called the Mexican Plateau. The plateau's lowest point is more than a half mile above sea level. Its highest point is close to two miles above sea level. The entire plateau spreads between two mountain ranges that rise still higher. One range, the Sierra Madre Oriental, lies in the east. The other, the Sierra Madre Occidental, lies in the west. Together, these two mountain ranges and another shorter one in southern Mexico make up the **Sierra Madre** (SYER-rah MAH-dray), or "mother range."

Between the two ranges in the south lies the Valley of Mexico. Mexico City, the country's capital, is located there. The mountains south of Mexico City include towering, snowcapped volcanoes. Volcanic eruptions, as well as earthquakes, are a threat there. The volcano Popocatépetl (poh-puh-cah-TE-pet-uhl) near Mexico City has been active as recently as 2010.

FOCUS ON READING
What do you think the text will discuss next?

Coastal Lowlands

From the highlands in central Mexico, the land slopes down to the coasts. Beautiful, sunny beaches stretch all along Mexico's eastern and western coasts. The plain that runs along the west coast is fairly wide in the north. It becomes narrower in the south. On the east side of the country, the Gulf coastal plain is wide and flat. The soils and climate there are good for farming.

The Yucatán Peninsula in the southeast is also mostly flat. Limestone rock underlies much of the area. Erosion there has created caves and sinkholes, steep-sided depressions that form when the roof of a cave collapses. Many of these sinkholes are filled with water.

ACADEMIC VOCABULARY

vary to be different

READING CHECK **Summarizing** What are Mexico's major physical features?

Climate and Vegetation

From snowcapped mountain peaks to warm, sunny beaches, Mexico has many different climates. You can see Mexico's climate regions on the map below. This great variety of climates results in several different types of vegetation.

In some areas, changes in elevation cause climates to **vary** widely within a short distance. For example, the areas of high elevation on the Mexican Plateau can have surprisingly cool temperatures. At times, freezing temperatures reach as far south as Mexico City—even though it is located in the tropics. Mexico's mountain valleys generally have mild climates, and many people have settled there.

The valleys along Mexico's southern coastal areas also have pleasant climates. Warm temperatures and a summer rainy season support the forests that cover about 25 percent of Mexico's land area. Tropical rain forests provide a home for jaguars, monkeys, anteaters, and other animals.

While most of southern Mexico is warm and humid, the climate in the northern part of the Yucatán Peninsula is hot and dry. The main vegetation there is scrub forest.

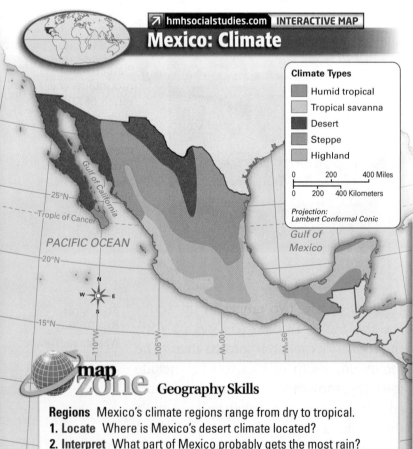

hmhsocialstudies.com **INTERACTIVE MAP**

Mexico: Climate

Climate Types
- Humid tropical
- Tropical savanna
- Desert
- Steppe
- Highland

0   200   400 Miles
0   200   400 Kilometers

Projection:
Lambert Conformal Conic

Gulf of California

25°N
Tropic of Cancer

PACIFIC OCEAN

20°N

N
W   E
S

15°N

110°W 105°W 100°W 95°W

Gulf of Mexico

map zone **Geography Skills**

Regions Mexico's climate regions range from dry to tropical.
1. **Locate** Where is Mexico's desert climate located?
2. **Interpret** What part of Mexico probably gets the most rain?

A Tropical Climate
A tropical savanna climate supports lush vegetation along Mexico's southern beaches.

Like the Yucatán Peninsula in the south, most of northern Mexico is dry. The deserts in Baja California and the northern part of the plateau get little rainfall. Desert plants and dry grasslands are common in the north. Cougars, coyotes, and deer live in some areas of the desert.

READING CHECK **Analyzing** Why does Mexico City sometimes experience freezing temperatures even though it is in the tropics?

Natural Resources

Mexico is rich in natural resources. One of its most important resources is petroleum, or oil. Oil reserves are found mainly under the southern and Gulf coastal plains as well as offshore in the Gulf of Mexico. Mexico sells much of its oil to the United States.

Before oil was discovered in Mexico, minerals were the country's most valuable resource. Some gold and silver mines that were begun many centuries ago are still in operation. In addition, new mines have been developed in Mexico's mountains. Today Mexico's mines produce more silver than any other country in the world. Mexican mines also yield large amounts of copper, gold, lead, and zinc.

Another important resource is water. The refreshing water surrounding Mexico draws many tourists to the country's scenic beaches. Unfortunately, water is limited in many parts of Mexico. Water scarcity is a serious issue.

READING CHECK **Finding Main Ideas** What is one of Mexico's most important resources?

SUMMARY AND PREVIEW The natural environments of Mexico range from arid plateaus in the north to humid, forested mountains in the south. Next, you will study the history and culture of Mexico.

Section 1 Assessment

hmhsocialstudies.com
ONLINE QUIZ

Reviewing Ideas, Terms, and Places

1. **a. Describe** What is the interior of Mexico like?
   b. Analyze Do you think the **Yucatán Peninsula** is a good place for farming? Explain your answer.
2. **a. Recall** What is the climate like in the northern part of the Yucatán Peninsula?
   b. Explain Why can climates sometimes vary widely within a short distance?
   c. Elaborate How do you think climate and vegetation affect where people live in Mexico?
3. **a. Identify** Where are Mexico's oil reserves located?
   b. Make Inferences What problems might water scarcity cause for Mexican citizens?
   c. Elaborate How are Mexico's location, climate, and physical features also natural resources?

Critical Thinking

4. **Categorizing** Draw a chart like the one here. Using your notes, list the geographical features found in northern Mexico and southern Mexico.

	Geography
Northern Mexico	
Southern Mexico	

FOCUS ON WRITING

5. **Telling What Mexico Looks Like** What features of Mexico's physical geography will you include in your "I Am" poem? Write notes about the physical features, climate and vegetation, and natural resources of Mexico.

History and Culture

What You Will Learn...

Main Ideas

1. Early cultures of Mexico included the Olmec, the Maya, and the Aztec.
2. Mexico's period as a Spanish colony and its struggles since independence have shaped its culture.
3. Spanish and native cultures have influenced Mexico's customs and traditions today.

The Big Idea

Native American cultures and Spanish colonization shaped Mexican history and culture.

Key Terms

empire, *p. 43*
mestizos, *p. 44*
missions, *p. 44*
haciendas, *p. 44*

hmhsocialstudies.com
TAKING NOTES

Use the graphic organizer online to organize your notes on Mexico's history and culture.

If **YOU** lived there...

You belong to one of the native Indian peoples in southern Mexico in the early 1500s. Years ago, the Aztec rulers went to war against your people. They took many captives. They have always treated you cruelly. Now some strangers have come from across the sea. They want your people to help them conquer the Aztecs.

**Will you help the strangers fight the Aztecs?
Why or why not?**

BUILDING BACKGROUND Mexico was home to several of the earliest advanced cultures in the Americas. Early farmers there developed crops that became staples in much of North America. Mexico also has valuable minerals, which drew Spanish conquerors and colonists. Spanish culture blended with native Mexican cultures.

Early Cultures

People first came to Mexico many thousands of years ago. As early as 5,000 years ago, they were growing beans, peppers, and squash. They also domesticated an early form of corn. Farming allowed these people to build the first permanent settlements in the Americas.

Early Cultures of Mexico

hmhsocialstudies.com
ANIMATED GEOGRAPHY

Olmec

- The Olmec made sculptures of giant stone heads.
- The heads may have represented rulers or gods.

Olmec

By about 1500 BC the Olmec people in Mexico were living in small villages. The Olmec lived on the humid southern coast of the Gulf of Mexico, where they built temples and giant statues. They also traded carved stones like jade and obsidian with other cultures in eastern Mexico.

Maya

A few hundred years later, the Maya built on the achievements of the Olmec. Between about AD 250 and 900, the Maya built large cities in Mexico and Central America. In these cities they built stone temples to worship their gods. They studied the stars and developed a detailed calendar. They also kept written records that scholars still study today to learn about Maya history. However, scholars do not fully understand why Maya civilization suddenly collapsed sometime after 900.

Aztec

After the decline of the Maya civilization, people called the Aztecs moved to central Mexico from the north. In 1325 they built their capital on an island in a lake. Known as Tenochtitlán (tay-nawch-teet-LAHN), this capital grew into one of the largest and most impressive cities of its time.

The Aztecs also built a large, powerful empire. An **empire** is a land with different territories and peoples under a single ruler.

CONNECTING TO **Technology**

hmhsocialstudies.com
ANIMATED GEOGRAPHY

Chinampas

The Aztecs practiced a form of raised-field farming in the swampy lake areas of central Mexico. They called these raised fields *chinampas*. To make them, Aztec farmers piled earth on rafts anchored to trees in the lake. There they grew the corn, beans, and squash that most people ate.

Analyzing Why do you think the Aztecs decided to build raised fields for their crops?

The Aztecs planted trees in the lake to anchor the rafts.

The Aztecs built their empire through conquest. They defeated their neighboring tribes in war. Then they forced the other people to pay taxes and to provide war captives for sacrifice to the Aztec gods.

READING CHECK **Summarizing** What were some achievements of Mexico's early cultures?

Maya

- The Maya had a trade network between cities.
- This Maya pyramid stands in Uxmal.

Aztec

- The Aztecs built the first empire in the Americas.
- Aztec artisans made art like this turquoise mask.

Colonial Mexico and Independence

FOCUS ON READING
What do you think will happen to the Aztec Empire?

In spite of its great size and power, the Aztec Empire did not last long after the first Europeans landed in Mexico. In 1519 Hernán Cortés, a Spanish soldier, arrived in Mexico with about 600 men. These conquistadors (kahn-KEES-tuh-dawrz), or conquerors, gained allies from other tribes in the region. They also had guns and horses, which the Aztecs had never seen before. The new weapons terrified the Aztecs and gave the Spanish an advantage.

The Spanish also unknowingly brought European diseases such as smallpox. The Aztecs had no resistance to these diseases, so many of them died. Greatly weakened by disease, the Aztecs were defeated. In 1521 Cortés claimed the land for Spain.

Colonial Times

After the conquest, Spanish and American Indian peoples and cultures mixed. This mixing formed a new Mexican identity. Spaniards called people of mixed European and Indian ancestry **mestizos** (me-STEE-zohs). When Africans were brought to America as slaves, they added to this mix of peoples. The Spaniards called people of mixed European and African ancestry mulattoes (muh-LAH-tohs). Africans and American Indians also intermarried.

Life in colonial Mexico was greatly influenced by the Roman Catholic Church. Large areas of northern Mexico were left to the church to explore and to rule. Church outposts known as **missions** were scattered throughout the area. Priests at the missions learned native languages and taught the Indians Spanish. They also worked to convert the American Indians to Catholicism.

In addition to spreading Christianity, the Spaniards wanted to find gold and silver in Mexico. American Indians and enslaved Africans did most of the hard physical labor in the mines. As a result, many died from disease and overwork.

Like mining, agriculture became an important part of the colonial economy. After the conquest, the Spanish monarch granted **haciendas** (hah-see-EN-duhs), or huge expanses of farm or ranch land, to some favored people of Spanish ancestry. Peasants, usually Indians, lived and worked on these haciendas. The haciendas made their owners very wealthy.

Hidalgo Calls for Independence

Miguel Hidalgo (center, in black) calls for independence from Spain in 1810. The famous Mexican painter Juan O'Gorman painted this image.

ANALYZING VISUALS What kinds of people joined Hidalgo in his revolt?

Independence

Spain ruled Mexico for almost 300 years before the people of Mexico demanded independence. The revolt against Spanish rule was led by a Catholic priest named Miguel Hidalgo. In 1810, he gave a famous speech calling for the common people to rise up against the Spanish. Hidalgo was killed in 1811, but fighting continued until Mexico won its independence in 1821.

Later Struggles

Fifteen years after Mexico gained its independence, a large area, Texas, broke away. Eventually, Texas joined the United States. As a result, Mexico and the United States fought over Texas and the location of their shared border. This conflict led to the Mexican-American War, in which Mexico lost nearly half its territory to the United States.

In the mid-1800s, Mexico faced other challenges. During this time, the popular president Benito Juárez helped Mexico survive a French invasion. He also made reforms that reduced the privileges of the church and the army.

In spite of these reforms, in the early 1900s the president helped the hacienda owners take land from peasants. Also, foreign companies owned huge amounts of land in Mexico and, in turn, influenced Mexican politics. Many Mexicans thought the president gave these large landowners too many privileges.

As a result, the Mexican Revolution broke out in 1910. The fighting lasted 10 years. One major result of the Mexican Revolution was land reform. The newly formed government took land from the large landowners and gave it back to the peasant villages.

READING CHECK **Sequencing** What events occurred after Mexico gained independence?

Culture

Mexico's history has **influenced** its culture. For example, one major influence from history is language. Most Mexicans speak Spanish because of the Spanish influence in colonial times. Another influence from Spain is religion. About 90 percent of all Mexicans are Roman Catholic.

However, Mexico's culture also reflects its American Indian heritage. For example, many people still speak American Indian languages. In Mexico, a person's language is tied to his or her ethnic group. Speaking an American Indian language identifies a person as Indian.

Mexicans also have some unique cultural practices that combine elements of Spanish influence with the influence of Mexican Indians. An example of this combining can be seen in a holiday called Day of the Dead. This holiday is a day to remember and honor dead ancestors.

ACADEMIC VOCABULARY

influence change or have an effect on

VIDEO
The Peasant Revolution

hmhsocialstudies.com

Day of the Dead

Everyone is sad when a loved one dies. But during Day of the Dead, Mexicans celebrate death as part of life. This attitude comes from the Mexican Indian belief that the souls of the dead return every year to visit their living relatives. To prepare for this visit, Mexican families gather in graveyards. They clean up around their loved one's grave and decorate it with flowers and candles. They also set out food and drink for the celebration. Favorite foods often include sugar candy skulls, chocolate coffins, and sweet breads shaped like bones.

Summarizing Why do Mexicans celebrate Day of the Dead?

Mexicans celebrate Day of the Dead on November 1 and 2. These dates are similar to the dates that the Catholic Church honors the dead with All Souls' Day. The holiday also reflects native customs and beliefs about hopes of life after death.

READING CHECK **Categorizing** What aspects of Mexican culture show the influence of Spanish rule?

SUMMARY AND PREVIEW Mexico's early cultures formed great civilizations, but after the conquest of the Aztec Empire, power in Mexico shifted to Spain. Spain ruled Mexico for nearly 300 years before Mexico gained independence. Mexico's history and its mix of Indian and Spanish backgrounds have influenced the country's culture. In the next section you will learn about life in Mexico today.

Section 2 Assessment

hmhsocialstudies.com
ONLINE QUIZ

Reviewing Ideas, Terms, and Places

1. **a. Recall** Where in Mexico did the Olmec live?
   b. Explain How did the Aztecs build and rule their empire?
   c. Elaborate Why do you think scholars are not sure what caused the end of Maya civilization?
2. **a. Identify** Who began the revolt that led to Mexico's independence?
   b. Explain What was Mexico like in colonial times?
   c. Predict How may history have been different if the Aztecs had defeated the Spanish?
3. **a. Identify** What Mexican holiday honors dead ancestors?
   b. Summarize How did Mexico's colonial past shape its culture?

Critical Thinking

4. **Sequencing** Draw a diagram like the one below. Then, using your notes, list the major events in Mexico's history in the order they happened.

Mexico gains independence

FOCUS ON WRITING

5. **Learning about History and Culture** Mexico's history is full of fascinating stories. In your notebook, jot down ideas about people and stories from Mexico's history.

Taking Notes

Learn

Taking notes can help you remember what you have learned from your textbook or in class. To be effective, your notes must be clear and organized. One good way to organize your notes is in a chart like the one here. Use the following steps to help you take useful notes:

- Before you read: Divide a page in your notebook into two columns as shown.

- While you read: Write down your notes in phrases or sentences in the large column on the right.

- After you read: Review your notes. Then in the small column on the left, jot down ideas, key terms, or questions in your own words based on the notes you took.

Recall	Notes
New Mexican identity	- Spanish and American Indian cultures mixed. - mestizos - Africans came as slaves.

Influence on Catholic Church	- Life in colonial Mexico was influenced by the Roman Catholic Church.
	  - missions
	    - Priests taught Spanish.

Economy: mining and agriculture	- Spaniards were interested in gold and silver.
	  - American Indians and enslaved Africans worked in mines.
	- Agriculture was important.
	  - haciendas

Practice

Answer the following questions about taking notes.

1 Where should you write your notes while you read or listen in class?

2 How can jotting down key ideas, terms, and questions help you clarify your notes after you take them?

Apply

Look back at Section 1 of this chapter. Divide your paper into two columns and take notes on the section using the suggestions above. Then answer the following questions.

1. What ideas or questions did you write in the Recall column on the left?

2. What are some advantages of taking notes?

Mexico Today

What You Will Learn...

Main Ideas

1. Government has tradition-ally played a large role in Mexico's economy.
2. Mexico has four distinct culture regions.

The Big Idea

Mexico has four culture regions that all play a part in the country's government and economy.

Key Terms and Places

inflation, *p. 48*
slash-and-burn agriculture, *p. 49*
cash crop, *p. 49*
Mexico City, *p. 50*
smog, *p. 50*
maquiladoras, *p. 51*

hmhsocialstudies.com
TAKING NOTES

Use the graphic organizer online to take notes on Mexico's govern-ment and economy.

If YOU lived there...

For many years, your family has lived in a small village in southern Mexico. Jobs are scarce there. Your older brother and sisters talk about moving to a larger city. Big cities may provide some more opportunities, but they can be crowded and noisy. Many people from your village have already gone to the city.

How do you feel about moving to the city?

> **BUILDING BACKGROUND** After Mexico gained independence, many government leaders did not rule democratically. For years the Mexican people had little say in their government. But changes in the 1990s and 2000s led toward more democracy and prosperity.

Government and Economy

Today people in Mexico can vote in certain elections for the first time. People can find jobs in cities and buy their families a home. More children are able to attend school. In recent years, changes in Mexico's government and economy have made improvements like these possible.

Government

Mexico has a democratic government. However, Mexico is not like the United States where different political parties have always competed for power. In Mexico the same political party controlled the government for 71 years. But this control ended in 2000 when Mexicans elected Vicente Fox their president. Fox represented a different political party.

For many years, Mexico's government controlled most of the country's economic activity. Today the government has less control of the economy.

Economy

Mexico is a developing country. It has struggled with debts to foreign banks, unemployment, and inflation. **Inflation** is a rise in prices that occurs when currency loses its buying power.

Although living standards in Mexico are lower than in many other countries, Mexico's economy is growing. The North American Free Trade Agreement (NAFTA), which took effect in 1994, has made trade among Mexico, the United States, and Canada easier. Mexico's agricultural and industrial exports have increased since NAFTA went into effect.

Agriculture Agriculture has long been a key part of the Mexican economy. This is true even though just 13 percent of the land is good for farming. Many farmers in southern Mexico practice **slash-and-burn agriculture**, which is the practice of burning forest in order to clear land for planting.

The high market demand for food in the United States has encouraged many farmers in Mexico to grow cash crops. A **cash crop** is a crop that farmers grow mainly to sell for a profit. Trucks bring cash crops like fruits and vegetables from Mexico to the United States.

Industry Oil is also an important export for Mexico. Many Mexicans work in the oil, mining, and manufacturing industries. These industries are growing.

The fastest-growing industrial centers in Mexico lie along the U.S. border. Because wages are relatively low in Mexico, many U.S. and foreign companies have built factories in Mexico. Mexican workers in these factories assemble goods for export to the United States and other countries. Some Mexican workers also come to the United States to look for jobs that pay more than they can make at home.

Tourism Tourism is another important part of Mexico's economy. Many tourists visit old colonial cities and Maya and Aztec monuments. Coastal cities and resorts such as Cancún and Acapulco are also popular with tourists.

READING CHECK **Summarizing** How is the government's role in the economy changing?

HISTORY

VIDEO
Mexico in the Modern Era

hmhsocialstudies.com

hmhsocialstudies.com

ANIMATED GEOGRAPHY
Resources and Products of Mexico

Satellite View

Smoke

Fire

Many people in Mexico are subsistence farmers. They do not own much land and grow only enough food to feed their families. To gain more land, farmers in southern Mexico burn patches of forest. The fires clear the trees and kill weeds, and ash from the fires fertilizes the soil. However, growing the same crops year after year drains valuable nutrients from the soil. The farmers then have to burn new forest land.

In the satellite image here, agricultural fires appear as red dots. As you can see, the fires create a lot of smoke. Wind then blows the smoke great distances. Every few years, when the conditions are right, smoke from agricultural fires in Mexico reaches as far as the southern United States. The smoke can cause health problems for some people.

Analyzing What direction was the wind blowing in this image?

Northern Mexico Northern Mexico's land is generally too dry to be much good for farming, but ranching is an important part of the region's economy.

ANALYSIS SKILL **ANALYZING INFORMATION**
How do you think life in greater Mexico City differs from life in northern Mexico?

Central Mexico The architecture and cobblestone streets of many towns in central Mexico reflect the region's Spanish colonial heritage.

Mexico's Culture Regions

Although all Mexicans share some cultural characteristics, we can divide Mexico into four regions based on regional differences. These four culture regions differ from each other in their population, resources, climate, and other features.

Greater Mexico City

Greater Mexico City includes the capital and about 50 smaller cities near it. With a population of more than 19 million, **Mexico City** is the world's second-largest city and one of the most densely populated urban areas. Thousands of people move there every year looking for work.

While this region does provide job and educational opportunities not so easily found in the rest of the country, its huge population causes problems. For example, Mexico City is very polluted. Factories and cars release exhaust and other pollutants into the air. The surrounding mountains trap the resulting **smog**—a mixture of smoke, chemicals, and fog. Smog can cause health problems like eye irritation and breathing difficulties.

Another problem that comes from crowding is poverty. Wealth and poverty exist side by side in Mexico City. The city has large urban slums. The slums often exist right next to modern office buildings, apartments, museums, or universities.

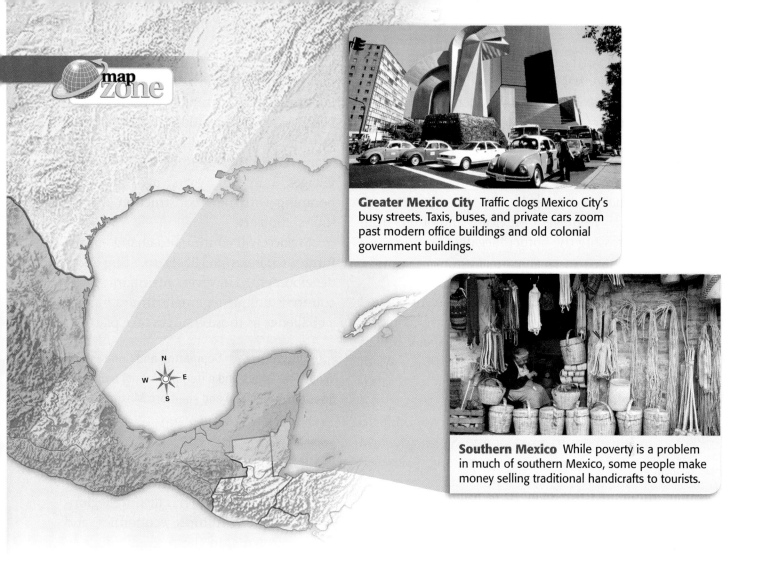

Greater Mexico City Traffic clogs Mexico City's busy streets. Taxis, buses, and private cars zoom past modern office buildings and old colonial government buildings.

Southern Mexico While poverty is a problem in much of southern Mexico, some people make money selling traditional handicrafts to tourists.

Central Mexico

North of greater Mexico City lies Mexico's central region. Many cities in this region were established as mining or ranching centers during the colonial period. Mexico's colonial heritage can still be seen today in these cities and towns. For example, small towns often have a colonial-style church near a main central square. The central square, or plaza, has served for hundreds of years as a community meeting spot and market area.

In addition to small colonial towns, central Mexico has many fertile valleys and small family farms. Farmers in this region grow vegetables, corn, and wheat for sale, mostly to cities in Mexico.

While central Mexico has always been a mining center, in recent years the region has also attracted new industries from overcrowded Mexico City. As a result, some cities in the region, such as Guadalajara, are growing rapidly.

Northern Mexico

Northern Mexico has become one of the country's richest and most modern areas. Trade with the United States has helped the region's economy grow. Monterrey and Tijuana are now major cities there. Many U.S.- and foreign-owned factories called **maquiladoras** (mah-kee-lah-DORH-ahs) have been built along Mexico's long border with the United States.

Northern Mexico's closeness to the border has **affected** the region's culture as well as its economy. American television, music, and other forms of entertainment are popular there. Many Mexicans cross the border to shop, work, or live in the United States. While many people cross the border legally, the U.S. government tries to prevent Mexicans and others from crossing the border illegally.

Southern Mexico

Southern Mexico is the least populated and industrialized region of the country. Many people in this region speak Indian languages and practice traditional ways of life. Subsistence farming and slash-and-burn agriculture are common.

However, southern Mexico is vital to the country's economy. Sugarcane and coffee, two major export crops, grow well in the region's warm, humid climate. Also, oil production along the Gulf coast has increased in recent years. The oil business has brought more industry and population growth to this coastal area of southern Mexico.

Another place in southern Mexico that has grown in recent years is the Yucatán Peninsula. Maya ruins, beautiful sunny beaches, and clear blue water have made tourism a major industry in this area. Many cities that were just tiny fishing villages only 20 years ago are now booming with new construction for the tourist industry.

Mexico will continue to change in the future. Changes are likely to bring more development. However, maintaining the country's unique regional cultures may be a challenge as those changes take place.

READING CHECK Comparing and Contrasting What similarities and differences exist between greater Mexico City and southern Mexico?

SUMMARY AND PREVIEW Mexico has a democratic government and a growing economy. It also has distinct regions with different cultures, economies, and environments. In the next chapter you will learn about the countries to the south of Mexico.

Section 3 Assessment

hmhsocialstudies.com
ONLINE QUIZ

Reviewing Ideas, Terms, and Places

1. a. Define What is the term for the practice of burning forest in order to clear land for planting?
b. Compare and Contrast How is Mexico's government similar to and different from the government of the United States?
2. a. Identify What is an environmental problem found in **Mexico City**?
b. Make Inferences What conditions in Mexico lead some Mexicans to cross the border into the United States?
c. Develop If you were to start a business in Mexico, what type of business would you start and where would you start it? Explain your decisions.

Critical Thinking

3. Finding Main Ideas Review your notes on Mexico's economy. Then use a chart like this one to show what parts of the economy are important in each region.

Greater Mexico City	Central Mexico	Northern Mexico	Southern Mexico

FOCUS ON WRITING

4. Describing Mexico Today Write some details about the four culture regions of Mexico. Which details will you include in your poem?

Chapter Review

Geography's Impact
video series
Review the video to answer the closing question:
Do you think emigration from Mexico to the United States hurts or helps Mexico? Why?

Visual Summary

Use the visual summary below to help you review the main ideas of the chapter.

QUICK FACTS

The physical geography of Mexico includes a high region of plateaus and mountains.

The Spanish conquered the Aztecs and ruled Mexico for about 300 years until the Mexicans gained independence.

Greater Mexico City, one of Mexico's four culture regions, is the center of Mexico's government and economy.

Reviewing Vocabulary, Terms, and Places

Unscramble each group of letters below to spell a term that matches the given definition.

1. **pmreie**—a land with different territories and peoples under a single ruler
2. **tflinnaoi**—a rise in prices that occurs when currency loses its buying power
3. **mogs**—a mixture of smoke, chemicals, and fog
4. **snipluane**—a piece of land surrounded on three sides by water
5. **ztosemsi**—people of mixed European and Indian ancestry
6. **hacs rpoc**—a crop that farmers grow mainly to sell for a profit
7. **ssnmiosi**—church outposts
8. **dqamiuarsloa**—U.S.- and foreign-owned factories in Mexico
9. **ndhceiasa**—expanses of farm or ranch land

Comprehension and Critical Thinking

SECTION 1 *(Pages 38–41)*

10. **a. Define** What is the Mexican Plateau? What forms its edges?

   b. Contrast How does the climate of Mexico City differ from the climate in the south?

   c. Evaluate What do you think would be Mexico's most important resource if it did not have oil? Explain your answer.

SECTION 2 *(Pages 42–46)*

11. **a. Recall** What early civilization did the Spanish conquer when they came to Mexico?

   b. Analyze How did Spanish rule influence Mexico's culture?

   c. Evaluate Which war—the war for independence, the Mexican War, or the Mexican Revolution—do you think changed Mexico the most? Explain your answer.

SECTION 3 (Pages 48–52)

12. **a. Describe** What are Mexico's four culture regions? Describe a feature of each.

   b. Analyze What regions do you think are the most popular with tourists? Explain your answer.

   c. Evaluate What are two major drawbacks of slash-and-burn agriculture?

Using the Internet 21ST CENTURY

13. **Activity: Writing a Description** Colorful textiles, paintings, and pottery are just some of the many crafts made throughout Mexico. Each region in Mexico has its own style of crafts and folk art. Through your online textbook, visit some of the different regions of Mexico and explore their arts and crafts. Pick a favorite object from each region. Learn about its use, its design, how it was made, and the people who made it. Then write a brief paragraph that describes each object and its unique characteristics.

hmhsocialstudies.com

Social Studies Skills

14. **Taking Notes** Look back at the information in Section 3 about Mexico's government and economy. Then use a chart like this one to take notes on the information in your book.

Recall	Notes

Map Activity 21ST CENTURY

15. **Mexico** On a separate sheet of paper, match the letters on the map with their correct labels.

   Gulf of Mexico   Baja California
   Río Bravo (Rio Grande)   Tijuana
   Yucatán Peninsula   Mexico City

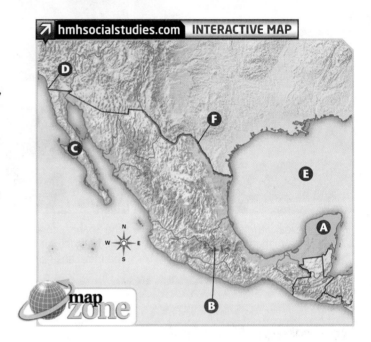
hmhsocialstudies.com   INTERACTIVE MAP

map zone

16. **Predicting** Now you can use your skills in predicting to think about events that might happen in the future. Reread the text in your book about Mexico's economy. Write three to four sentences about how you think the economy might change in the future.

17. **Writing an "I Am" Poem** Now it is time to write your poem. Title your poem "I am Mexico" and make it six lines long. Use each line to give details about Mexico, such as "I have towering, snowcapped volcanoes." Make sure at least one line deals with physical geography, one line with history and culture, and one line with Mexico today. Your poem does not need to rhyme, but you should try to use vivid language.

CHAPTER 2

Standardized Test Prep

DIRECTIONS: Read questions 1 through 6 and write the letter of the best response. Then read question 7 and write your own well-constructed response.

1 **What physical features make up much of central Mexico?**

A plateaus and mountains

B peninsulas

C beaches and lowlands

D sinkholes

2 **What early culture in Mexico did the Spanish conquer?**

A Olmec

B Maya

C Aztec

D conquistador

3 **Which of the following was a way in which the Spanish affected Mexico during colonial times?**

A granted land to the native people

B set up missions and taught about Christianity

C started the Mexican Revolution

D gave away half of Mexico to the United States

4 **Where are Mexico's fastest-growing industrial centers?**

A on the Gulf coast

B in Mexico City

C on the Yucatán Peninsula

D along the U.S. border

5 **What factor helps classify Mexico as a developing country?**

A high unemployment

B few political parties

C an economy based on oil and tourism

D relatively high living standards

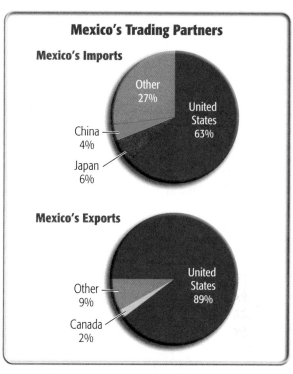

Mexico's Trading Partners

Mexico's Imports

Other 27%
China 4%
Japan 6%
United States 63%

Mexico's Exports

Other 9%
Canada 2%
United States 89%

Source: *World Almanac and Book of Facts,* 2005

6 **Based on the graphs above, which of the following statements is false?**

A The United States is Mexico's biggest trading partner.

B The United States imports 63% of its goods from Mexico.

C 89% of Mexico's exports go to the United States.

D Imports from Japan make up 6% of Mexico's total imports.

7 **Extended Response** Look at the graphs above and the information in Section 3. Then write a brief essay explaining how NAFTA has influenced Mexico.

Mexico

Teotihuacán, established around 200 B.C., was the first great civilization of ancient Mexico. At its height around the middle of the first millennium A.D., the "City of the Gods" was one of the largest cities in the world. It covered 12 square miles and was home to some 200,000 people. The Pyramid of the Sun, above, was the largest building in Teotihuacán.

For centuries after the fall of Teotihuacán, present-day Mexico was home to a number of great empires, including the highly sophisticated Aztec civilization. The arrival of the Spanish in the early 1500s forever changed life for Mexico's ancient peoples, and Mexican culture today is dominated by a blend of indigenous and Spanish cultures.

Explore the history of Mexico from ancient to modern times online. You can find a wealth of information, video clips, primary sources, activities, and more at ⏃ hmhsocialstudies.com .

The Arrival of the Spanish
Watch the video to learn how the arrival of the conquistadors led to the fall of the Aztec Empire.

Miguel Hidalgo's Call to Arms
Watch the video to learn about Miguel Hidalgo's path from priest to revolutionary leader.

Mexico in the Modern Era
Watch the video to learn about the role of oil in the industrialization of Mexico's economy.

Mexico's Ancient Civilizations
Watch the video to learn about the great civilizations that arose in ancient Mexico.

Central America and the Caribbean

Essential Question How have Central America and the Caribbean been shaped by geography and history?

? What You Will Learn...

In this chapter you will learn about the beautiful physical landscapes of Central America and the Caribbean. You will also study the history of the region along with the people who live there and the way they live today.

FOCUS ON READING & WRITING

Understanding Comparison-Contrast When you compare, you look for ways in which things are alike. When you contrast, you look for ways in which things are different. As you read the chapter, look for ways you can compare and contrast information. **See the lesson, Understanding Comparison-Contrast, on page 196.**

Creating a Travel Guide People use travel guides to learn more about places they want to visit. As you read about Central America and the Caribbean in this chapter, you will collect information about places tourists might visit. Then you will create your own travel guide for visitors to one of these vacation spots.

Gulf of Mexico

MEXICO

Belmopan
BELIZE

GUATEMALA
Guatemala
City
Motagua R.
HONDURAS
Tegucigalpa
Coco River

San Salvador
EL SALVADOR
PACIFIC
OCEAN
Managua
NICARAGUA
San
Juan
River

COSTA RICA
San José

○ National capital

0   100   200 Miles
0   100   200 Kilometers

Projection: Azimuthal Equal-Area

History The Spanish built forts like this one in Puerto Rico to defend their islands and protect the harbors from pirates.

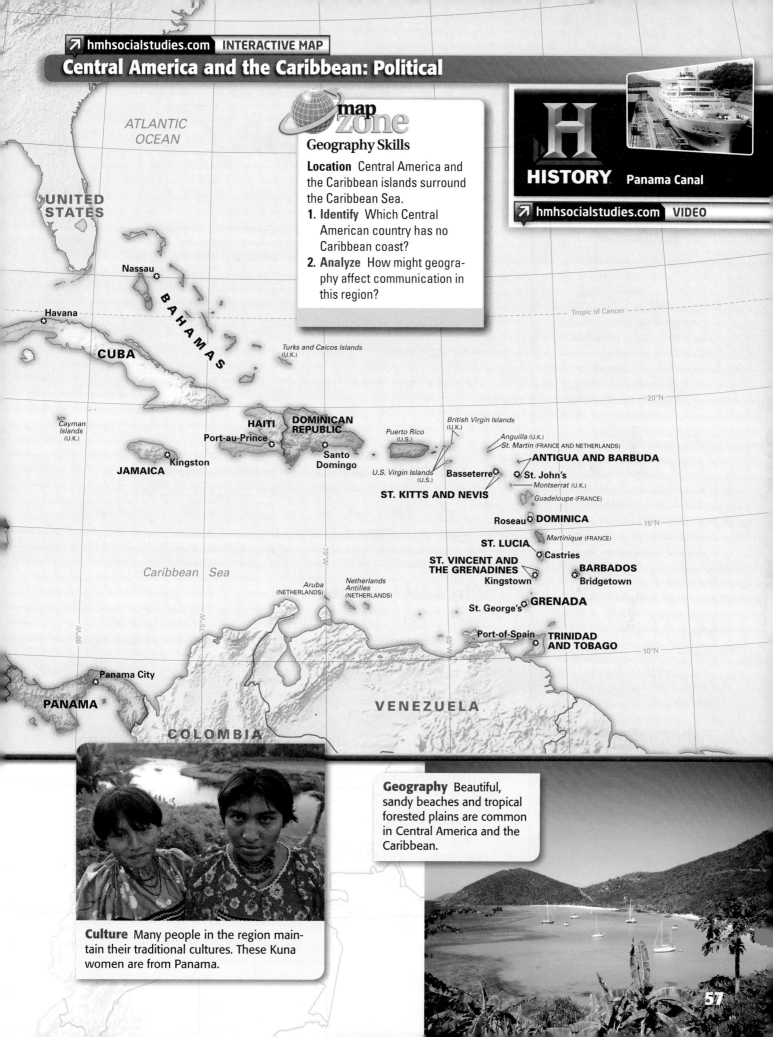

Central America and the Caribbean: Political

map zone

Geography Skills

Location Central America and the Caribbean islands surround the Caribbean Sea.

1. **Identify** Which Central American country has no Caribbean coast?
2. **Analyze** How might geography affect communication in this region?

HISTORY Panama Canal

↗ hmhsocialstudies.com **VIDEO**

ATLANTIC OCEAN

UNITED STATES

Nassau ✪

BAHAMAS

Havana ⊙

CUBA

Turks and Caicos Islands (U.K.)

Tropic of Cancer

Cayman Islands (U.K.)

HAITI

Port-au-Prince ⊙

DOMINICAN REPUBLIC ✪

Puerto Rico (U.S.)

British Virgin Islands (U.K.)

Anguilla (U.K.)
St. Martin (FRANCE AND NETHERLANDS)

20°N

Kingston ✪

JAMAICA

Santo Domingo

U.S. Virgin Islands (U.S.)

Basseterre ✪

ANTIGUA AND BARBUDA

St. John's ✪

ST. KITTS AND NEVIS

Montserrat (U.K.)

Guadeloupe (FRANCE)

Roseau ✪ DOMINICA

15°N

ST. LUCIA

Martinique (FRANCE)

Castries ✪

Caribbean Sea

ST. VINCENT AND THE GRENADINES

Kingstown ✪

BARBADOS
Bridgetown

Aruba (NETHERLANDS)

Netherlands Antilles (NETHERLANDS)

St. George's ✪ GRENADA

80°W 75°W 70°W 65°W

Port-of-Spain ✪

TRINIDAD AND TOBAGO

10°N

Panama City ✪

PANAMA

VENEZUELA

COLOMBIA

Culture Many people in the region maintain their traditional cultures. These Kuna women are from Panama.

Geography Beautiful, sandy beaches and tropical forested plains are common in Central America and the Caribbean.

57

Physical Geography

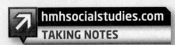
If YOU lived there...

You live in San José, the capital of Costa Rica. But now you are visiting a tropical forest in one of the country's national parks. You make your way carefully along a swinging rope bridge in the forest canopy—40 feet above the forest floor! You see a huge green iguana making its way along a branch. A brilliantly colored parrot flies past you.

What other creatures might you see in the forest?

BUILDING BACKGROUND Nearly all the countries of Central America and the Caribbean lie in the tropics. That means they generally have warm climates and tropical vegetation. Many people like to visit these countries because of their physical beauty.

Physical Features

Sandy beaches, volcanic mountains, rain forests, clear blue water—these are images many people have of Central America and the Caribbean islands. This region's physical geography is beautiful. This beauty is one of the region's greatest resources.

Central America

The region called Central America is actually the southern part of North America. Seven countries make up this region: Belize, Guatemala, Honduras, El Salvador, Nicaragua, Costa Rica, and Panama. As you can see on the map, Central America is an **isthmus**, or a narrow strip of land that connects two larger land areas. No place on this isthmus is more than about 125 miles (200 km) from either the Pacific Ocean or the **Caribbean Sea**.

A chain of mountains and volcanoes separates the Pacific and Caribbean coastal plains, and only a few short rivers flow through Central America. The ruggedness of the land and the lack of good water routes make travel in the region difficult.

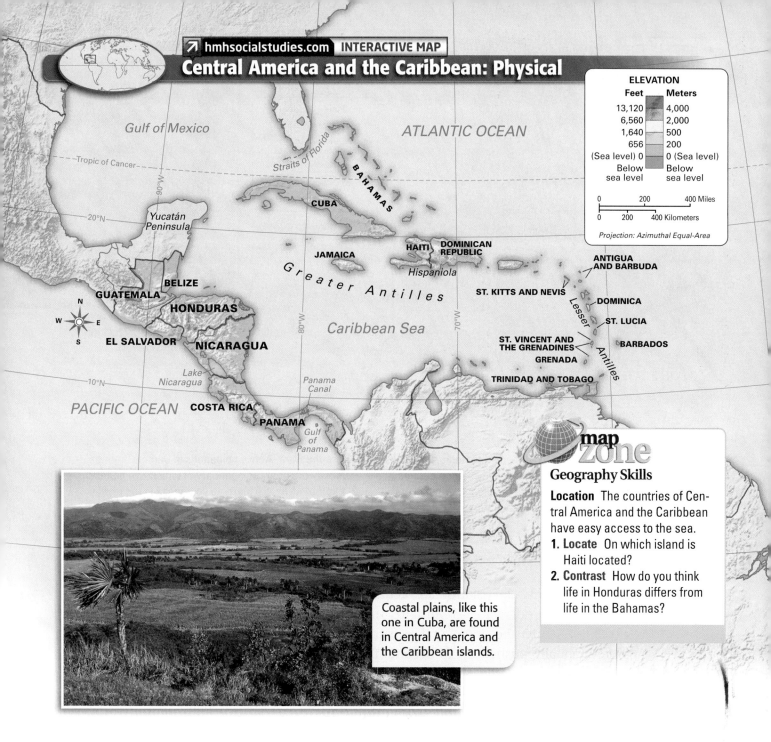

Gulf of Mexico

ATLANTIC OCEAN

Tropic of Cancer

Straits of Florida

BAHAMAS

CUBA

20°N

Yucatán Peninsula

90°W

JAMAICA

HAITI

DOMINICAN REPUBLIC

Hispaniola

ANTIGUA AND BARBUDA

Greater Antilles

ST. KITTS AND NEVIS

DOMINICA

BELIZE

GUATEMALA

HONDURAS

80°W

Caribbean Sea

70°W

Lesser Antilles

ST. LUCIA

BARBADOS

EL SALVADOR

NICARAGUA

ST. VINCENT AND THE GRENADINES

GRENADA

Lake Nicaragua

Panama Canal

TRINIDAD AND TOBAGO

10°N

PACIFIC OCEAN

COSTA RICA

PANAMA

Gulf of Panama

N W E S

ELEVATION

Feet		Meters
13,120		4,000
6,560		2,000
1,640		500
656		200
(Sea level) 0		0 (Sea level)
Below sea level		Below sea level

0   200   400 Miles

0   200   400 Kilometers

Projection: Azimuthal Equal-Area

Coastal plains, like this one in Cuba, are found in Central America and the Caribbean islands.

map zone

Geography Skills

Location The countries of Central America and the Caribbean have easy access to the sea.

1. **Locate** On which island is Haiti located?
2. **Contrast** How do you think life in Honduras differs from life in the Bahamas?

The Caribbean Islands

Across the Caribbean Sea from Central America lie hundreds of islands known as the Caribbean islands. They make up an **archipelago** (ahr-kuh-PE-luh-goh), or large group of islands. Arranged in a long curve, the Caribbean islands stretch from the southern tip of Florida to northern South America. They divide the Caribbean Sea from the Atlantic Ocean.

There are two main island groups in the Caribbean. The four large islands of Cuba, Jamaica, Hispaniola, and Puerto Rico make up the **Greater Antilles** (an-TI-leez). Many smaller islands form the **Lesser Antilles**. They stretch from the Virgin Islands to Trinidad and Tobago. A third island group, the Bahamas, lies in the Atlantic Ocean southeast of Florida. It includes nearly 700 islands and thousands of reefs.

FOCUS ON READING

How are the Greater and Lesser Antilles different?

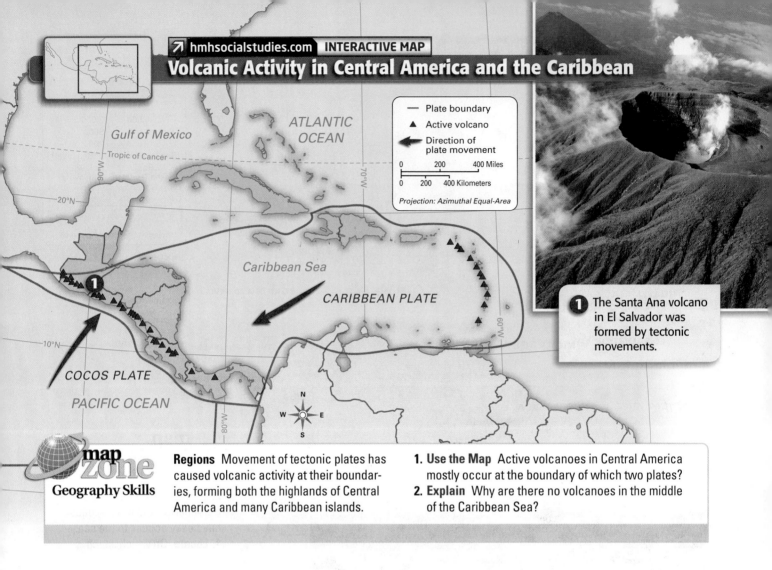

Volcanic Activity in Central America and the Caribbean

ATLANTIC OCEAN

Gulf of Mexico

Tropic of Cancer

20°N

Caribbean Sea

CARIBBEAN PLATE

10°N

COCOS PLATE

PACIFIC OCEAN

— Plate boundary
▲ Active volcano
← Direction of plate movement

0   200   400 Miles
0 200 400 Kilometers

Projection: Azimuthal Equal-Area

1 The Santa Ana volcano in El Salvador was formed by tectonic movements.

map zone
Geography Skills

Regions Movement of tectonic plates has caused volcanic activity at their boundaries, forming both the highlands of Central America and many Caribbean islands.

1. Use the Map Active volcanoes in Central America mostly occur at the boundary of which two plates?
2. Explain Why are there no volcanoes in the middle of the Caribbean Sea?

Many Caribbean islands are actually the tops of underwater mountains and volcanoes. Others began as coral reefs that were gradually pushed up to become flat limestone islands. Colliding tectonic plates have pushed this region's land up out of the sea over several million years. You can see these tectonic plates on the map above. Notice how the land follows the boundaries of the plates. Earthquakes and volcanic eruptions occur frequently as these plates shift. When such events do occur, they can cause great damage to the region and its people.

READING CHECK **Comparing** What physical features do Central America and the Caribbean islands have in common?

Climate and Vegetation

Central America and the Caribbean islands are generally sunny and warm. Humid tropical and tropical savanna climates are common in the islands and on Central America's coastal plains. On the Pacific coast, much of the area's original savanna vegetation has been cleared. It has been replaced by plantations and ranches. The opposite coast, along the Caribbean, has areas of tropical rain forest.

Inland mountain areas contain cool, humid climates. Some mountainous parts of Central America are covered with dense cloud forest. A **cloud forest** is a moist, high-elevation tropical forest where low clouds are common. These forests are home to numerous plant and animal species.

Temperatures in most of Central America and the Caribbean do not change much from day to night or from summer to winter. Instead, the change in seasons is marked by a change in rainfall. Winters in the region are generally dry, while it rains nearly every day during the summers.

From summer to fall, hurricanes are a threat in the region. These tropical storms bring violent winds, heavy rain, and high seas. Most hurricanes occur between June and November. Their winds and flooding can cause destruction and loss of life.

READING CHECK **Generalizing** Where would one find the coolest temperatures in the region?

Resources

The region's best resources are its land and climate. These factors make tourism an important industry. They also influence agriculture. Agriculture in the region can be profitable where volcanic ash has enriched the soil. Coffee, bananas, sugarcane, and cotton grow well and are major crops. Timber is exported from the rain forests.

Although its land and climate make good agricultural resources, the region has few mineral resources. Energy resources are also limited. Central America and the Caribbean islands must rely on energy imports, which limits their development.

READING CHECK **Analyzing** Why would having few energy resources limit economic development?

SUMMARY AND PREVIEW Central America and the Caribbean islands share volcanic physical features and a warm, tropical climate good for agriculture. In the next section you will learn about the history and culture of Central America.

Satellite View

Strong hurricane winds spin around a calm center point called the eye.

Hurricane Isabel

Hurricanes are rotating storms that bring heavy rain and winds that can reach speeds higher than 155 miles per hour (249 kph). This image shows Hurricane Isabel sweeping through the Caribbean Sea in 2003. Strong hurricanes like this one can shatter houses and hurl cars through the air.

Analyzing How can you tell the storm is rotating?

Section 1 Assessment

hmhsocialstudies.com
ONLINE QUIZ

Reviewing Ideas, Terms, and Places
1. **a. Define** What is an **isthmus**?
   b. Explain How has tectonic activity affected Central America and the Caribbean islands?
2. **a. Describe** What is a **cloud forest**?
   b. Make Inferences Why do temperatures in the region change little from summer to winter?
3. **a. Recall** What crops grow well in the region?
   b. Evaluate Do you think tourists who want to go to the beach are more likely to visit Guatemala or the Bahamas? Explain your answer.

Critical Thinking
4. **Categorizing** Draw a diagram like the one here. Using your notes, write descriptive phrases about the physical features, climate, and resources of both places.

Central America	Caribbean Islands

FOCUS ON WRITING

5. **Writing about Geography** What information about the physical geography of the region might interest readers of your travel guide? Jot down some ideas.

Central America

If YOU lived there...

You live in El Salvador, in a town that is still living with the effects of a civil war 20 years ago. Your parents and your older neighbors still speak about those years with fear. One effect of the war was damage to the economy. Many people have gone to Mexico to try to make a better life. Now your parents are talking about going there to look for work. But you are not sure.

How do you feel about leaving your home?

BUILDING BACKGROUND All the countries of Central America were once colonies of European nations. Years of colonial rule made it hard for most of these countries to establish strong economies or democratic governments. Today things are slowly improving.

History

Many countries of Central America have a shared history. This shared history has been influenced by the Maya, the Spanish, and the United States.

Early History

In several Central American countries, the Maya were building large cities with pyramids and temples by about AD 250. The Maya abandoned most of their cities around 900, but the ruins of many ancient cities still stand in the region today. People of Maya descent still live in Guatemala and Belize. In fact, many ancient Maya customs still influence modern life there.

Hundreds of years later, in the early 1500s, most of Central America came under European control. Spain claimed most of the region. Britain claimed what is now Belize and also occupied part of Nicaragua's coast. The Spanish established large plantations in their colonies to grow crops like tobacco and sugarcane. They made Central American Indians work on the plantations or in gold mines elsewhere in the Americas. In addition, Europeans brought many enslaved Africans to the region to work on plantations and in mines.

One-Crop Economies

The economies of many Central American countries relied on only one crop—bananas. The U.S.-based United Fruit Company was the biggest banana exporter and the largest employer in the region for many years. The old photo below shows the company's hiring hall in Guatemala.

ANALYZING VISUALS Why do workers place cushions between bananas?

Central America Since Independence

The Spanish colonies of Central America declared independence from Spain in 1821, but much of the region remained joined together as the United Provinces of Central America. The countries of Costa Rica, Nicaragua, Honduras, El Salvador, and Guatemala separated from each other in 1838 to 1839. Panama remained part of Colombia until 1903. Belize did not gain independence from Britain until 1981.

For most countries in Central America, independence brought little change. The Spanish officials left, but wealthy landowners continued to run the countries and their economies. The plantation crops of bananas and coffee supported Central American economies.

In the early to mid-1900s, one landowner in particular, the U.S.-based United Fruit Company, controlled most of the banana production in Central America. To help its business, the company developed railroads and port facilities. This kind of development helped transportation and communications in the region.

Many people resented the role of foreign companies, however. They thought it was wrong that only a few people should own so much land while many people struggled to make a living. In the mid- to late 1900s, demands for reforms led to armed struggles in Guatemala, El Salvador, and Nicaragua. Only in recent years have these countries achieved peace.

READING CHECK **Evaluating** How did Spain influence the region's history?

Culture

Central America's colonial history has influenced its culture. The region's people, languages, religion, and festivals reflect both Spanish and native practices.

People and Languages

Most of the people in Central America are mestizos, or people of mixed European and Indian ancestry. Various Indian peoples descended from the ancient Maya live in places such as the Guatemalan Highlands.

People of African ancestry also make up a significant minority in this region. They live mostly along the Caribbean coast.

In some countries in Central America, many people still speak the native Indian languages. In places that were colonized by England, English is spoken. For example, it is the official language of Belize. In most countries, however, Spanish is the official language. The Spanish colonization of Central America left this lasting mark on the region.

Close-up

A Market in Guatemala

Villages in Guatemala and all over Central America hold weekly markets. On market day, people come from all around to buy and sell food and other items. The market is also an important gathering spot for the community. Scenes like this one are typical in the region.

The Catholic church is a major influence in most towns.

Patterns on women's clothing are unique to the village where the woman lives.

Religion, Festivals, and Food

Many Central Americans practice a religion brought to the region by Europeans. Most people are Roman Catholic because Spanish missionaries taught the Indians about Catholicism. However, Indian traditions have influenced Catholicism in return. Also, Protestant Christians are becoming a large minority in places such as Belize.

Religion has influenced celebrations in towns throughout the region. For example, to celebrate special saints' feast days, some people carry images of the saint in parades through the streets. Easter is a particularly important holiday. Some towns decorate whole streets with designs made of flowers and colorful sawdust.

During festivals, people eat **traditional** foods. Central America shares some of its traditional foods, like corn, with Mexico. The region is also known for tomatoes, hot peppers, and cacao (kuh-KOW), which is the source of chocolate.

READING CHECK **Contrasting** How is Belize culturally different from the rest of the region?

ACADEMIC VOCABULARY

traditional
customary, time-honored

Tourists contribute to the local economy when they buy crafts.

People often spend all day at the market and need to eat lunch there.

ANALYSIS SKILL **ANALYZING VISUALS**

How do the contributions of tourists and Guatemalans affect the local economy differently?

Central America Today

The countries of Central America share similar histories and cultures. However, they all face their own economic and political challenges today. In 2005 Costa Rica, the Dominican Republic, El Salvador, Guatemala, Honduras, and Nicaragua signed the Central American Free Trade Agreement (CAFTA) with the United States to help increase trade among the countries.

Guatemala

Guatemala is the most populous country in Central America. More than 13 million people live there. About 60 percent of Guatemalans are mestizo and European. About 40 percent are Central American Indians. Many speak Maya languages.

Most people in Guatemala live in small villages in the highlands. Fighting between rebels and government forces there killed some 200,000 people between 1960 and 1996. Guatemalans are still recovering from this conflict.

Coffee, which grows well in the cool highlands, is Guatemala's most important crop. The country also is a major producer of cardamom, a spice used in Asian foods.

Belize

Belize has the smallest population in Central America. The country does not have much land for agriculture, either. But **ecotourism**—the practice of using an area's natural environment to attract tourists—has become popular lately. Tourists come to see the country's coral reefs, Maya ruins, and coastal resorts.

Honduras

Honduras is a mountainous country. Most people live in mountain valleys and along the northern coast. The rugged land makes transportation difficult and provides little land where crops can grow. However, citrus fruits and bananas are important exports.

El Salvador

In El Salvador, a few rich families own much of the best land while most people live in poverty. These conditions were a reason behind a long civil war in the 1980s. A **civil war** is a conflict between two or more groups within a country. The war killed many people and hurt the economy.

El Salvador's people have been working to rebuild their country since the end of the war in 1992. One advantage they have in this rebuilding effort is the country's fertile soil. People are able to grow and export crops such as coffee and sugarcane.

Nicaragua

Nicaragua has also been rebuilding since the end of a civil war. In 1979, a group called the Sandinistas overthrew a dictator.

Many Nicaraguans supported the Sandinistas, but rebel forces aided by the United States fought the Sandinistas for power. The civil war ended in 1990 when elections ended the rule of the Sandinistas. Nicaragua is now a democracy.

Costa Rica

Unlike most other Central American countries, Costa Rica has a history of peace. It also has a stable, democratic government. The country does not even have an army. Peace has helped Costa Rica make progress in reducing poverty.

Agricultural products like coffee and bananas are important to Costa Rica's economy. Also, many tourists visit Costa Rica's rich tropical rain forests.

Panama

Panama is the narrowest, southernmost country of Central America. Most people live in areas near the **Panama Canal**. Canal fees and local industries make the canal area the country's most prosperous region.

The Panama Canal provides a link between the Pacific Ocean, the Caribbean Sea, and the Atlantic Ocean. The United States finished building the canal in 1914. For years the Panama canal played an important role in the economy and politics of the region. The United States controlled the canal until 1999. Then, as agreed to in a treaty, Panama finally gained full control of the canal.

READING CHECK Drawing Inferences Why do you think Panama might want control of the canal?

FOCUS ON READING
What word in the paragraphs on Costa Rica signals contrast?

SUMMARY AND PREVIEW Native peoples, European colonizers, and the United States have influenced Central America's history and culture. Today most countries are developing stable governments. Their economies rely on tourism and agriculture. In the next section you will learn about the main influences on the Caribbean islands and life there today.

Section 2 Assessment

Reviewing Ideas, Terms, and Places

1. **a. Recall** What parts of Central America did the British claim?
   b. Analyze How did independence affect most Central American countries?
   c. Elaborate What benefits and drawbacks might there be to the United Fruit Company's owning so much land?
2. **a. Identify** What language do most people in Central America speak?
   b. Explain How have native cultures influenced cultural practices in the region today?
3. **a. Define** What is a **civil war,** and where in Central America has a civil war been fought?
   b. Explain Why might some people practice **ecotourism**?
   c. Elaborate Why is the **Panama Canal** important to Panama? Why is it important to other countries?

Critical Thinking

4. **Summarizing** Copy the graphic organizer below. Using your notes, write at least one important fact about each Central American country today.

Guatemala	
Belize	
Honduras	
El Salvador	
Nicaragua	
Costa Rica	
Panama	

FOCUS ON WRITING

5. **Describing Central America** Note details about the history, culture, and life today of people in Central America. Which details will appeal to people who are thinking of visiting the region?

The Panama Canal

The Panama Canal links the Atlantic and Pacific oceans. Built in the early 1900s, workers on the canal faced tropical diseases and the dangers of blasting through solid rock. The result of their efforts was an amazing feat of engineering. Today some 13,000 to 14,000 ships pass through the canal each year.

Routes Before and After the Panama Canal

map zone

San Francisco
New York

NORTH AMERICA

ATLANTIC OCEAN

5,200 MILES (8,368 KM)

Panama Canal

13,000 MILES (20,921 KM)

PACIFIC OCEAN

SOUTH AMERICA

— Route around South America

— Route through the Panama Canal

| 0 | 750 | 1,500 Miles |

| 0 | 750 | 1,500 Kilometers |

Projection: Azimuthal Equal-Area

N W E S

The Panama Canal shortens a trip from the east coast of the United States to the west coast by about 8,000 miles (15,000 km).

Crossing a Continent

The Panama Canal takes ships from sea level, across a mountain range, and back to sea level.

Caribbean Sea

Gatún Locks

Pedro Miguel Locks

Miraflores Locks

Gatún Lake

Pacific Ocean

Trains help guide large ships through the canal.

These locks act as doors to different compartments of the canal. Underground pumps raise and lower the water in each compartment like an elevator.

HISTORY VIDEO Panama Canal

↗ hmhsocialstudies.com

ANALYSIS SKILL **ANALYZING VISUALS**

1. Why was Panama a good location for a canal?
2. Why must ships be raised and lowered in order to get through the canal?

The Caribbean Islands

What You Will Learn...

Main Ideas

1. The history of the Caribbean islands includes European colonization followed by independence.
2. The culture of the Caribbean islands shows signs of past colonialism and slavery.
3. Today the Caribbean islands have distinctive governments with economies that depend on agriculture and tourism.

The Big Idea

The Caribbean islands have a rich history and culture influenced by European colonization.

Key Terms and Places

dialect, *p. 72*
commonwealth, *p. 73*
refugee, *p. 73*
Havana, *p. 74*
cooperative, *p. 74*

hmhsocialstudies.com
TAKING NOTES

Use the graphic organizer online to organize your notes on the Caribbean islands.

If YOU lived there...

You are a young sailor on Christopher Columbus's second voyage to the New World. The year is 1493. Now that your ship is in the Caribbean Sea, you are sailing from island to island. You have seen volcanoes and waterfalls and fierce natives. Columbus has decided to establish a trading post on one of the islands. You are part of the crew who will stay there.

What do you expect in your new home?

BUILDING BACKGROUND In the late 1400s and early 1500s, European nations began to compete for colonies. Sailing for Spain, Christopher Columbus made four voyages to the Americas. He and his men discovered and explored many islands.

History

When Christopher Columbus discovered America in 1492, he actually discovered the Caribbean islands. These islands now include 13 independent countries. The countries themselves show the influence of those first European explorers.

Early History

Christopher Columbus first sailed into the Caribbean Sea from Spain in 1492. He thought he had reached the Indies, or the islands near India. Therefore, he called the Caribbean islands the West Indies and the people who lived there Indians.

Spain had little interest in the smaller Caribbean islands, but the English, French, Dutch, and Danish did. In the 1600s and 1700s, these countries established colonies on the islands. They built huge sugarcane plantations that required many workers. Most Caribbean Indians had died from disease, so Europeans brought Africans to work as slaves. Soon Africans and people of African descent outnumbered Europeans on many islands.

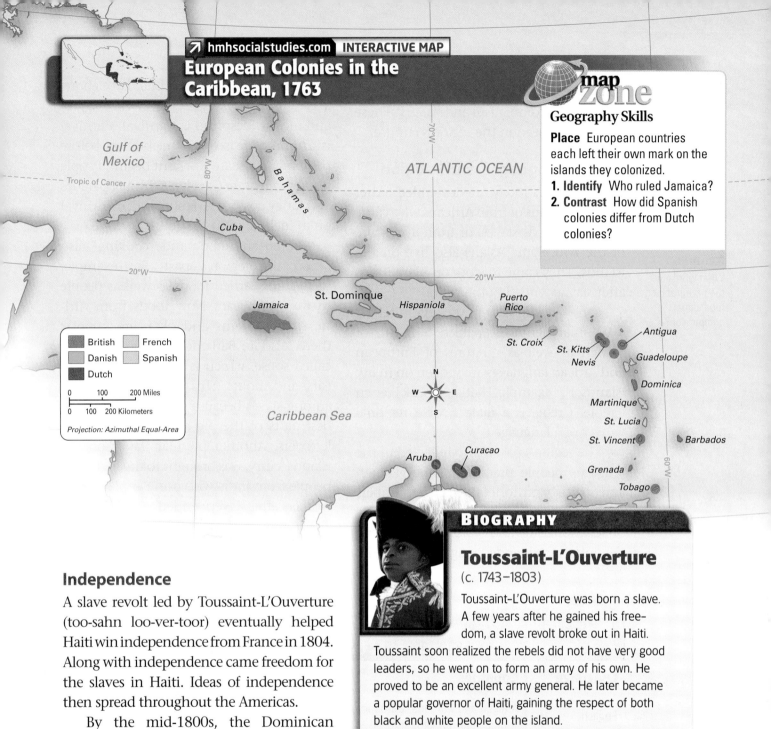

European Colonies in the Caribbean, 1763

↗ hmhsocialstudies.com **INTERACTIVE MAP**

Gulf of Mexico

Tropic of Cancer

ATLANTIC OCEAN

Bahamas

Cuba

Jamaica

St. Dominque

Hispaniola

Puerto Rico

St. Croix

St. Kitts
Nevis

Antigua

Guadeloupe

Dominica

Martinique

St. Lucia

St. Vincent

Barbados

Grenada

Tobago

Aruba

Curacao

Caribbean Sea

Legend:
- British
- French
- Danish
- Spanish
- Dutch

0   100   200 Miles
0   100   200 Kilometers
Projection: Azimuthal Equal-Area

map zone

Geography Skills

Place European countries each left their own mark on the islands they colonized.
1. **Identify** Who ruled Jamaica?
2. **Contrast** How did Spanish colonies differ from Dutch colonies?

Independence

A slave revolt led by Toussaint-L'Ouverture (too-sahn loo-ver-toor) eventually helped Haiti win independence from France in 1804. Along with independence came freedom for the slaves in Haiti. Ideas of independence then spread throughout the Americas.

By the mid-1800s, the Dominican Republic had gained independence. The United States won Cuba from Spain, but Cuba gained independence in 1902. The other Caribbean countries did not gain independence until more than 40 years later, after World War II. At that time, the Europeans transferred political power peacefully to most of the islands.

Many Caribbean islands still are not independent countries. For example, the islands of Martinique and Guadeloupe are still French possessions. Each has its own elected government and is also represented in the French government. Most people on these islands seem not to wish for independence from their ruling countries.

BIOGRAPHY

Toussaint-L'Ouverture
(c. 1743–1803)

Toussaint-L'Ouverture was born a slave. A few years after he gained his freedom, a slave revolt broke out in Haiti. Toussaint soon realized the rebels did not have very good leaders, so he went on to form an army of his own. He proved to be an excellent army general. He later became a popular governor of Haiti, gaining the respect of both black and white people on the island.

READING CHECK **Identifying Points of View**
Why might an island's people not be interested in gaining independence?

Culture

Today nearly all Caribbean islands show signs of past colonialism and slavery. These signs can be seen in the region's culture.

People, Languages, and Religion

FOCUS ON READING
What words in the paragraph on food signal comparison?

Most islanders today are descended either from Europeans or from Africans who came to the region as slaves, or from a mixture of the two. Some Asians also live on the islands. They came to work on plantations after slavery ended in the region.

Languages spoken in the region reflect a colonial heritage. Spanish, English, or French as well as mixtures of European and African languages are spoken on many islands. For example, Haitians speak French Creole. Creole is a **dialect**, or a regional variety of a language.

The region's past is also reflected in the religions people practice. Former French and Spanish territories have large numbers of Catholics. People also practice a blend of Catholicism and traditional African religions. One blended religion is Santería.

Festivals and Food

People on the Caribbean islands celebrate a variety of holidays. One of the biggest and most widespread is Carnival. Carnival is a time of feasts and celebration before the Christian season of Lent begins. People usually celebrate Carnival with big parades and fancy costumes. Festivals like Carnival often include great music.

Caribbean food and cooking also reflect the region's past. For example, slave ships carried foods as well as people to the Caribbean. Now foods from Africa, such as yams and okra, are popular there. Also, in Barbados, people eat a dish called souse, which is made of pigs' tails, ears, and snouts. This dish was developed among slaves because slaveholders ate the best parts of the pig and gave slaves the leftovers. Another popular flavor on the islands, curry, was brought to the region by people from India who came as plantation workers after slavery ended.

READING CHECK **Generalizing** How does Caribbean culture reflect African influences?

THE WORLD ALMANAC Facts about Countries: Languages of the Caribbean

Language	Countries
English	Antigua and Barbuda, Barbados, Trinidad and Tobago
Creole English	Saint Kitts and Nevis, Grenada, Jamaica, Bahamas
Creole French	Haiti, Dominica, Saint Lucia
Spanish	Cuba, Puerto Rico, Dominican Republic

Interpreting Charts What language do people speak in Barbados?

BIBLIOTHEQUE UNIVERSITAIRE

hmhsocialstudies.com

CONNECTING TO the Arts

Caribbean Music

The Caribbean islands have produced many unique styles of music. For example, Jamaica is famous as the birthplace of reggae. Merengue is the national music and dance of the Dominican Republic. Trinidad and Tobago is the home of steel-drum and calypso music.

Here, a band in the Grenadines performs on steel drums. Steel-drum bands can include as few as 4 or as many as 100 musicians. The instruments are actually metal barrels like the kind used for shipping oil. The end of each drum is hammered into a curved shape with multiple grooves and bumps. Hitting different-sized bumps results in different notes.

Drawing Inferences What role might trade have played in the development of steel-drum music?

The Caribbean Islands Today

Many Caribbean islands share a similar history. Still, each island has its own economy, government, and culture.

Puerto Rico

Once a Spanish colony, Puerto Rico today is a U.S. commonwealth. A **commonwealth** is a self-governing territory associated with another country. Puerto Ricans are U.S. citizens, but they do not have voting representation in Congress.

Overall, Puerto Rico's economy has benefitted from U.S. aid and investment. Still, wages are lower and unemployment is higher on the island than in the United States. Many Puerto Ricans have moved to the United States for better paying jobs. Today, Puerto Ricans debate whether their island should remain a U.S. commonwealth, become an American state, or become an independent nation.

Haiti

Haiti occupies the western part of the island of Hispaniola. Haiti's capital, Port-au-Prince, is the center of the nation's limited industry. Most Haitians farm small plots. Coffee and sugarcane are among Haiti's main exports.

Haiti is the poorest country in the Americas. Its people have suffered under a string of corrupt governments during the last two centuries. Violence, political unrest, and poverty have created many political refugees. A **refugee** is someone who flees to another country, usually for political or economic reasons. Many Haitian refugees have come to the United States.

On January, 12, 2010, a catastrophic earthquake struck close to Port-au-Prince. The quake devastated Haiti, leaving about 230,000 Haitians dead, 300,000 injured, and over a million homeless. Today, many Haitians continue working to rebuild their lives and nation.

Dominican Republic

The Dominican Republic occupies the eastern part of Hispaniola. The capital is Santo Domingo. Santo Domingo was the first permanent European settlement in the Western Hemisphere.

The Dominican Republic is not a rich country. However, its economy, health care, education, and housing are more developed than Haiti's. Agriculture is the basis of the economy in the Dominican Republic. The country's tourism industry has also grown in recent years. Beach resorts along the coast are popular with many tourists from Central and South America as well as from the United States.

Cuba

Cuba is the largest and most populous country in the Caribbean. It is located just 92 miles (148 km) south of Florida. **Havana**, the capital, is the country's largest and most important city.

Cuba has been run by a Communist government since Fidel Castro came to power in 1959. At that time, the government took over banks, large sugarcane plantations, and other businesses. Many of these businesses were owned by U.S. companies. Because of the takeovers, the U.S. government banned trade with Cuba and restricted travel there by U.S. citizens.

Today the government still controls the economy. Most of Cuba's farms are organized as cooperatives or government-owned plantations. A **cooperative** is an organization owned by its members and operated for their mutual benefit.

Besides controlling the economy, Cuba's government also controls all the newspapers, television, and radio stations. While many Cubans support these policies, others oppose them. Some people who oppose the government have become refugees in the United States. Many Cuban refugees have become U.S. citizens.

Cubans Divided

Government-sponsored rallies are a part of Cuban life. Meanwhile, some Cubans try to flee their country on tiny rafts.

ANALYZING VISUALS How can you tell that the people in the raft are trying to flee Cuba?

Other Islands

The rest of the Caribbean islands are small countries. Jamaica is the largest of the remaining Caribbean countries. The smallest country is Saint Kitts and Nevis. It is not even one-tenth the size of Rhode Island, the smallest U.S. state!

A number of Caribbean islands are not independent countries but territories of other countries. These territories include the U.S. and British Virgin Islands. The Netherlands and France also still have some Caribbean territories.

Some of these islands have enough land to grow some coffee, sugarcane, or spices. However, most islands' economies are based on tourism. Hundreds of people on the islands work in restaurants and hotels visited by tourists. While tourism has provided jobs and helped economies, not all of its effects have been positive. For example, new construction sometimes harms the same natural environment tourists come to the islands to enjoy.

READING CHECK **Contrasting** How are the governments of Puerto Rico and Cuba different?

Caribbean Tourism

Tourism has helped Caribbean economies. New developments, like this hotel in Saint Martin, have also changed many islands' landscapes.

SUMMARY AND PREVIEW The Caribbean islands were colonized by European countries, which influenced the culture of the islands. Today the islands have different types of governments but similar economies. Next, you will read about countries in South America that are also located near the Caribbean Sea.

Section 3 Assessment

Reviewing Ideas, Terms, and Places

1. **a. Describe** What crop was the basis of the colonial economy on the Caribbean islands?
   b. Make Inferences Why do you think most smaller Caribbean countries were able to gain independence peacefully?
2. **a. Define** What is a **dialect**?
   b. Explain In what ways have African influences shaped Caribbean culture?
3. **a. Recall** What is a **refugee**, and from what Caribbean countries have refugees come?
   b. Make Inferences Why do you think many Cubans support their government's policies?
   c. Evaluate What would be the benefits and drawbacks for Puerto Rico if it became a U.S. state?

Critical Thinking

4. **Summarizing** Look over your notes. Then use a diagram like this one to note specific influences on the region and where they came from in each circle. You may add more circles if you need to.

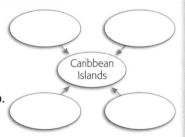

Caribbean Islands

FOCUS ON WRITING

5. **Telling about the Caribbean Islands** These islands have a fascinating history and a rich culture. Take notes about them for your travel guide.

Social Studies Skills

Interpreting a Climate Graph

Learn

A climate graph is a visual representation of the climate in a certain region. The graph shows the average precipitation and average temperature for each month of the year.

Use the following tips to help you interpret a climate graph:

- The months of the year are labeled across the bottom of the graph.
- The measurements for monthly average temperatures are found on the left side of the graph.
- The measurements for monthly average precipitation are found on the right side of the graph.

Practice

Use the climate graph here to answer the following questions.

1 What four months get the highest amount of precipitation?

2 What months get fewer than two inches of precipitation?

3 What is the average temperature in February?

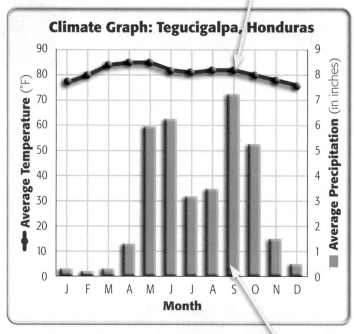

A line shows the average temperature each month.

Climate Graph: Tegucigalpa, Honduras

Source: The Weather Channel Interactive, Inc.

Bars show the average precipitation each month.

Apply

Using the Internet, an almanac, or a newspaper, look up the monthly average temperatures and precipitation for your home town. Then make your own climate graph using that information.

Chapter Review

Geography's Impact
video series
Review the video to answer the closing question:
Why do so many visitors to the Caribbean come from the United States and Canada?

Visual Summary

Use the visual summary below to help you review the main ideas of the chapter.

QUICK FACTS

The region's landscapes include warm coastal lowlands and cool highland regions with tropical forests.

Native cultures still influence Central America. Today governments and economies there are changing.

The Caribbean islands have a history of colonial rule. Today many countries' economies there depend on tourism.

Reviewing Vocabulary, Terms, and Places

Choose one word from each word pair to correctly complete each sentence below.

1. A(n) _____ is a narrow strip of land that connects two larger land areas. **(archipelago/ isthmus)**

2. A _____ is a self-governing territory associated with another country. **(commonwealth/ cooperative)**

3. A _____ is someone who flees to another country, usually for political or economic reasons. **(traditional/refugee)**

4. The United States controlled the _____ until 1999. **(Caribbean Sea/Panama Canal)**

5. The large islands of Cuba, Jamaica, Hispaniola, and Puerto Rico make up the _____. **(Greater Antilles/Lesser Antilles)**

6. _____ is found in the mountainous part of Central America. **(Cloud forest/Havana)**

Comprehension and Critical Thinking

SECTION 1 *(Pages 58–61)*

7. **a. Describe** What process has formed many of the Caribbean islands? Describe the effect this process has on the region today.

   b. Compare and Contrast How are summer and winter similar in Central America and the Caribbean? How are the seasons different?

   c. Elaborate What kinds of damage might hurricanes cause? What damage might earthquakes and volcanic eruptions cause?

SECTION 2 *(Pages 62–67)*

8. **a. Identify** In what Central American country is English the official language?

   b. Make Inferences Why do you think people of African ancestry live mainly along the coast?

   c. Elaborate How might recent political conflict have affected development in some countries?

SECTION 3 (Pages 70–75)

9. a. Recall What country was the first to gain independence? Who led the revolt that led to independence?

b. Analyze How does tourism impact the smaller islands of the Caribbean?

c. Evaluate What might be some benefits and drawbacks of working for a cooperative?

Social Studies Skills

Interpreting a Climate Graph *Use the climate graph below to answer the questions that follow.*

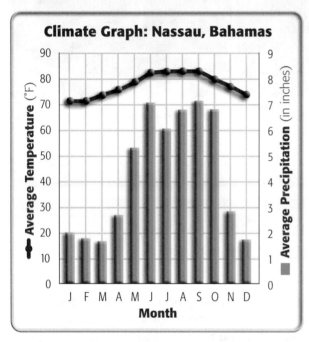

Source: The Weather Channel Interactive, Inc.

10. What two months get the most rainfall?

11. What is the average temperature in December?

Using the Internet 21ST CENTURY

12. Activity: Taking an Ecotour Ecotourism is all about visiting places to appreciate the environment. Through your online textbook, take your own Internet ecotour of Central America and the Caribbean islands. Visit the Web sites to learn more about some of the people and places you have read about in this chapter. Then create a postcard from a place you visited on your trip.

Map Activity 21ST CENTURY

13. Central America and the Caribbean On a separate sheet of paper, match the letters on the map with their correct labels.

Guatemala	Caribbean Sea
Panama	Puerto Rico
Havana, Cuba	Lesser Antilles

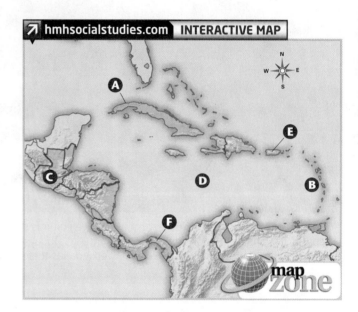

FOCUS ON READING AND WRITING

14. Understanding Comparison-Contrast Look back over the section on physical geography. Then write a paragraph comparing and contrasting Central America with the Caribbean islands. Consider their physical features, climates, landscapes, and resources.

15. Creating a Travel Guide Choose one place in this region to be the subject of your travel guide. Then look over your notes for facts about that place to interest your reader. Your guide should begin with a paragraph describing the outstanding physical features of the place. Your second paragraph should identify interesting details about its history and culture. End with a sentence that might encourage your readers to visit. Include two images in your guide to show off the features of the place you have chosen.

Standardized Test Prep

DIRECTIONS: Read questions 1 through 7 and write the letter of the best response. Then read question 8 and write your own well-constructed response.

1 **Which country is an example of an isthmus?**

A Guatemala

B Bahamas

C Panama

D Cuba

2 **Which European country established the most colonies in the Greater Antilles?**

A France

B Spain

C England

D Netherlands

3 **Which country has a Communist government?**

A Cuba

B Puerto Rico

C Dominican Republic

D Haiti

4 **Which of the following countries has remained at peace since independence?**

A Guatemala

B El Salvador

C Nicaragua

D Costa Rica

5 **Which of the following sentences about the region's economy is false?**

A Coffee and bananas are major export crops.

B The region has good energy resources.

C The region's climate, land, and history attract many tourists.

D Most countries have limited economic development.

Languages of Central America

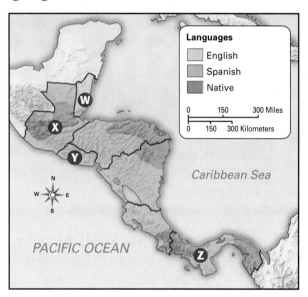

6 **On the map above, which letter represents the country where English is spoken?**

A W

B X

C Y

D Z

7 **On the map above, which letters represent countries whose people speak either Spanish or a native language?**

A W and X

B X and Y

C Y and Z

D X and Z

8 **Extended Response** Using the map above and your knowledge of Central America, write a description of influences on culture in Central America today.

Caribbean South America

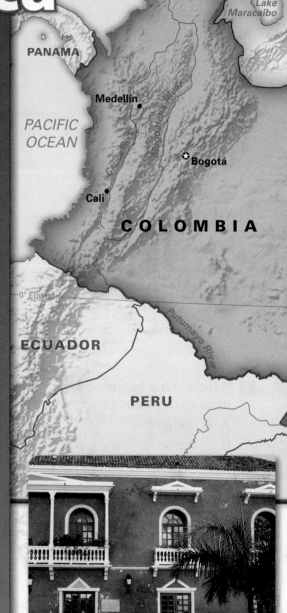

Caribbean Sea

Barranquilla
Cartagena
Maracaibo
Lake Maracaibo

PANAMA

Medellín

PACIFIC OCEAN

Bogotá

Cali

COLOMBIA

0° Equator

ECUADOR

PERU

Essential Question What challenges have the countries of Caribbean South America faced since gaining their independence?

? What You Will Learn...

In this chapter you will learn about the physical geography, history, and cultures of Colombia, Venezuela, Guyana, Suriname, and French Guiana. These countries make up the region of Caribbean South America.

FOCUS ON READING AND WRITING

Identifying Supporting Details Supporting details are the facts and examples that provide information to support the main ideas of a chapter, section, or paragraph. At the beginning of each section in this book, there is a list of main ideas. As you read this chapter, look for the details that support each section's main ideas. **See the lesson, Identifying Supporting Details, on page 197.**

Writing a Letter You live in a country in Caribbean South America. Your pen pal in the United States has asked you to write a letter telling her about life in your region. As you read this chapter, collect details to include in your letter. Your friend will want to know about your country as well as the whole region.

History The architecture of Cartagena, Colombia, reflects the city's Spanish colonial past.

Caribbean South America: Political

- ✪ National capital
- ★ Other capitals
- • Other cities

0   100   200 Miles
0   100   200 Kilometers
Projection: Azimuthal Equal-Area

ATLANTIC OCEAN

60°W

Caracas ✪
Valencia •

TRINIDAD AND TOBAGO

V E N E Z U E L A

Orinoco River

Georgetown ✪

Paramaribo ✪

Cayenne ★

G U Y A N A

FRENCH GUIANA
(FRANCE)

S U R I N A M E

Orinoco River

50°W

Rio Negro

B R A Z I L

Amazon River

map zone

Geography Skills

Place Most of Caribbean South America is located on the Caribbean Sea.

1. **Identify** What is the capital of Venezuela?
2. **Contrast** How is Colombia's location different from Venezuela's location?

Culture Cowboys called llaneros work on the plains of Venezuela.

Geography Dense rain forest covers much of Suriname.

81

Physical Geography

What You Will Learn...

Main Ideas

1. Caribbean South America has a wide variety of physical features and wildlife.
2. The region's location and elevation both affect its climate and vegetation.
3. Caribbean South America is rich in resources, such as farmland, oil, timber, and rivers for hydroelectric power.

The Big Idea

Caribbean South America is a region with diverse physical features, wildlife, climates, and resources.

Key Terms and Places

Andes, *p. 82*
cordillera, *p. 82*
Guiana Highlands, *p. 83*
Llanos, *p. 83*
Orinoco River, *p. 84*

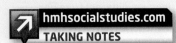

hmhsocialstudies.com
TAKING NOTES

Use the graphic organizer online to take notes on the physical geography of Caribbean South America.

If **YOU** lived there...

You live in Caracas, Venezuela, but this is your first visit to the great Orinoco River. You've heard about the fierce creatures that live in the river, so you think your guide is kidding when he says he's going to catch a piranha. You're expecting a monster and are surprised when he pulls up a small orange fish. It has many sharp teeth, but it's only seven inches long!

What other animals might you see in the region?

BUILDING BACKGROUND The narrow Isthmus of Panama joins the continent of South America at its northwestern corner, the country of Colombia. Like the countries of Central America, the five countries in Caribbean South America border the Caribbean Sea. They all vary in landscape, climate, and culture and have large rivers and rugged mountains.

Physical Features and Wildlife

If you were traveling through the region of Caribbean South America, you might see the world's highest waterfall, South America's largest lake, and even the world's largest rodent! As you can see on the map, the geography of this region includes rugged mountains, highlands, and plains drained by huge river systems.

Mountains and Highlands

The highest point in the region is in Colombia, a country larger than California and Texas combined. On the western side of Colombia the **Andes** (AN-deez) reach 18,000 feet (5,490 m). The Andes form a **cordillera** (kawr-duhl-YER-uh), a mountain system made up of roughly parallel ranges. Some of the Andes' snowcapped peaks are active volcanoes. Eruptions and earthquakes shake these mountains frequently.

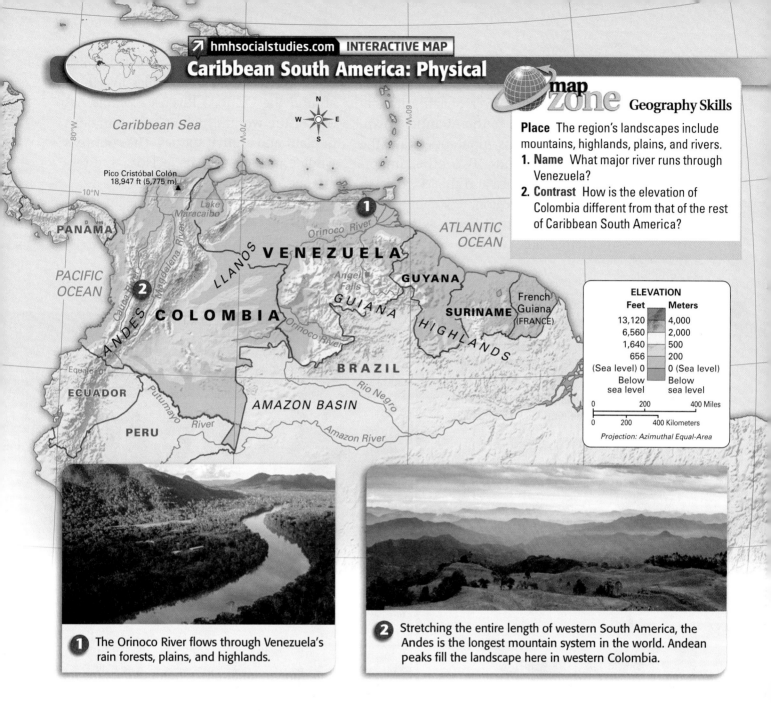

map zone Geography Skills

Place The region's landscapes include mountains, highlands, plains, and rivers.
1. **Name** What major river runs through Venezuela?
2. **Contrast** How is the elevation of Colombia different from that of the rest of Caribbean South America?

Caribbean Sea

Pico Cristóbal Colón
18,947 ft (5,775 m) ▲

Lake Maracaibo

PANAMA

PACIFIC OCEAN

VENEZUELA

LLANOS

Orinoco River

Angel Falls

GUYANA

ATLANTIC OCEAN

Magdalena River

Cauca River

COLOMBIA

G U I A N A H I G H L A N D S

SURINAME

French Guiana (FRANCE)

ANDES

Orinoco River

BRAZIL

Equator 0°

ECUADOR

Putumayo River

Rio Negro

AMAZON BASIN

PERU

Amazon River

ELEVATION
Feet		Meters
13,120		4,000
6,560		2,000
1,640		500
656		200
(Sea level) 0		0 (Sea level)
Below sea level		Below sea level

0   200   400 Miles
0   200   400 Kilometers
Projection: Azimuthal Equal-Area

1 The Orinoco River flows through Venezuela's rain forests, plains, and highlands.

2 Stretching the entire length of western South America, the Andes is the longest mountain system in the world. Andean peaks fill the landscape here in western Colombia.

Lying on the Caribbean coast, Venezuela is located in the middle of the other countries in the region. Venezuela's highest elevation is in the **Guiana Highlands**, which stretch into Guyana and Suriname. For millions of years, wind and rain have eroded these highlands' plateaus. However, some of the steep-sided plateaus are capped by sandstone layers that have resisted erosion. These unusual flat-topped formations are sometimes called *tepuís* (tay-PWEEZ). The *tepuís* create a dramatic landscape as they rise about 3,000 to 6,000 feet (900 to 1,800 m) above the surrounding plains.

Plains, Rivers, and Wildlife

As you look at the map above, notice how much the elevation drops between the highlands and the Andes. This region of plains is known as the **Llanos** (YAH-nohs). The Llanos is mostly grassland with few trees. At a low elevation and not much vegetation, these plains flood easily.

CARIBBEAN SOUTH AMERICA **83**

FOCUS ON READING

What details in this paragraph support this section's first main idea?

Flowing for about 1,600 miles (2,575 km), the **Orinoco** (OHR-ee-NOH-koh) **River** is the region's longest river. Snaking its way through Venezuela to the Atlantic Ocean, the Orinoco and its tributaries drain the plains and highlands. Two other important rivers, the Cauca and the Magdalena, drain the Andean region.

Caribbean South America is home to some remarkable wildlife. For example, hundreds of bird species, meat-eating fish called piranhas, and crocodiles live in or around the Orinoco River. Colombia has one of the world's highest concentrations of plant and animal species. The country's wildlife includes jaguars, ocelots, and several species of monkeys.

READING CHECK **Summarizing** What are the region's major physical features?

Venezuela's Canaima National Park

Covering almost 3 million acres of eastern Venezuela, Canaima National Park is one of the largest national parks in the world.

ANALYZING VISUALS What do you think attracts millions of people from around the world to visit Canaima National Park?

GUYANA

Angel Falls

Canaima National Park

Mt. Roraima ▲

Caroní River

VENEZUELA

BRAZIL

Dropping more than 3,200 feet (975 m), Angel Falls is the world's highest waterfall.

A rocky *tepuí* rises from the park's flat plains. Hundreds of these flat-topped mountains are scattered throughout the park.

The red-billed toucan is among the almost 500 species of birds that live in the park.

Climate and Vegetation

Caribbean South America's location near the equator means that most of the region has warm temperatures year-round. However, temperatures do vary with elevation. For example, in the Andes, as you go up in elevation, the temperature can drop rapidly—about four degrees Fahrenheit every 1,000 feet (305 m).

In contrast, the vast, flat landscape of the Llanos region has a tropical savanna climate. Here, both the wet and dry seasons provide favorable conditions for grasslands to grow.

Rain forests, another type of landscape, thrive in the humid tropical climate of southern Colombia. This area is a part of the Amazon Basin. Here, rain falls throughout the year, watering the forest's huge trees. These trees form a canopy where the vegetation is so dense that sunlight barely shines through to the jungle floor.

READING CHECK Analyzing What causes the region's temperatures to vary?

Resources

Good soil and moderate climates help make most of Caribbean South America a rich agricultural region. Major crops include rice, coffee, bananas, and sugarcane.

In addition, the region has other valuable resources, such as oil, iron ore, and coal. Both Venezuela and Colombia have large oil-rich areas. Forests throughout the region provide timber. While the seas provide plentiful fish and shrimp, the region's major rivers are used to generate hydroelectric power.

READING CHECK Summarizing How do geographic factors affect economic activities in Caribbean South America?

SUMMARY AND PREVIEW In this section you learned that the physical geography of Caribbean South America includes mountains, highlands, plains, and rivers. The region's location near the equator and its elevation affect the region's climate. In the next section you will learn about Colombia's history, people, and economy. You will also learn about the challenges Colombia is facing today, which include a civil war.

Section 1 Assessment

hmhsocialstudies.com
ONLINE QUIZ

Reviewing Ideas, Terms, and Places

1. **a. Recall** Where are the **Andes** located?
   b. Explain How are the rock formations called *tepuís* unusual?
   c. Elaborate Why do the **Llanos** in Colombia and Venezuela flood easily?
2. **a. Describe** In the Andes, how does the temperature change with elevation?
   b. Make Inferences How does the region's location near the equator affect its climate?
3. **a. Identify** What is a major resource in both Venezuela and Colombia?
   b. Explain Which resource provides hydroelectric power?

Critical Thinking

4. **Categorizing** Use your notes to identify four types of physical features in the region. Write each type in one of the small circles of the diagram.

Physical Features

FOCUS ON WRITING

5. **Describing Physical Geography** Take notes about the physical features, wildlife, climate, vegetation, and resources of the region. After you decide which country you are living in, collect more details about it.

Colombia

If YOU lived there...

You live in the beautiful colonial city of Cartagena, on the coast of the Caribbean. Your family runs a small restaurant there. You're used to the city's wide beaches and old colonial buildings with wooden balconies that overhang the street. Now you are on your way to visit your cousins. They live on a cattle ranch on the inland plains region called the Llanos.

How do you think life on the ranch is different from yours?

BUILDING BACKGROUND Like most of the countries of Central and South America, Colombia was once a colony of Spain. Colombians gained their independence from Spain in 1819. The new country was then named after the explorer Christopher Columbus.

Colombia's History

Giant mounds of earth, mysterious statues, and tombs—these are the marks of the people who lived in Colombia more than 1,500 years ago. Colombia's history begins with these people. It also includes conquest by Spain and, later, independence.

The Chibcha

Have you heard of the legend of El Dorado (el duh-RAH-doh), or the Golden One? That legend about

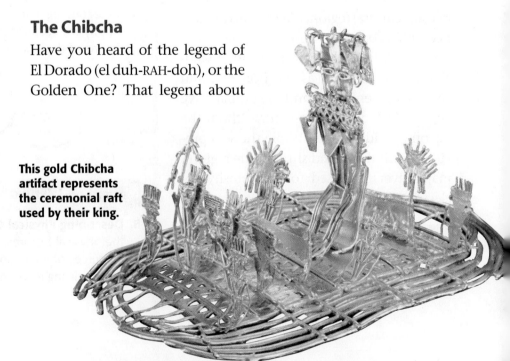

This gold Chibcha artifact represents the ceremonial raft used by their king.

a land rich in gold was inspired by the Chibcha culture in Colombia. The Chibcha covered their new rulers in gold dust. Then they took each ruler to a lake to wash the gold off. As the new ruler washed, the Chibcha threw gold and emerald objects into the water. A well-developed civilization, they practiced pottery making, weaving, and metalworking. Their gold objects were among the finest in ancient America.

Spanish Conquest

In about 1500 Spanish explorers arrived on the Caribbean coast of South America. The Spaniards wanted to expand Spain's new empire. In doing so, the Spanish conquered the Chibcha and seized much of their treasure. Soon after claiming land for themselves, the Spaniards founded a colony and cities along the Caribbean coast.

One colonial city, **Cartagena**, was a major naval base and commercial port in the Spanish empire. By the 1600s Spaniards and their descendants had set up large estates in Colombia. Spanish estate owners forced South American Indians and enslaved Africans to work the land.

Independence

In the late 1700s people in Central and South America began struggling for independence from Spain. After independence was achieved, the republic of Gran Colombia was created. It included Colombia, Ecuador, Panama, and Venezuela. In 1830 the republic dissolved, and New Granada, which included Colombia and Panama, was created.

After independence, two different groups of Colombians debated over how Colombia should be run. One group wanted the Roman Catholic Church to participate in government and education. On the other hand, another group did not want the church involved in their lives.

CONNECTING TO History

Cartagena's Spanish Fort

Imagine you are a Spanish colonist living in Cartagena, Colombia, in the 1600s. Your city lies on the Caribbean coast and has been attacked by English pirates several times. They have stolen tons of silver and gold that were waiting shipment to Spain. How do you protect your city from these pirates? Build an enormous fort, of course! You make sure to design the fort's walls to deflect the cannonballs that the pirates shoot from their ships. Today this fort still stands on a peninsula outside Cartagena. A statue commemorates one of the heroes that defended the city from attack.

Drawing Conclusions Why did the Spanish want to defend Cartagena from the pirates?

Outbreaks of violence throughout the 1800s and 1900s killed thousands. Part of the problem had to do with the country's rugged geography, which isolated people in one region from those in another region. As a result, they developed separate economies and identities. Uniting these different groups into one country was hard.

READING CHECK **Drawing Conclusions** How did Spanish conquest shape Colombia's history and culture?

Different regions of Colombia are home to diverse ethnic groups.

ANALYZING VISUALS What are some of the goods sold in this market?

Colombians of African descent unload their goods at a local market near the Pacific coast.

Colombia Today

Colombia is Caribbean South America's most populous country. The national capital is **Bogotá**, a city located high in the eastern Andes. Although Colombia is rich in culture and resources, more than 40 years of civil war have been destructive to the country's economy.

People and Culture

FOCUS ON READING

In the first paragraph under Economy, find at least three details to support the idea stated in the first sentence.

Most Colombians live in the fertile valleys and river basins among the mountain ranges, where the climate is moderate and good for farming. Rivers, such as the Cauca and the Magdalena, flow down from the Andes to the Caribbean Sea. These rivers provide water and help connect settlements located between the mountains and the coast. Other Colombians live on cattle ranches scattered throughout the Llanos. Few people live in the tropical rainforest regions in the south.

Because the physical geography of Colombia isolates some regions of the country, the people of Colombia are often known by the region where they live. For example, those who live along the Caribbean coast are known for songs and dances influenced by African traditions.

Colombian culture is an interesting mix of influences:

- Music: traditional African songs and dances on the Caribbean coast and South American Indian music in remote areas of the Andes
- Sports: soccer, as well as a traditional Chibcha ring-toss game called *tejo*
- Religion: primarily Roman Catholicism
- Official language: Spanish
- Ethnic groups: 58 percent mestizo; also Spanish, African, and Indian descent

Economy

Colombia's economy relies on several valuable resources. Rich soil, steep slopes, and tall shade trees produce world-famous Colombian coffee. Other major export crops include bananas, sugarcane, and cotton. Many farms in Colombia produce flowers that are exported around the world. In fact, 80 percent of the country's flowers are shipped to the United States.

Colombia's economy depends on the country's valuable natural resources. Recently oil has become Colombia's major export. Other natural resources include iron ore, gold, and coal. Most of the world's emeralds also come from Colombia.

Students from a school in Colombia's capital, Bogotá, take a break from their classes.

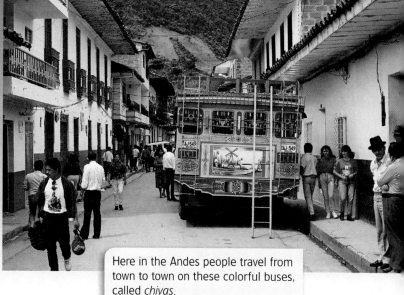

Here in the Andes people travel from town to town on these colorful buses, called *chivas*.

Civil War

Civil war is a major problem in Colombia today. Many different groups have waged war with each other and with Colombia's government. For more than 40 years, these heavily armed militant groups have controlled large areas of the country.

One of these groups is an army of **guerrillas**, or members of an irregular military force. These guerrillas want to overthrow the government. The guerrillas, as well as other militant groups, have forced farmers off their land and caused thousands of Colombians to flee the country. All of these groups are also involved in growing crops of the illegal coca plant. This plant is used to make cocaine, a dangerous drug.

Because of the instability caused by civil war, the future of Colombia is uncertain. However, the Colombian government has passed new laws that make it harder for the guerrillas and other militant groups to operate freely. In addition, the United States provides assistance to Colombia's government. Colombia is one of the top recipients of U.S. foreign aid.

READING CHECK **Drawing Conclusions** How do you think civil war affects daily life in Colombia?

SUMMARY AND PREVIEW Colombia's history includes the Chibcha, Spanish conquest, and independence. Today, Colombia's people are dealing with a long civil war. Next, you will learn about Colombia's neighbor, Venezuela.

Section 2 Assessment

hmhsocialstudies.com
ONLINE QUIZ

Reviewing Ideas, Terms, and Places

1. **a. Recall** Who were the Chibcha?
   b. Draw Conclusions Why did Spain want land in Colombia?
2. **a. Describe** What factors make Colombia ideal for growing coffee?
   b. Interpret In what part of the country do most Colombians live?
   c. Predict How might Colombia solve the problem of **guerrillas** trying to control the country?

Critical Thinking

3. **Analyzing** Using your notes, write a sentence about the topic of each box in a diagram like this one.

Music	→	
Sports	→	
Religion	→	
Language	→	

FOCUS ON WRITING

4. **Writing about Colombia** What information about the history, culture, and daily life of Colombia might your pen pal like to learn? Add these details to your notes.

Venezuela and the Guianas

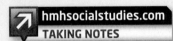
If YOU lived there...

You've come from your home in eastern Venezuela to visit the nearby country of Suriname. Your visit is full of surprises. As you walk along the streets of the country's capital, Paramaribo, people are not speaking Spanish, but Dutch, English, and some languages you don't even recognize. You see Hindu temples and Muslim mosques alongside Christian churches.

Why is Suriname so different from Venezuela?

BUILDING BACKGROUND Venezuela, like Colombia, was once a Spanish colony, but the Guianas were colonized by other nations—Great Britain, the Netherlands, and France. When these countries gained independence, British Guiana became Guyana and Dutch Guiana became Suriname.

History and Culture of Venezuela

Venezuela was originally the home of many small tribes of South American Indians. Those groups were conquered by the Spanish in the early 1500s. Though Venezuela became independent from Spain in the early 1800s, those three centuries of Spanish rule shaped the country's history and culture.

Spanish Settlement and Colonial Rule

The Spanish came to Venezuela hoping to find gold and pearls. They forced the native Indians to search for these treasures, but they finally realized there was little gold to be found. Then the Spanish turned to agriculture, once again forcing the Indians to do the work. They grew indigo (IN-di-goh), a plant used to make a deep blue dye. Because the work was very hard, many of the Indians died. Then the Spanish began bringing enslaved Africans to take the Indians' places. Eventually, some of the slaves escaped, settling in remote areas of the country.

Venezuela's Independence

Each year, Venezuelans celebrate Simon Bolívar's efforts in achieving Venezuela's independence. Independence Day is filled with parades and parties.

Simon Bolívar
(1783–1830)

Known as the "George Washington of South America," Simon Bolívar was a revolutionary general. In the early 1800s he led the liberation of several South American countries from Spanish rule.

Beginning in 1811 Bolívar helped free his native Venezuela. He was president of Gran Colombia (present-day Venezuela, Colombia, Panama, and Ecuador) and then Peru. Because Bolívar also helped free Bolivia, the country was named in his honor. People across South America admire Bolívar for his determination in achieving independence for the former Spanish colonies. Today in both Venezuela and Bolivia, Bolívar's birthday is a national holiday.

Drawing Inferences Why do you think Bolívar is often compared to George Washington?

Independence and Self-Rule

Partly because the colony was so poor, some people in Venezuela revolted against Spain. Simon Bolívar helped lead the fight against Spanish rule. Bolívar is considered a hero in many South American countries because he led wars of independence throughout the region. Bolívar helped win Venezuelan independence from Spain by 1821. However, Venezuela did not officially become independent until 1830.

Throughout the 1800s Venezuelans suffered from dictatorships and civil wars. Venezuela's military leaders ran the country. After oil was discovered in the early 1900s, some leaders kept the country's oil money for themselves. As a result, the people of Venezuela did not benefit from their country's oil wealth.

People and Culture

The people of Venezuela are descended from native Indians, Europeans, and Africans. The majority of Venezuelans are of mixed Indian and European descent. Indians make up only about 2 percent of the population. People of European descent tend to live in the large cities. People of African descent tend to live along the coast. Most Venezuelans are Spanish-speaking Roman Catholics, but the country's Indians speak 25 different languages and follow the religious practices of their ancestors.

Venezuelan culture includes dancing and sports. Venezuela's national dance, the *joropo*, is a lively foot-stomping couples' dance. Large crowds of Venezuelans attend rodeo events. Baseball and soccer are also popular throughout Venezuela.

READING CHECK **Summarizing** How did the Spanish contribute to Venezuela's history?

FOCUS ON
READING

In the paragraphs under Venezuela Today, what details support the main idea that oil production plays a large role in Venezuela's economy and government?

Venezuela Today

Many Venezuelans make a living by farming and ranching. However, most wealthy Venezuelans have made money in the country's oil industry. In addition, Venezuela's government has also benefited from oil wealth.

Agriculture and Ranching

Rural areas of Venezuela are dotted by farms and ranches. Northern Venezuela has some small family farms as well as large commercial farms. **Llaneros** (yah-NAY-rohs)—or Venezuelan cowboys—herd cattle on the many ranches of the Llanos region. However, some small communities of Indians practice traditional agriculture.

Economy and Natural Resources

In the 1960s Venezuela began earning huge sums of money from oil production. This wealth allowed part of the population to buy luxuries. However, the vast majority of the population still lived in poverty. Many of Venezuela's poor people moved to the cities to try to find work. Some settled on the outskirts in communities of shacks. They had no running water, sewers, or electricity.

Venezuela's wealth attracted many immigrants from Europe and other South American countries. These immigrants, like most other Venezuelans, suffered in the 1980s when the price of oil dropped sharply. Without the money provided by high oil prices, the economy couldn't support the people. Oil prices recovered in the 1990s, and the Venezuelan economy continues to be based on oil production.

As you can see on the map on the next page, the Orinoco River basin and **Lake Maracaibo** (mah-rah-KY-boh) are rich in oil. Venezuela is the only South American member of the Organization of Petroleum

FOCUS ON CULTURE

The Feast of Corpus Christi

One day each summer, men dressed as devils dance in the streets of the Venezuelan town of San Francisco de Yare. On this day, people here honor the Roman Catholic feast day of Corpus Christi. Spanish settlers brought the tradition of dressing up as devils to Venezuela. This tradition includes the making of elaborate, colorful masks that the dancers wear. These masks usually resemble pigs or jaguars. Dancing through the town's streets to the beat of drums, the dancers shake musical instruments called maracas. They believe their dancing, music, and scary masks will keep evil away from their town.

Summarizing How do some Venezuelans celebrate the Feast of Corpus Christi?

Venezuela's Major Resources

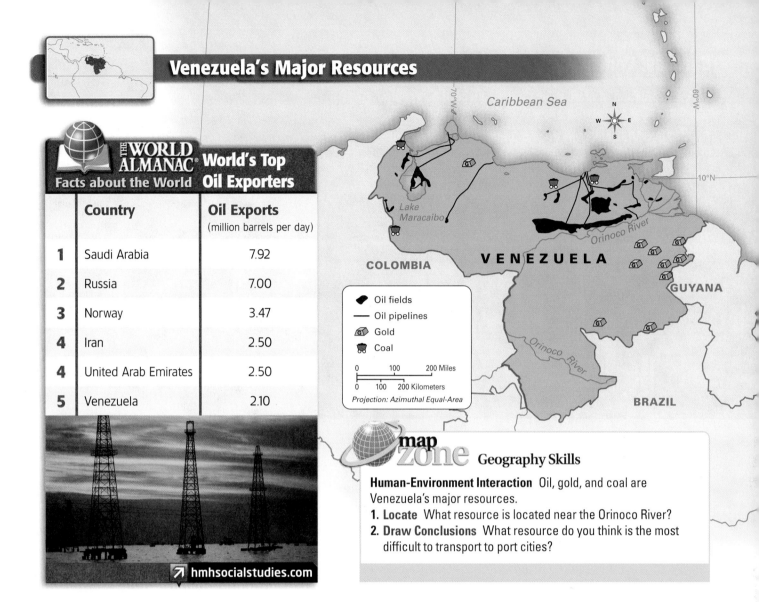

THE WORLD ALMANAC® Facts about the World — **World's Top Oil Exporters**

	Country	Oil Exports (million barrels per day)
1	Saudi Arabia	7.92
2	Russia	7.00
3	Norway	3.47
4	Iran	2.50
4	United Arab Emirates	2.50
5	Venezuela	2.10

hmhsocialstudies.com

map@zone Geography Skills

Human-Environment Interaction Oil, gold, and coal are Venezuela's major resources.
1. **Locate** What resource is located near the Orinoco River?
2. **Draw Conclusions** What resource do you think is the most difficult to transport to port cities?

Exporting Countries (OPEC). The member countries in this organization attempt to control world oil production and keep oil prices from falling too low.

The Guiana Highlands in the southeast are rich in other minerals, such as iron ore for making steel. Gold is also mined in remote areas of the highlands. Dams on tributaries of the Orinoco River produce hydroelectricity.

Caracas (kah-RAH-kahs) is Venezuela's capital and the economic and cultural center of the country. It is a large city with a modern subway system, busy expressways, and tall office buildings. Still, neither Caracas nor Venezuela has escaped poverty.

Caracas is encircled by slums, and many Venezuelans living in the rural areas of the country are also poor.

Government

After years of suffering under military dictatorships, the people of Venezuela elected their first president in 1959. Since then, Venezuela's government has dealt with economic turmoil and political protests.

In 2002 Venezuela's president, Hugo Chavez, started to distribute the country's oil income equally among all Venezuelans. Before Chavez's presidency, only a small percentage of wealthy Venezuelans benefited from the country's oil income.

With a population of more than 4 million, Venezuela's capital city, Caracas, is the country's financial and cultural center.

ANALYZING VISUALS Why do you think Caracas is located in this mountain valley?

Millions of Venezuelans went on strike to protest the president's actions. A **strike** is a group of workers stopping work until their demands are met. The strike lasted for about two months. The protestors wanted Chavez to resign, but he refused. As a result of the strike, Venezuela's economy suffered and oil exports fell dramatically.

Many Venezuelans opposed to President Chavez called for a **referendum**, or recall vote. The referendum was defeated. In 2006 about 63 percent of Venezuelans re-elected Chavez president. In his second term, Chavez adopted new **policies** aimed at bringing an end to poverty, illiteracy, and hunger. Chavez has also supported changing his nation's constitution to end presidential term limits. Many Venezuelans fear that Chavez has grown too powerful and might rule indefinitely.

ACADEMIC VOCABULARY
policy rule, course of action

READING CHECK Identifying Cause and Effect What effect did the workers' strike have on Venezuela's economy?

The Guianas

The countries of Guyana, Suriname, and French Guiana are together known as the Guianas (gee-AH-nuhz). Dense tropical rain forests cover much of this region, which lies east of Venezuela.

Guyana

Guyana (gy-AH-nuh) comes from a South American Indian word that means "land of waters." About one-third of the country's population lives in Georgetown, the capital. Nearly all of Guyana's agricultural lands are located on the flat, fertile plains along the coast. Guyana's most important agricultural products are rice and sugar.

Guyana's population is diverse. About half of its people are descended from people who migrated to Guyana from India. These immigrants came to Guyana to work on the country's sugar plantations. Most Guyanese today farm small plots of land or run small businesses. About one-third of the population is descended from former African slaves. These people operate large businesses and hold most of the government positions.

Suriname

The resources and economy of Suriname (soohr-uh-NAHM) are similar to those of Guyana. Like Guyana, Suriname has a diverse population. The country's population includes South Asians, Africans, Chinese, Indonesians, and Creoles—people of mixed heritage. The capital, Paramaribo (pah-rah-MAH-ree-boh), is home to nearly half of the country's people.

French Guiana

French Guiana (gee-A-nuh) is a territory of France and sends representatives to the government in Paris. French Guiana's roughly 200,000 people live mostly in coastal areas. About two-thirds of the people are of African descent. Other groups include Europeans, Asians, and South American Indians. The country depends heavily on imports for its food and energy.

READING CHECK **Contrasting** How is French Guiana different from the rest of the Guianas?

Creole women carry gifts to a party in downtown Paramaribo. About 30 percent of Suriname's population is Creole.

SUMMARY AND PREVIEW In this section, you learned that Venezuela's history was largely shaped by Spanish settlement. Today Venezuela's economy is based on oil. You also learned that to the east, the Guianas are home to a diverse population. In the next chapter, you will learn about the history and people of Atlantic South America.

Section 3 Assessment

hmhsocialstudies.com ONLINE QUIZ

Reviewing Ideas, Terms, and Places

1. **a. Recall** What did Spanish settlers hope to find in Venezuela?
   b. Explain Who led Venezuela's revolt against Spain?
2. **a. Describe** What does the landscape of **Caracas** include?
   b. Explain How is oil important to Venezuela's economy?
   c. Elaborate Why did some Venezuelans go on **strike**?
3. **a. Describe** What are Guyana's agricultural lands and products like?
   b. Contrast How is population of the Guianas different from that of Colombia and Venezuela?

Critical Thinking

4. **Identifying Cause and Effect** Using your notes on Venezuela's natural resources and this diagram, list the effects of oil production on Venezuela's people, economy, and government.

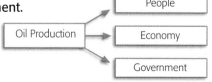

Oil Production → People
Oil Production → Economy
Oil Production → Government

FOCUS ON WRITING

5. **Writing about Venezuela and the Guianas** Collect details about Venezuela and the Guianas for your letter. What is interesting about these cultures?

Social Studies Skills

Chart and Graph | Critical Thinking | Geography | Study

Using Latitude and Longitude

Learn

The pattern of imaginary lines that circle the globe in east-west and north-south directions is called a grid. Geographers measure the distances between the lines of the grid in degrees.

Look at the diagram to the right. As you can see, lines that run east to west are lines of latitude. These lines measure distance north and south of the equator. Lines that run north to south are lines of longitude. These lines measure distance east and west of the prime meridian.

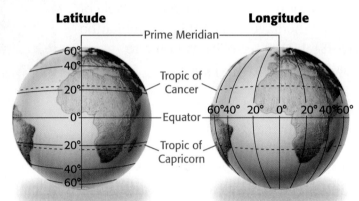

Practice

Look at the world map to the right. Use these guidelines to read latitude and longitude.

❶ Pick a city on the map.

❷ To find the latitude of the city you picked, first look at the equator. From there, look at the city's location. Then find the closest line of latitude to see how many degrees the city is north or south of the equator.

❸ To find the longitude of the city, first look at the prime meridian. Then find the closest line of longitude to see how many degrees the city is east or west of the prime meridian.

World: Political

Apply

Using an atlas, find a map of the United States and a map of the world. On the map of the United States, find the line of latitude that is located near your hometown. Then look at a world map and follow this line of latitude across the world. Which countries share the same latitude as your hometown?

Chapter Review

Geography's Impact
video series
Review the video to answer the closing question:
What are some advantages and disadvantages of industries along the Orinoco River?

Visual Summary

Use the visual summary below to help you review the main ideas of the chapter.

QUICK FACTS

Caribbean South America's physical features include rivers, plains, mountains, and the world's highest waterfall.

A country rich in history and culture, Colombia is enduring a civil war today.

Venezuela is an oil-rich nation that has a population of mostly mixed Indian and European descent.

Reviewing Vocabulary, Terms, and Places

For each statement below, write T if it is true and F if it is false.

1. The Andes is a river system.

2. The Orinoco River flows 1,300 miles (2,100 km) through Venezuela.

3. Caribbean South America's location near the equator means that the region is very cold.

4. The Chibcha were the first people to settle Colombia.

5. Colombian culture includes traditional African songs and dances.

6. Most Venezuelans are of mixed Indian and European descent.

7. Venezuela gained its independence from France.

8. Venezuela's economy depends on oil production.

Comprehension and Critical Thinking

SECTION 1 *(Pages 82–85)*

9. **a. Recall** What is the region's longest river?

   b. Analyze How does the temperature vary in the Andes?

   c. Evaluate Why do you think it would be hard to live in the rain forest of Colombia?

SECTION 2 *(Pages 86–89)*

10. **a. Describe** How did the Chibcha treat their ruler?

    b. Draw Conclusions What created a problem for all Colombians after independence?

    c. Elaborate Why do most Colombians live in fertile valleys and river basins?

SECTION 3 *(Pages 90–95)*

11. **a. Define** What is a strike?

b. Draw Conclusions Why did people from India immigrate to Guyana?

c. Predict Do you think Venezuela's government will continue to use oil wealth to help the country's people? Explain your answer.

Using the Internet

12. Activity: Writing a Journal Entry Ride with the llaneros! Pack your bags and prepare for a trek through the South American countryside. Explore the vast grasslands, visit villages, and learn about the life and work of the cowboys, or llaneros, of the Venezuelan plains. Through your online textbook, research and take notes that will help you describe your adventure. Use the interactive template to write your journal entry. Describe what you have learned about the people and places you visited.

hmhsocialstudies.com

Social Studies Skills

13. Using Latitude and Longitude Look at the physical map in Section 1. Find the lines of latitude and longitude. What line of latitude, shown on the map, runs through both Venezuela and Colombia? Which country in Caribbean South America is partly located on the equator?

Map Activity

14. Caribbean South America On a separate sheet of paper, match the letters on the map with their correct labels.

Llanos   Andes

Guiana Highlands Orinoco River

Lake Maracaibo

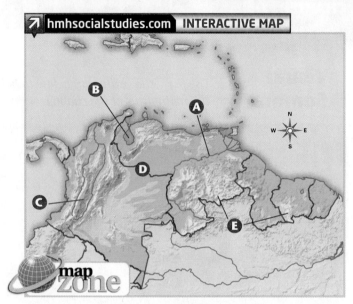

hmhsocialstudies.com   **INTERACTIVE MAP**

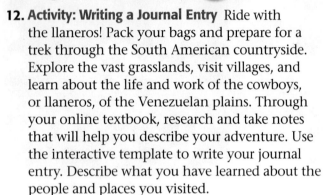

FOCUS ON READING AND WRITING

15. Identifying Supporting Details Look back over Section 2 on Colombia. Then make a list of details you find to support the section's main ideas. Make sure you include details about the Spanish conquest, independence, culture, resources, and civil war.

16. Writing a Letter By now you have information about the region and the country you have chosen to live in. Begin your letter to your pen pal by describing the most interesting physical and cultural features of the whole region. Then write a second paragraph telling your pen pal about the special physical and cultural features of the country you've chosen to live in. Try to keep your pen pal interested in reading by including fascinating details and descriptions.

CHAPTER 4

Standardized Test Prep

DIRECTIONS: *Read questions 1 through 7 and write the letter of the best response. Then read question 8 and write your own well-constructed response.*

1 Temperatures in Caribbean South America remain warm year-round because of the region's location near the

A equator.

B Caribbean Sea.

C Amazon Basin.

D Tropic of Cancer.

2 What valuable natural resource were the Chibcha known for using?

A silver

B gold

C copper

D iron

3 What Colombian city was a major naval base and commercial port in the Spanish empire?

A Bogotá

B Cali

C Caracas

D Cartagena

4 Venezuela's economy is based on

A oil production.

B flower exports.

C small farms.

D silver mining.

5 Simon Bolívar helped several South American countries gain independence from

A Britain.

B Brazil.

C Spain.

D Mexico.

Volcanoes of Colombia

6 Based on the map above, active volcanoes are located in Colombia's

A rivers.

B mountains.

C plains.

D coastal areas.

7 The physical geography of the Guianas includes

A dense rain forests.

B deserts.

C the Orinoco River.

D the Andes.

8 **Extended Response** Look at the table of the world's oil exporters and the map of Venezuela's major resources in Section 3. Write a paragraph explaining why oil is Venezuela's most important resource. Identify at least two reasons.

CHAPTER 5

Atlantic South America

Essential Question How have the nations of Atlantic South America addressed economic and environmental challenges?

What You Will Learn...

In this chapter you will learn about the plains and rain forest of Atlantic South America. You will also study the histories of the different countries and how different influences have shaped their cultures. In addition, you will learn about life, landscapes, and issues in Brazil, Argentina, Uruguay, and Paraguay today.

FOCUS ON READING AND WRITING

Using Context Clues As you read, you may find some unknown words. You can usually figure out what a word means by using context clues. Look at the words and sentences around the unknown word—its context—to figure out the definition. **See the lesson, Using Context Clues, on page 198.**

Creating a Web Site You are a Web designer at a travel agency. Read this chapter and then use what you learn to create a Web site about Atlantic South America. The goal of your Web site will be to convince viewers to visit the region.

PACIFIC OCEAN

⚙ National capital
● Other cities

0 ___ 300 ___ 600 Miles
0 ___ 300 ___ 600 Kilometers

Projection:
Lambert Azimuthal Equal-Area

110°W
100°W
0° Equator
20°S

map zone

Geography Skills

Place Brazil and Argentina are South America's largest countries.
1. **Identify** What city lies on the Amazon River?
2. **Analyze** What would be some benefits of the location of Buenos Aires?

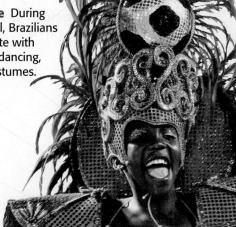

Culture During Carnival, Brazilians celebrate with music, dancing, and costumes.

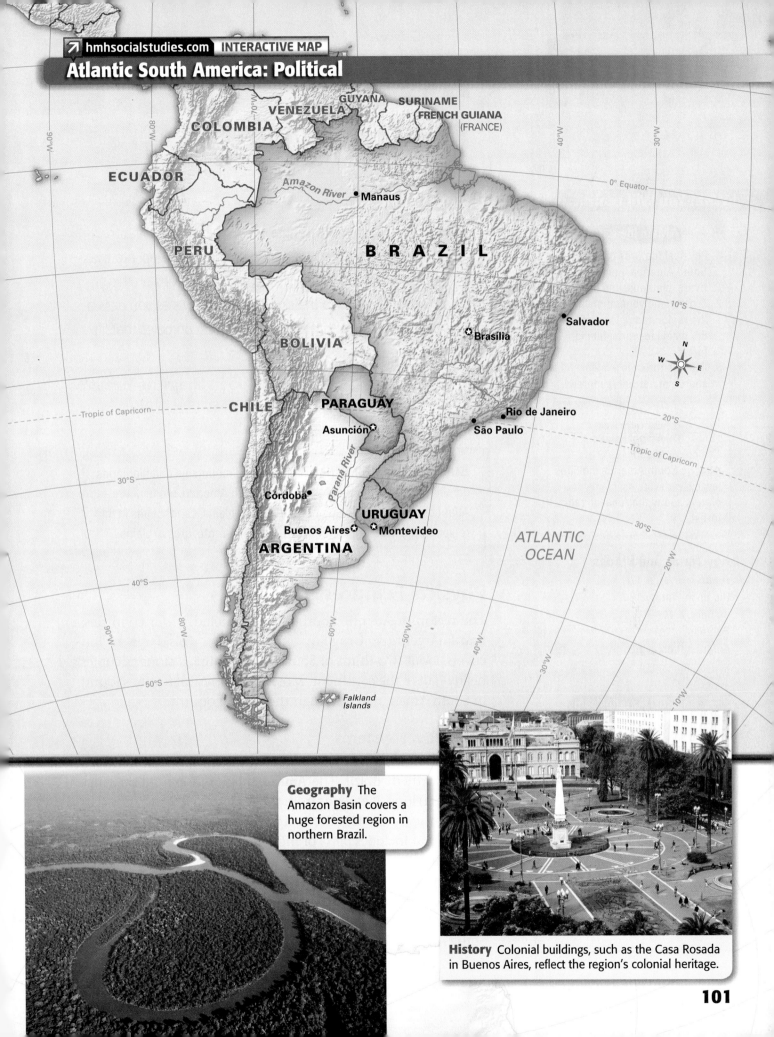

COLOMBIA
VENEZUELA
GUYANA
SURINAME
FRENCH GUIANA
(FRANCE)

ECUADOR

Amazon River • Manaus

PERU

B R A Z I L

BOLIVIA

Salvador

✪ Brasília

CHILE

PARAGUAY

Rio de Janeiro

Asunción ✪

São Paulo

Córdoba •

URUGUAY

Buenos Aires ✪

✪ Montevideo

ARGENTINA

ATLANTIC
OCEAN

Paraná River

Tropic of Capricorn

Falkland
Islands

Geography The Amazon Basin covers a huge forested region in northern Brazil.

History Colonial buildings, such as the Casa Rosada in Buenos Aires, reflect the region's colonial heritage.

101

Physical Geography

What You Will Learn...

Main Ideas

1. Physical features of Atlantic South America include large rivers, plateaus, and plains.
2. Climate and vegetation in the region range from cool, dry plains to warm, humid forests.
3. The rain forest is a major source of natural resources.

The Big Idea

The physical geography of Atlantic South America includes large river systems, plains and plateaus, and the Amazon rain forest.

Key Terms and Places

Amazon River, *p. 102*
Río de la Plata, *p. 103*
estuary, *p. 103*
Pampas, *p. 103*
deforestation, *p. 105*
soil exhaustion, *p. 105*

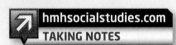
hmhsocialstudies.com
TAKING NOTES

Use the graphic organizer online to take notes on the physical geography of Atlantic South America.

If **YOU** lived there...

You live on the coast of Brazil, near the mouth of the Amazon River. Now you are taking your first trip up the river deep into the rain forest. The river is amazingly wide and calm. Trees on the riverbanks seem to soar to the sky. Your boat slows as you pass a small village. You notice that all the houses rest on poles that lift them 8 to 10 feet out of the water.

What would it be like to live in the rain forest?

BUILDING BACKGROUND While rugged mountains and highlands dominate the lansdcape of Caribbean South America, much of the Atlantic region is made up of broad interior plains. Landscapes in this region range from tropical rain forest to temperate, grassy plains.

Physical Features

The region of Atlantic South America includes four countries: Brazil, Argentina, Uruguay, and Paraguay. This large region covers about two-thirds of South America. Brazil alone occupies nearly half of the continent. Most of the physical features found in South America are found in these four countries.

Major River Systems

The world's largest river system, the Amazon, flows eastward across northern Brazil. The **Amazon River** is about 4,000 miles (6,440 km) long. It extends from the Andes Mountains in Peru to the Atlantic Ocean. Hundreds of tributaries flow into it, draining an area that includes parts of most South American countries.

Because of its huge drainage area, the Amazon carries more water than any other river in the world. About 20 percent of the water that runs off Earth's surface flows down the Amazon. Where it meets the Atlantic, this freshwater lowers the salt level of the Atlantic for more than 100 miles (160 km) from shore.

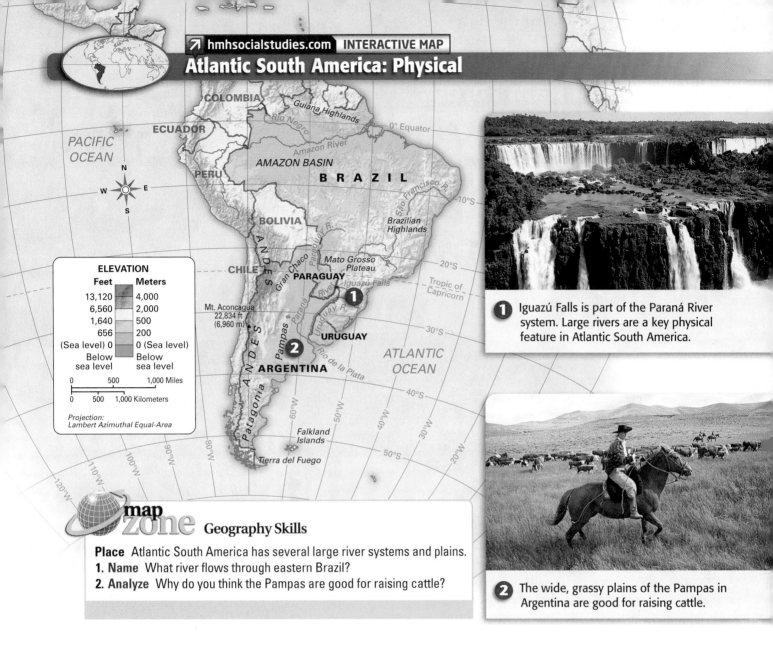

Atlantic South America: Physical

COLOMBIA

ECUADOR

PACIFIC OCEAN

Guiana Highlands

Rio Negro

0° Equator

Amazon River

AMAZON BASIN

B R A Z I L

PERU

São Francisco R.

10°S

Brazilian Highlands

BOLIVIA

ELEVATION

Feet	Meters
13,120	4,000
6,560	2,000
1,640	500
656	200
(Sea level) 0	0 (Sea level)
Below sea level	Below sea level

0   500   1,000 Miles

0   500   1,000 Kilometers

Projection: Lambert Azimuthal Equal-Area

CHILE

Mt. Aconcagua 22,834 ft (6,960 m)

Gran Chaco

Paraguay R.

Mato Grosso Plateau

PARAGUAY

Iguazú Falls

20°S

Tropic of Capricorn

Uruguay R.

Paraná River

Pampas

URUGUAY

30°S

Río de la Plata

ATLANTIC OCEAN

ARGENTINA

Patagonia

40°S

60°W

50°W

40°W

30°W

20°W

Falkland Islands

50°S

Tierra del Fuego

110°W 100°W 90°W 80°W

map zone Geography Skills

Place Atlantic South America has several large river systems and plains.
1. Name What river flows through eastern Brazil?
2. Analyze Why do you think the Pampas are good for raising cattle?

1 Iguazú Falls is part of the Paraná River system. Large rivers are a key physical feature in Atlantic South America.

2 The wide, grassy plains of the Pampas in Argentina are good for raising cattle.

The Paraná (pah-rah-NAH) River drains much of the central part of South America. Water from the Paraná River eventually flows into the **Río de la Plata** (REE-oh day lah PLAH-tah) and the Atlantic Ocean beyond. The Río de la Plata is an estuary. An **estuary** is a partially enclosed body of water where freshwater mixes with salty seawater.

Plains and Plateaus

As you can see on the map, this region's landforms mainly consist of plains and plateaus. The Amazon Basin in northern Brazil is a giant, flat floodplain. South of the Amazon Basin are the Brazilian

Highlands, a rugged region of old, eroded mountains, and another area of high plains called the Mato Grosso Plateau.

Farther south, a low plains region known as the Gran Chaco (grahn CHAH-koh) stretches across parts of Paraguay and northern Argentina. In central Argentina are the wide, grassy plains of the **Pampas**. South of the Pampas is Patagonia—a region of dry plains and plateaus. All of these southern plains rise in the west to form the high Andes Mountains.

READING CHECK **Summarizing** What are the region's major landforms and rivers?

FOCUS ON READING

Where can you find the definition of *Pampas*?

Close-up
The Amazon Rain Forest

The Amazon rain forest covers more than one-third of South America. Seen from the air, it looks like a big, green carpet. The top level of tree branches is called the canopy. Most action in the forest takes place in the canopy, but plenty of life also exists below.

↗ hmhsocialstudies.com
ANIMATED GEOGRAPHY

Animals such as monkeys and sloths can spend their entire lives in the canopy.

People have cleared parts of the rain forest for farming, ranching, and logging.

Parts of the forest are flooded for half the year, and trees stand in water up to 40 feet (12 m) deep.

ANALYSIS
SKILL ANALYZING VISUALS
What kinds of animals could not survive living in the canopy?

Climate and Vegetation

Atlantic South America has many climates. Generally, cool climates in southern and highland areas give way to tropical, moist climates in northern and coastal areas.

In southern Argentina Patagonia has a cool, desert climate. North of Patagonia, rich soils and a humid subtropical climate make parts of the Pampas good for farming. Farther north in Argentina, the Gran Chaco has a humid tropical climate. There, summer rains can turn some parts of the plains into marshlands.

North of Argentina, in Brazil, a large part of the central region has a tropical savanna climate with warm grasslands. The northeastern part of the country has a hot, dry climate, while the southeast is cooler and more humid.

In northern Brazil the Amazon Basin's humid tropical climate supports the world's largest tropical rain forest. Rain falls almost every day in this region. The Amazon rain forest contains the world's greatest variety of plant and animal life.

READING CHECK **Finding Main Ideas** What is the climate like in the rain forest?

Natural Resources

The Amazon rain forest is one of the region's greatest natural resources. It provides food, wood, rubber, plants for medicines, and other products. In recent years **deforestation**, or the clearing of trees, has become an issue in the forest.

The region's land is also a resource for commercial farming, which is found near coastal areas of Atlantic South America. In some areas, however, planting the same crop every year has caused **soil exhaustion**, which means the soil is infertile because it has lost nutrients needed by plants.

Atlantic South America also has good mineral and energy resources such as gold, silver, copper, iron, and oil. Dams on some of the region's large rivers also provide hydroelectric power.

READING CHECK **Summarizing** What resources does the rain forest provide?

SUMMARY AND PREVIEW Physical features of Atlantic South America include great river systems and plains. The Amazon rain forest makes up a huge part of the region. Next you will learn about Brazil, the country of the Amazon.

Section 1 Assessment
hmhsocialstudies.com
ONLINE QUIZ

Reviewing Ideas, Terms, and Places
1. **a. Define** What is an **estuary**?
   b. Explain How does the **Amazon River** affect the Atlantic Ocean at the river's mouth?
   c. Elaborate What benefits do you think the rivers might bring to Atlantic South America?
2. **a. Recall** What kind of climate does Patagonia have?
   b. Make Inferences Why are temperatures in the south generally cooler than temperatures in the north?
3. **a. Identify** What resources does the rain forest provide?
   b. Analyze What is one benefit and one drawback of practicing commercial agriculture in the rain forest?
   c. Elaborate **Soil exhaustion** might lead to what kinds of additional problems?

Critical Thinking
4. **Categorizing** Look back over your notes. Then use a table like this one to organize the physical geography of Atlantic South America by country.

	Geography
Brazil	
Argentina	

FOCUS ON WRITING

5. **Describing Physical Geography** Jot down notes about the physical features, climate and vegetation, landscapes, and resources of this area. Identify one or two images you could use for your Web site.

Brazil

What You Will Learn...

Main Ideas

1. Brazil's history has been affected by Brazilian Indians, Portuguese settlers, and enslaved Africans.
2. Brazil's society reflects a mix of people and cultures.
3. Brazil today is experiencing population growth in its cities and new development in rain forest areas.

The Big Idea

The influence of Brazil's history can be seen all over the country in its people and culture.

Key Terms and Places

São Paulo, *p. 108*
megacity, *p. 108*
Rio de Janeiro, *p. 108*
favelas, *p. 109*
Brasília, *p. 109*
Manaus, *p. 109*

hmhsocialstudies.com
TAKING NOTES

Use the graphic organizer online to take notes on Brazil.

If **YOU** lived there...

You live in Rio de Janeiro, Brazil's second-largest city. For months your friends have been preparing for Carnival, the year's biggest holiday. During Carnival, people perform in glittery costumes and there is dancing all day and all night in the streets. The city is packed with tourists. It can be fun, but it is hectic! Your family is thinking of leaving Rio during Carnival so they can get some peace and quiet, but you may stay in Rio with a friend if you like.

Would you stay for Carnival? Why or why not?

BUILDING BACKGROUND Carnival is a tradition that is not unique to Brazil, but it has come to symbolize certain parts of Brazilian culture. Brazilian culture differs from cultures in the rest of South America in many ways. Brazil's unique history in the region is responsible for most of the cultural differences.

History

Brazil is the largest country in South America. Its population of more than 188 million is larger than the population of all of the other South American countries combined. Most Brazilians are descended from three groups of people who contributed in different ways throughout Brazil's history.

Colonial Brazil

The first people in Brazil were American Indians. They arrived in the region many thousands of years ago and developed a way of life based on hunting, fishing, and small-scale farming.

In 1500 Portuguese explorers became the first Europeans to find Brazil. Soon Portuguese settlers began to move there. Good climates and soils, particularly in the northeast, made Brazil a large sugar-growing colony. Colonists brought a third group of people—Africans—to work as slaves on the plantations. Sugar plantations made Portugal rich, but they also eventually replaced forests along the Atlantic coast.

Other parts of Brazil also contributed to the colonial economy. Inland, many Portuguese settlers created cattle ranches. In the late 1600s and early 1700s, people discovered gold and precious gems in the southeast. A mining boom drew people to Brazil from around the world. Finally, in the late 1800s southeastern Brazil became a major coffee-producing region.

Brazil Since Independence

Brazil gained independence from Portugal without a fight in 1822. However, independence did not change Brazil's economy much. For example, Brazil was the last country in the Americas to end slavery.

Since the end of Portuguese rule, Brazil has been governed at times by dictators and at other times by elected officials. Today the country has an elected president and legislature. Brazilians can participate in politics through voting.

READING CHECK **Summarizing** What was Brazil's colonial economy like?

People and Culture

The people who came to Brazil over the years brought their own traditions. These traditions blended to create a unique Brazilian culture.

People

More than half of Brazilians consider themselves of European descent. These people include descendants of original Portuguese settlers along with descendants of more recent immigrants from Spain, Germany, Italy, and Poland. Nearly 40 percent of Brazil's people are of mixed African and European descent. Brazil also has the largest Japanese population outside of Japan.

Because of its colonial heritage, Brazil's official language is Portuguese. In fact, since Brazil's population is so huge, there are more Portuguese-speakers in South America than there are Spanish-speakers, even though Spanish is spoken in almost every other country on the continent. Other Brazilians speak Spanish, English, French, Japanese, or native languages.

FOCUS ON READING
What context clues in this paragraph help you understand the meaning of *descent?*

FOCUS ON CULTURE

Soccer in Brazil

To Brazilians, soccer is more than a game. It is part of being Brazilian. Professional stars are national heroes. The national team often plays in Rio de Janeiro, home of the world's largest soccer stadium. Some fans beat drums all through the games. But it is not just professional soccer that is popular. People all over Brazil play soccer—in cleared fields, on the beach, or in the street. Here, boys in Rio practice their skills.

Analyzing Why do you think soccer is so popular in Brazil?

Regions of Brazil

Brazil's regions differ from each other in their people, climates, economies, and landscapes.

ANALYZING VISUALS Which region appears to be the wealthiest?

1 The southeast has the country's largest cities, such as Rio de Janeiro.

hmhsocialstudies.com

ANIMATED GEOGRAPHY
Present-Day Brazil

Religion

Brazil has the largest population of Roman Catholics of any country in the world. About 75 percent of Brazilians are Catholic. In recent years Protestantism has grown in popularity, particularly among the urban poor. Some Brazilians practice macumba (mah-KOOM-bah), a religion that combines beliefs and practices of African and Indian religions with Christianity.

Festivals and Food

ACADEMIC VOCABULARY

aspects parts

Other **aspects** of Brazilian life also reflect the country's mix of cultures. For example, Brazilians celebrate Carnival before the Christian season of Lent. The celebration mixes traditions from Africa, Brazil, and Europe. During Carnival, Brazilians dance the samba, which was adapted from an African dance.

Immigrant influences can also be found in Brazilian foods. In parts of the country, an African seafood dish called vatapá (vah-tah-PAH) is popular. Many Brazilians also enjoy eating feijoada (fay-ZHWAH-dah), a stew of black beans and meat.

READING CHECK **Analyzing** How has cultural borrowing affected Brazilian culture?

Brazil Today

Brazil's large size creates opportunities and challenges for the country. For example, Brazil has the largest economy in South America and has modern and wealthy areas. However, many Brazilians are poor.

While some of the same issues and characteristics can be found throughout Brazil, other characteristics are unique to a particular region of the country. We can divide Brazil into four regions based on their people, economies, and landscapes.

The Southeast

Most people in Brazil live in the southeast. **São Paulo** is located there. Almost 19 million people live in and around São Paulo. It is the largest urban area in South America and the fourth largest in the world. São Paulo is considered a **megacity**, or a giant urban area that includes surrounding cities and suburbs.

Rio de Janeiro, Brazil's second-largest city, lies northeast of São Paulo. Almost 12 million people live there. The city was the capital of Brazil from 1822 until 1960. Today Rio de Janeiro remains a major port city. Its spectacular setting and exciting culture are popular with tourists.

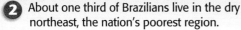
About one third of Brazilians live in the dry northeast, the nation's poorest region.

Rivers provide resources and transportation for people living in the Amazon region.

In addition to having the largest cities, the southeast is also Brazil's richest region. It is rich in natural resources and has most of the country's industries and productive farmland. It is one of the major coffee-growing regions of the world.

Although the southeast has a strong economy, it also has poverty. Cities in the region have huge slums called **favelas** (fah-VE-lahz). Many people who live in favelas have come to cities of the southeast from other regions of Brazil in search of jobs.

The Northeast

Immigrants to Brazil's large cities often come from the northeast, which is Brazil's poorest region. Many people there cannot read, and health care is poor. The region often suffers from droughts, which make farming and raising livestock difficult. The northeast has also had difficulty attracting industry. However, the region's beautiful beaches do attract tourists.

Other tourist attractions in northeastern Brazil are the region's many old colonial cities. These cities were built during the days of the sugar industry. They have brightly painted buildings, cobblestone streets, and elaborate Catholic churches.

The Interior

The interior region of Brazil is a frontier land. Its abundant land and mild climate could someday make it an important area for agriculture. For now, few people live in this region, except for those who reside in the country's capital, **Brasília**.

In the mid-1950s government officials hoped that building a new capital city in the Brazilian interior would help develop the region. Brasília has modern buildings and busy highways. More than 2 million people live in Brasília, although it was originally designed for only 500,000.

The Amazon

The Amazon region covers the northern part of Brazil. **Manaus**, which lies 1,000 miles (1,600 km) from the mouth of the Amazon, is a major port and industrial city. More than 1 million people live there. They rely on the river for transportation and communication.

Isolated Indian villages are scattered throughout the region's dense rain forest. Some of Brazil's Indians had little contact with outsiders until recently. Now, logging, mining, and new roads are bringing more people and development to this region.

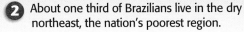
About one third of Brazilians live in the dry northeast, the nation's poorest region.

Rivers provide resources and transportation for people living in the Amazon region.

In addition to having the largest cities, the southeast is also Brazil's richest region. It is rich in natural resources and has most of the country's industries and productive farmland. It is one of the major coffee-growing regions of the world.

Although the southeast has a strong economy, it also has poverty. Cities in the region have huge slums called **favelas** (fah-VE-lahz). Many people who live in favelas have come to cities of the southeast from other regions of Brazil in search of jobs.

The Northeast

Immigrants to Brazil's large cities often come from the northeast, which is Brazil's poorest region. Many people there cannot read, and health care is poor. The region often suffers from droughts, which make farming and raising livestock difficult. The northeast has also had difficulty attracting industry. However, the region's beautiful beaches do attract tourists.

Other tourist attractions in northeastern Brazil are the region's many old colonial cities. These cities were built during the days of the sugar industry. They have brightly painted buildings, cobblestone streets, and elaborate Catholic churches.

The Interior

The interior region of Brazil is a frontier land. Its abundant land and mild climate could someday make it an important area for agriculture. For now, few people live in this region, except for those who reside in the country's capital, **Brasília**.

In the mid-1950s government officials hoped that building a new capital city in the Brazilian interior would help develop the region. Brasília has modern buildings and busy highways. More than 2 million people live in Brasília, although it was originally designed for only 500,000.

The Amazon

The Amazon region covers the northern part of Brazil. **Manaus**, which lies 1,000 miles (1,600 km) from the mouth of the Amazon, is a major port and industrial city. More than 1 million people live there. They rely on the river for transportation and communication.

Isolated Indian villages are scattered throughout the region's dense rain forest. Some of Brazil's Indians had little contact with outsiders until recently. Now, logging, mining, and new roads are bringing more people and development to this region.

Satellite View

Deforestation in the Amazon

Deforestation is changing the landscape of the Amazon rain forest. This satellite image shows new roads and cleared areas where people have taken resources from the forest.

Many people depend on the industries that result in deforestation. For example, people need wood for building and making paper. Also, farmers, loggers, and miners need to make a living. However, deforestation in the Amazon also threatens the survival of many plant and animal species. It also threatens hundreds of unique ecosystems.

Making Inferences What do you think might be some effects of building roads in the rain forest?

This new development provides needed income for some people. But it destroys large areas of the rain forest. It also creates tensions among the Brazilian Indians, new settlers, miners, and the government.

READING CHECK **Contrasting** How does the northeast of Brazil differ from the southeast?

SUMMARY AND PREVIEW In this section you read about Brazil—a huge country of many contrasts. Brazil reflects the mixing of people and cultures from its history. In the next section you will learn about Brazil's neighbors—Argentina, Uruguay, and Paraguay.

Section 2 Assessment

hmhsocialstudies.com
ONLINE QUIZ

Reviewing Ideas, Terms, and Places

1. **a. Recall** What European country colonized Brazil?
   b. Make Inferences Why did the colonists bring Africans to work on plantations as slaves?
   c. Elaborate Why do you think the main basis of Brazil's colonial economy changed over the years?

2. **a. Identify** What religion is most common in Brazil?
   b. Explain Why is so much of Brazil's culture influenced by African traditions?

3. **a. Define** What is a **megacity**, and what is an example of a megacity in Brazil?
   b. Make Inferences Why might development in the Amazon cause tensions between Brazilian Indians and new settlers?
   c. Elaborate How might life change for a person who moves from the northeast to the southeast?

Critical Thinking

4. **Finding Main Ideas** Review your notes on Brazil. Then, write a main idea statement about each region. Use a graphic organizer like this one.

	Main Idea
The Southeast	
The Northeast	
The Interior	
The Amazon	

FOCUS ON WRITING

5. **Writing about Brazil** What information about the history, people, and culture of Brazil will draw readers to the country? What regions do you think they would like to visit? List details and ideas for possible images for your Web site.

Connecting Ideas

Learn

You have already used several types of graphic organizers in this book. Graphic organizers are drawings that help you organize information and connect ideas.

One type of graphic organizer is a word web. A word web like the one at right helps you organize specific facts and details around a main topic. Notice that information gets more detailed as it gets farther away from the main topic.

Practice

Use the word web here to answer the following questions. You may also want to look back at the information on Brazilian culture in your textbook.

1 How can a graphic organizer help you connect ideas?

2 What is the main topic of this word web?

3 What three main ideas does this graphic organizer connect?

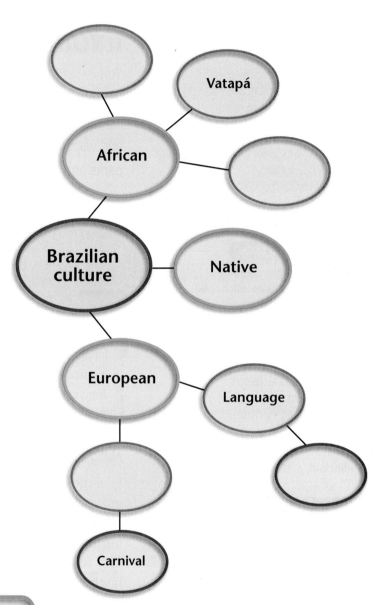

Apply

Copy the graphic organizer shown here in your notebook. Use the information on Brazilian culture in your textbook to fill in the blank circles with additional details about the main topic.

SECTION 3

Argentina, Uruguay, and Paraguay

What You Will Learn...

Main Ideas

1. European immigrants have dominated the history and culture of Argentina.
2. Argentina's capital, Buenos Aires, plays a large role in the country's government and economy today.
3. Uruguay has been influenced by its neighbors.
4. Paraguay is the most rural country in the region.

The Big Idea

Argentina, Uruguay, and Paraguay have been influenced by European immigration, a tradition of ranching, and large urban populations.

Key Terms and Places

gauchos, *p. 113*
Buenos Aires, *p. 114*
Mercosur, *p. 114*
informal economy, *p. 115*
landlocked, *p. 116*

hmhsocialstudies.com
TAKING NOTES

Use the graphic organizer online to organize your notes on Argentina, Uruguay, and Paraguay.

If **YOU** lived there...

You live in Montevideo, the capital of Uruguay. On weekends you like to visit the old part of the city and admire its beautiful buildings. You also enjoy walking along the banks of the Río de la Plata and watching fishers bring in their catch. Sometimes you visit the parks and beaches along the banks of the river.

How do you think the river has influenced Montevideo?

BUILDING BACKGROUND The southern countries of Atlantic South America—Argentina, Uruguay, and Paraguay—have all been influenced by their locations and European culture. Neither Spanish influence nor Indian culture is as strong in the southern part of South America as in other parts of the continent.

Argentina's History and Culture

Like most of South America, Argentina was originally home to groups of Indians. Groups living in the Pampas hunted wild game, while farther north Indians built irrigation systems for farming. However, unlike most of South America, Argentina has very few native peoples remaining. Instead, Argentina's culture has been mostly influenced by Europeans.

Early History

The first Europeans to come to Argentina were the Spanish. In the 1500s Spanish conquerors spread from the northern part of the continent into southern South America in search of silver and gold. They named the region Argentina. *Argentina* means "land of silver" or "silvery one."

Gauchos on the Pampas

Gauchos were a popular subject in Argentine art. In this painting from 1820, gauchos gather to watch a horse race.

ANALYZING VISUALS Why would horses be important to a gaucho?

The Spanish soon built settlements in Argentina. The Spanish monarch granted land to the colonists, who in turn built the settlements. These landowners were also given the right to force the Indians living there to work.

During the colonial era, the Pampas became an important agricultural region. Argentine cowboys, called **gauchos** (GOW-chohz), herded cattle and horses on the open grasslands. Although agriculture is still important on the Pampas, very few people in Argentina live as gauchos today.

In the early 1800s Argentina fought for independence from Spain. A period of violence and instability followed. Many Indians were killed or driven away by fighting during this time.

Modern Argentina

As the Indians were being killed off, more European influences dominated the region. New immigrants arrived from Italy, Germany, and Spain. Also, the British helped build railroads across the country. Railroads made it easier for Argentina to transport agricultural products for export to Europe. Beef exports, in particular, made the country rich.

Argentina remained one of South America's richest countries throughout the 1900s. However, the country also struggled under dictators and military governments during those years.

Some political leaders, like Eva Perón, were popular. But many leaders abused human rights. During the "Dirty War" in the 1970s, they tortured and killed many accused of disagreeing with the government. Both the country's people and its economy suffered. Finally, in the 1980s, Argentina's last military government gave up power to an elected government.

BIOGRAPHY

Eva Perón
(1919–1952)

Known affectionately as Evita, Eva Perón helped improve the living conditions of people in Argentina, particularly the poor. As the wife of Argentina's president, Juan Perón, Evita established thousands of hospitals and schools throughout Argentina. She also helped women gain the right to vote. After years of battling cancer, Evita died at age 33. All of Argentina mourned her death for weeks.

Analyzing Why was Eva Perón able to help many people?

People and Culture

Argentina's historical ties to Europe still affect its culture. Most of Argentina's roughly 40 million people are descended from Spanish, Italian, or other European settlers. Argentine Indians and mestizos make up only about 3 percent of the population. Most Argentines are Roman Catholic.

Beef is still a part of Argentina's culture. A popular dish is parrilla (pah-REE-yah), which includes grilled sausage and steak. Supper is generally eaten late.

READING CHECK **Generalizing** What kind of governments did Argentina have in the 1900s?

Argentina Today

Today many more of Argentina's people live in **Buenos Aires** (BWAY-nohs EYE-rayz) than in any other city. Buenos Aires is the country's capital. It is also the second-largest urban area in South America. Much of Argentina's industry is located in and around Buenos Aires. Its location on the coast and near the Pampas has contributed to its economic development.

The Pampas are the country's most developed agricultural region. About 11 percent of Argentina's labor force works in agriculture. Large ranches and farms there produce beef, wheat, and corn for export to other countries.

Argentina's economy has always been affected by government policies. In the 1990s government leaders made economic reforms to help businesses grow. Argentina joined **Mercosur**—an organization that promotes trade and economic cooperation among the southern and eastern countries of South America. By the late 1900s and early 2000s, however, heavy debt and government spending brought Argentina into an economic crisis.

Argentina: Population

PARAGUAY

Tropic of Capricorn

CHILE

San Miguel de Tucumán

30°S

Córdoba

Mendoza

Rosario

BRAZIL

URUGUAY

Buenos Aires

PACIFIC OCEAN

ARGENTINA

ATLANTIC OCEAN

40°S

50°S

- 10,000 people

0   300   600 Miles
0   300   600 Kilometers

Projection: Lambert Azimuthal Equal-Area

map zone Geography Skills

Place Buenos Aires is home to nearly a third of all Argentines.
1. **Interpreting Graphs** How many times bigger is Buenos Aires than Argentina's second-largest city?
2. **Analyze** What might be a benefit and a drawback of having most of the country's population in one area?

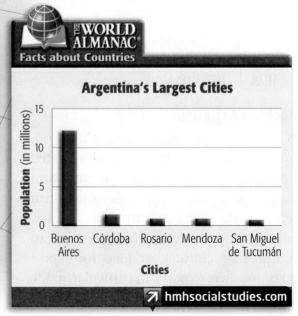

THE WORLD ALMANAC
Facts about Countries

Argentina's Largest Cities

Population (in millions)

15

10

5

0

Buenos Aires   Córdoba   Rosario   Mendoza   San Miguel de Tucumán

Cities

↗ hmhsocialstudies.com

Buenos Aires

Buenos Aires is a huge, modern city. Its main street is said to be the widest avenue in the world.

ANALYZING VISUALS What do the wide street and trees suggest about the people who built this city?

The economic crisis caused a political crisis. As a result, during 2001, Argentina's government changed hands four times as its leaders tried to solve the problems. By 2003 the economy had stabilized somewhat, but thousands of people's lives had changed forever. The crisis caused many people who once had professional careers to lose their jobs and join the informal economy. The **informal economy** is a part of the economy based on odd jobs that people perform without government regulation through taxes. Today many Argentines are still searching for ways to improve their economy.

READING CHECK Comparing and Contrasting What are some similarities and differences between Buenos Aires and the Pampas?

Uruguay

Tucked between Argentina and Brazil lies Uruguay. Its capital, Montevideo (mawn-tay-vee-DAY-oh), is located on the north shore of the Río de la Plata, not far from Buenos Aires. Uruguay has always been influenced by its larger neighbors.

Portugal claimed Uruguay during the colonial era, but the Spanish took over in the 1770s. By that time, few Uruguayan Indians remained. A few years later, in 1825, Uruguay declared independence from Spain. Since then, military governments have ruled Uruguay off and on. In general, however, the country has a strong tradition of respect for political freedom. Today Uruguay is a democracy.

People

As in Argentina, people of European descent make up the majority of Uruguay's population. Only about 12 percent of the population is mestizo, Indian, or of African descent. Roman Catholicism is the main religion in the country. Spanish is the official language, but many people also speak Portuguese because of Uruguay's location near Brazil.

More than 90 percent of Uruguay's people live in urban areas. More than a third of Uruguayans live in and near Montevideo. The country has a high literacy rate. In addition, many people there have good jobs and can afford a wide range of consumer goods and travel to Europe. However, many young people leave Uruguay to explore better economic opportunities elsewhere.

Economy

FOCUS ON
READING
Where can you
find the definition
of *landlocked*?

Just as Uruguay's culture is tied to its neighbors, its economy is tied to the economies of Brazil and Argentina. In fact, more than half of Uruguay's foreign trade is with these two Mercosur partners. Beef is an important export. As in Argentina, ranchers graze livestock on inland plains.

Agriculture, along with some limited manufacturing, is the basis of Uruguay's economy. Uruguay has few mineral resources. One important source of energy is hydroelectric power. Developing poor rural areas in the interior, where resources are in short supply, is a big challenge.

READING CHECK **Compare** In what ways is Uruguay similar to Argentina?

Paraguay

Paraguay shares borders with Bolivia, Brazil, and Argentina. It is a landlocked country. **Landlocked** means completely surrounded by land with no direct access to the ocean. The Paraguay River divides the country into two regions. East of the river is the country's most productive farmland. Ranchers also graze livestock in some parts of western Paraguay.

Paraguay was claimed by Spanish settlers in the mid-1530s. It remained a Spanish colony until 1811, when it won independence. From independence until 1989, Paraguay was ruled off and on by dictators. Today the country has elected leaders and a democratic government.

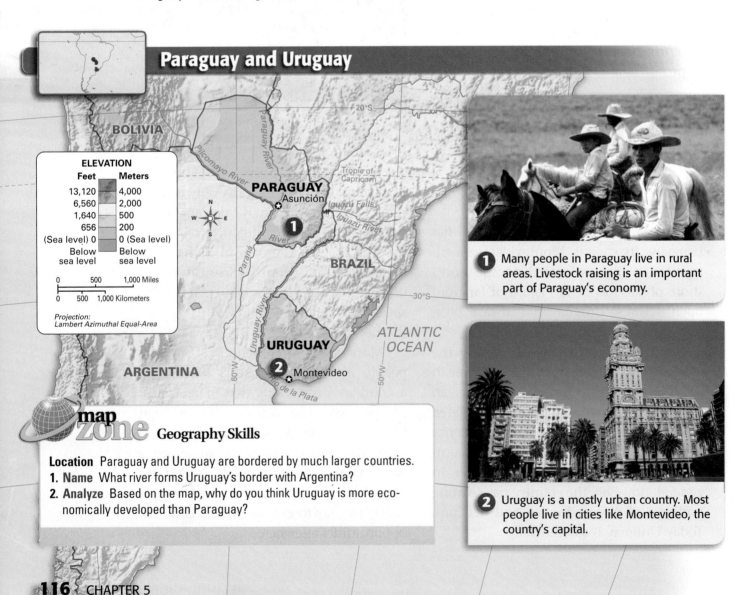

Paraguay and Uruguay

ELEVATION

Feet	Meters
13,120	4,000
6,560	2,000
1,640	500
656	200
(Sea level) 0	0 (Sea level)
Below sea level	Below sea level

0   500   1,000 Miles
0   500   1,000 Kilometers

Projection:
Lambert Azimuthal Equal-Area

BOLIVIA

Pilcomayo River

Paraguay River

20°S

Tropic of Capricorn

PARAGUAY
Asunción ①

Iguazú Falls

Iguazú River

Paraná River

BRAZIL

Uruguay River

30°S

ARGENTINA

URUGUAY
② Montevideo

Río de la Plata

ATLANTIC OCEAN

60°W   50°W

map zone **Geography Skills**

Location Paraguay and Uruguay are bordered by much larger countries.
1. **Name** What river forms Uruguay's border with Argentina?
2. **Analyze** Based on the map, why do you think Uruguay is more economically developed than Paraguay?

① Many people in Paraguay live in rural areas. Livestock raising is an important part of Paraguay's economy.

② Uruguay is a mostly urban country. Most people live in cities like Montevideo, the country's capital.

People

A great majority—about 95 percent—of Paraguayans are mestizos. Indians and people of mostly European descent make up the rest of the population. Paraguay has two official languages. Almost all people in Paraguay speak both Spanish and Guarani (gwah-ruh-NEE), an Indian language. As in Uruguay, most people are Roman Catholic.

Paraguay's capital and largest city is Asunción (ah-soon-SYOHN). The city is located along the Paraguay River near the border with Argentina.

Economy

Much of Paraguay's wealth is controlled by a few rich families and companies. These families and companies have tremendous influence over the country's government.

Agriculture is an important part of the economy. In fact, nearly half of the country's workers are farmers. Many of these farmers grow just enough food to feed themselves and their families. They grow crops such as corn, cotton, soybeans, and sugarcane. Paraguay also has many small businesses but not much industry.

Paraguay's future may be promising as the country learns how to use its resources more effectively. For example, the country has built large hydroelectric dams on the Paraná River. These dams provide more power than Paraguay needs, so Paraguay is able to sell the surplus electricity to Brazil and Argentina.

READING CHECK **Contrast** How are the people of Paraguay different from the people of Argentina and Uruguay?

SUMMARY AND PREVIEW The people of Paraguay, Argentina, and Uruguay share some aspects of their European heritage. Their economies are also closely tied. In the next chapter you will learn about these countries' neighbors to the west.

Section 3 Assessment

Reviewing Ideas, Terms, and Places

1. **a. Define** What is a **gaucho**?
   b. Explain Why is Argentina's population mostly of European descent?
2. **a. Identify** What is Argentina's biggest city?
   b. Make Inferences What benefits do you think being part of **Mercosur** brings to Argentina?
   c. Elaborate What are some benefits the **informal economy** provides, and what are some of its drawbacks?
3. **a. Recall** Where is Uruguay's capital located?
   b. Summarize How has Uruguay's location influenced its culture?
4. **a. Define** What does it mean to say a country is **landlocked**?
   b. Explain What is Paraguay's economy like?
   c. Predict What are some possible ways Paraguay may be able to improve its economy in the future?

Critical Thinking

5. **Comparing and Contrasting** Look over your notes on Uruguay and Paraguay. Then draw a diagram like the one here and use it to show similarities and differences between the two countries.

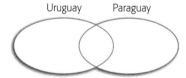

Uruguay   Paraguay

Focus on Writing

6. **Thinking about Argentina, Uruguay, and Paraguay** Add details about these countries to your notes for your Web site. What information on history, culture, and specific locations will you include? For each country, think of one image that would best illustrate it.

from
The Gaucho Martín Fierro

by José Hernández

About the Reading *José Hernández spent part of his childhood on Argentina's Pampas. The gauchos lived freely on the plains there, herding cattle. In 1872 he published an epic poem about his days as an Argentine cowboy. The passage below is an excerpt.*

AS YOU READ Notice the emotion with which Hernández writes.

Gauchos spent a lot of time alone on the plains, but sometimes they got together for games and amusement.

GUIDED READING

WORD HELP

lassoing catching with a rope
steers cattle
keen happy, eager

❶ Notice Hernández's description of the Pampas.

❷ Hernández describes the work of gauchos.

What were some activities of gauchos?

Even the poorest gaucho
had a string of matching horses;
he could always afford some amusement,
and people were ready for anything . . .
Looking out across the land
you'd see nothing but cattle and sky. ❶

When the branding-time came round
that was work to warm you up!
What a crowd! lassoing the running steers
and keen to hold and throw them . . . ❷
What a time that was! in those days surely
there were champions to be seen . . .

And the games that would get going
when we were all of us together!
We were always ready for them,
as at times like those
a lot of neighbors would turn up
to help out the regular hands.

Connecting Literature to Geography

1. **Identifying Points of View** Hernández had happy memories of his days as a gaucho. What words and phrases demonstrate how Hernández felt?

2. **Analyzing** Although few people still work as gauchos, they are popular subjects in Argentine literature. What aspects of gaucho life do you think modern readers find appealing?

Chapter Review

Geography's Impact
video series
Review the video to answer the closing question:
What are some arguments for and against deforestation?

Visual Summary

Use the visual summary below to help you review the main ideas of the chapter.

QUICK FACTS

The lush Amazon rain forest covers a huge part of the region.

Brazil has many large cities as well as large rural areas.

Argentina, Uruguay, and Paraguay have large plains that are good for ranching.

Reviewing Vocabulary, Terms, and Places

For each group of terms below, write a sentence that shows how all the terms in the group are related.

1. estuary
   Río de la Plata
   Buenos Aires
2. megacity
   favelas
   aspects
3. gauchos
   Pampas
4. soil exhaustion
   deforestation
   Amazon River
5. Rio de Janeiro
   São Paulo
   Manaus

Comprehension and Critical Thinking

SECTION 1 *(Pages 102–105)*

6. **a. Recall** What kind of climate does the Amazon Basin have?

   b. Contrast How are northern Brazil and southern Argentina different?

   c. Elaborate How might the region's major physical features have influenced development and daily life in Atlantic South America?

SECTION 2 *(Pages 106–111)*

7. **a. Describe** What parts of Brazilian culture reflect African influences?

   b. Analyze What factors lead people from the northeast of Brazil to move to the southeast?

   c. Evaluate Is deforestation of the Amazon rain forest necessary? Explain your answer. What arguments might someone with a different opinion use?

8. a. Describe How is Argentina's culture different from other South American countries?

b. Contrast What is one difference between Uruguay and Paraguay?

c. Predict As Argentina's economy improves, what might happen to its informal economy?

Social Studies Skills

9. Connecting Ideas Draw a graphic organizer to help you organize information about the economy in Atlantic South America. One has been started for you below. You will need to add more ovals to contain the information.

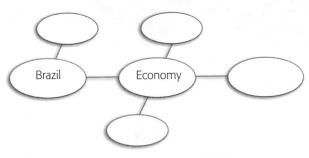

Using the Internet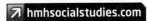

10. Activity: Creating a Poster The Amazon River is the world's second-longest river. Through your online textbook, explore the many aspects of the river, including its wildlife, the rain forest it cuts through, the people who live alongside it, and the environmental issues surrounding it. Use the information you find and the interactive template provided to create a poster about the amazing Amazon River.

↗ **hmhsocialstudies.com**

Map Activity

11. Atlantic South America On a separate sheet of paper, match the letters on the map with their correct labels.

São Paulo	Pampas	Patagonia
Paraná River	Río de la Plata	Amazon River

↗ **hmhsocialstudies.com** INTERACTIVE MAP

FOCUS ON READING AND WRITING

12. Using Context Clues Look through the chapter and pick out two difficult words that you had to figure out by using context clues. Then, note the context clues you used to help you figure out the definitions of the difficult words.

13. Creating a Web Site You can create a real Web site or a paper version of a Web site. First, look back through your notes and choose key ideas about each country to include. In designing your site, first include a home page that briefly describes the region. Indicate links for pages about each of the countries in the region. Each of your country pages should include one short paragraph and one image. Remember to keep the pages simple—too much text might overwhelm your readers and send them off to another site!

Standardized Test Prep

DIRECTIONS: *Read questions 1 through 7 and write the letter of the best response. Then read question 8 and write your own well-constructed response.*

1 **In which country do most people speak Portuguese?**

A Brazil

B Argentina

C Uruguay

D Paraguay

2 **What major river flows through northwestern Brazil?**

A Río de la Plata

B Uruguay River

C Paraná River

D Amazon River

3 **Which of the following statements about Argentina is true?**

A Most people are mestizos.

B Most people in Argentina live on the Pampas.

C Argentina is a member of Mercosur.

D Argentina has had a stable government and economy since 2000.

4 **Which of the following was an effect of the "Dirty War" in Argentina?**

A The country's economy suffered.

B Eva Perón became a popular political leader.

C Many Indians were killed on the Pampas.

D People elected military leaders to rule their country.

5 **What is the most important part of the economy of Paraguay?**

A mining

B agriculture

C manufacturing

D logging

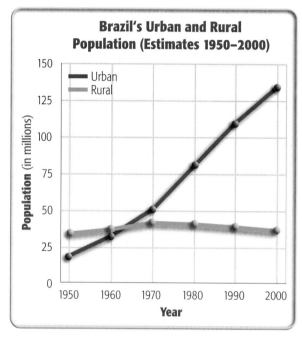

Brazil's Urban and Rural Population (Estimates 1950–2000)

Source: Instituto Brasileiro de Geografia e Estatística

6 **Based on the graph above, which of the following statements is false?**

A Brazil's urban population is increasing while the rural population is decreasing.

B By 1960 more people in Brazil lived in urban areas than in rural areas.

C In 1950 more people in Brazil lived in rural areas than in urban areas.

D Brazil's total population is growing.

7 **Based on the graph above, about how many people lived in urban areas of Brazil in 1990?**

A 20 million

B 135 million

C 110 million

D 40 million

8 **Extended Response** Study the graph above and the information in your book about Brazil today. Then write a brief essay explaining how urban and rural landscapes in Brazil are changing. You will also want to discuss the causes and effects of this change.

Pacific South America

Essential Question How has political unrest shaped the nations of Pacific South America?

? What You Will Learn...

In this chapter you will learn about the Andes mountains that dominate the physical geography of Pacific South America. You will also study the history and culture of the region. In addition, you will learn about some of the struggles and progress happening today in Ecuador, Peru, Bolivia, and Chile.

FOCUS ON READING AND SPEAKING

Making Inferences An inference is a kind of guess. Sometimes an author does not give you complete information, and you have to make an inference. As you read, try to fill in gaps in information. Make guesses about things the writer does not tell you directly. **See the lesson, Making Inferences, on page 199.**

Interviewing Interviews with experts are a great way to learn new information. As you read about Pacific South America, you will identify questions for an interview. Then, with a partner, you will create a script for an interview about the region. One of you will play the role of the interviewer, and one will play the regional expert.

0° Equator — Galápagos Islands (ECUADOR)

10°S

PACIFIC OCEAN

20°S

Tropic of Capricorn

map zone

Geography Skills

Location The countries of Pacific South America lie on the western side of South America.

1. **Identify** Which country is landlocked?
2. **Analyze** How do you think Chile's shape affects life in that country?

30°S

40°S

Physical Geography The Andes are the second-highest mountain range in the world. These peaks are in a national park in Chile.

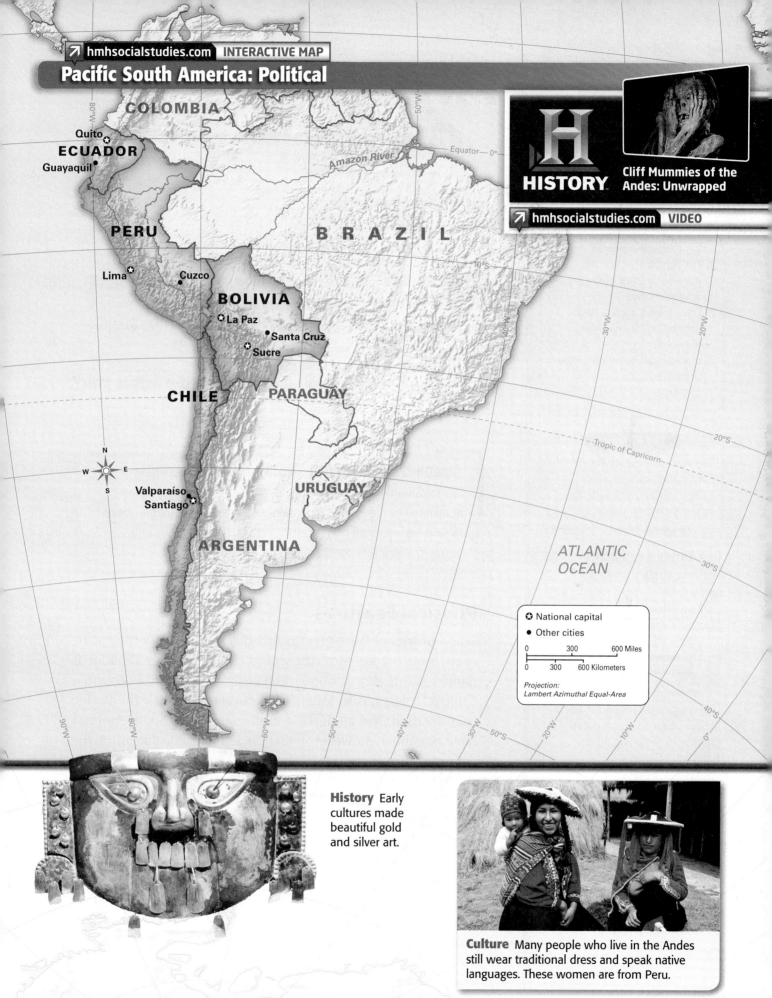

Pacific South America: Political

COLOMBIA

Quito ✪
ECUADOR
Guayaquil •

PERU

Lima ✪   Cuzco •

BOLIVIA
✪ La Paz
• Santa Cruz
✪ Sucre

CHILE   PARAGUAY

BRAZIL

Amazon River

Equator — 0°

10°S

Valparaíso •
Santiago ✪

URUGUAY

Tropic of Capricorn

20°S

ARGENTINA

ATLANTIC
OCEAN

30°S

40°S

✪ National capital
• Other cities

0   300   600 Miles
0   300   600 Kilometers

Projection:
Lambert Azimuthal Equal-Area

HISTORY
Cliff Mummies of the
Andes: Unwrapped

↗ hmhsocialstudies.com VIDEO

History Early
cultures made
beautiful gold
and silver art.

Culture Many people who live in the Andes
still wear traditional dress and speak native
languages. These women are from Peru.

Physical Geography

What You Will Learn...

Main Ideas

1. The Andes are the main physical feature of Pacific South America.
2. The region's climate and vegetation change with elevation.
3. Key natural resources in the region include lumber, oil, and minerals.

The Big Idea

The Andes dominate Pacific South America's physical geography and influence the region's climate and resources.

Key Terms and Places

altiplano, *p. 125*
strait, *p. 125*
Atacama Desert, *p. 127*
El Niño, *p. 127*

hmhsocialstudies.com
TAKING NOTES

Use the graphic organizer online to take notes on the physical geography of Pacific South America.

If **YOU** lived there...

You and your family fish for herring in the cold waters off the coast of Peru. Last year, however, an event called El Niño changed both the weather and the water. El Niño made the nearby ocean warmer. Without cold water, all the herring disappeared. You caught almost no fish at all. El Niño also caused terrible weather on the mainland.

How might another El Niño affect you?

BUILDING BACKGROUND Although most of the countries of Pacific South America lie along the coast, their landscapes are dominated by the rugged mountain range called the Andes. These mountains influence climates in the region. Ocean winds and currents also affect coastal areas here.

Physical Features

The countries of Pacific South America stretch along the Pacific coast from the equator, for which the country of Ecuador is named, south almost to the Arctic Circle. One narrow country, Chile (CHEE-lay), is so long that it covers about half the Pacific coast by itself. Not all of the countries in Pacific South America have coastlines, however. Bolivia is landlocked. But all of the countries in this region do share one major physical feature— the high Andes mountains.

Mountains

The Andes run through Ecuador, Peru, Bolivia, and Chile. Some ridges and volcanic peaks in the Andes rise more than 20,000 feet (6,800 m) above sea level. Because two tectonic plates meet at the region's edge, earthquakes and volcanoes are a constant threat. Sometimes these earthquakes disturb Andean glaciers, sending ice and mud rushing down mountain slopes.

Landscapes in the Andes differ from south to north. In southern Chile, rugged mountain peaks are covered by ice caps. In the north, the Andes are more rounded than rugged, and there the range splits into two ridges. In southern Peru and Bolivia these ridges are quite far apart. A broad, high plateau called the **altiplano** lies between the ridges of the Andes.

Water and Islands

Andean glaciers are the source for many tributaries of the Amazon River. Other than the Amazon tributaries, the region has few major rivers. Rivers on the altiplano have no outlet to the sea. Water collects in two large lakes. One of these, Lake Titicaca, is the highest lake in the world that large ships can cross.

At the southern tip of the continent, the Strait of Magellan links the Atlantic and Pacific oceans. A **strait** is a narrow body of water connecting two larger bodies of water. The large island south of the strait is Tierra del Fuego, or "land of fire."

Chile and Ecuador both control large islands in the Pacific Ocean. Ecuador's volcanic Galápagos Islands have wildlife not found anywhere else in the world.

READING CHECK Contrasting How do the Andes differ from north to south?

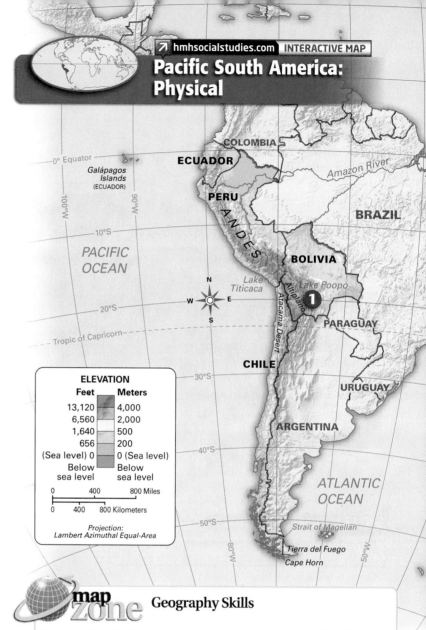

hmhsocialstudies.com **INTERACTIVE MAP**

Pacific South America: Physical

ELEVATION

Feet	Meters
13,120	4,000
6,560	2,000
1,640	500
656	200
(Sea level) 0	0 (Sea level)
Below sea level	Below sea level

0   400   800 Miles

0   400   800 Kilometers

Projection:
Lambert Azimuthal Equal-Area

map zone **Geography Skills**

Regions The Andes stretch all through the countries of Pacific South America.
1. **Identify** To what country do the Galápagos Islands belong?
2. **Interpret** How do you think the Andes affect life in the region?

1 Llamas graze on the high, dry altiplano. The climate on the altiplano is too dry for trees to grow.

125

Close-up

Climate Zones in the Andes

Five climate zones exist in the Andes. The different elevations support different types of plant and animal life.

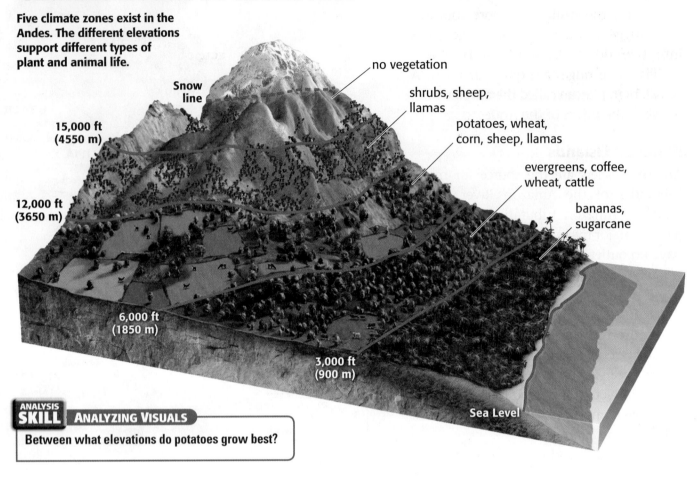

- no vegetation
- shrubs, sheep, llamas
- potatoes, wheat, corn, sheep, llamas
- evergreens, coffee, wheat, cattle
- bananas, sugarcane

Snow line

15,000 ft (4550 m)

12,000 ft (3650 m)

6,000 ft (1850 m)

3,000 ft (900 m)

Sea Level

ANALYSIS SKILL ANALYZING VISUALS

Between what elevations do potatoes grow best?

Climate and Vegetation

FOCUS ON READING

What can you infer about the location of mountains in Ecuador?

Climate, vegetation, and landscapes all vary widely in Pacific South America. We usually think of latitude as the major factor that affects climate. However, in Pacific South America, elevation has the biggest effect on climate and vegetation.

Elevation

Mountain environments change with elevation. For this reason, we can identify five different climate zones in the Andes. You can see these different climate zones on the diagram above.

The lowest zone includes the hot and humid lower elevations near sea level. Crops such as sugarcane and bananas grow well there. This first zone is often found along the coast, but it is also found inland in eastern Ecuador and Peru and northern Bolivia. These regions are part of the Amazon basin. They have a humid tropical climate with thick, tropical rain forests.

As elevation increases, the air becomes cooler. The second elevation zone has moist climates with mountain forests. This zone is good for growing coffee. In addition, many of Pacific South America's large cities are located in this zone.

Higher up the mountains is a third, cooler zone of forests and grasslands. Farmers grow potatoes and wheat there. Many people in Pacific South America live and farm in this climate zone.

126 CHAPTER 6

At a certain elevation, the climate becomes too cool for trees to grow. This fourth climate zone above the tree line contains alpine meadows with grasslands and hardy shrubs. The altiplano region between the two ridges of the Andes lies mostly in this climate zone.

The fifth climate zone, in the highest elevations, is very cold. No vegetation grows in this zone because the ground is almost always covered with snow and ice.

Deserts

Pacific South America also has some climates that are not typical of any of the five climate zones. Instead of hot and humid climates, some coastal regions have desert climates.

Northern Chile contains the **Atacama Desert**. This desert is about 600 miles (965 km) long. Rain falls there less than five times a century, but fog and low clouds are common. They form when a cold current in the Pacific Ocean chills the warmer air above the ocean's surface. Cloud cover keeps the air near the ground from being warmed by the sun. As a result, coastal Chile is one of the cloudiest—and driest—places on Earth.

In Peru, some rivers cut through the dry coastal region. They bring snowmelt down from the Andes. Because they rely on melting snow, some of these rivers only appear at certain times of the year. The rivers have made some small settlements possible in these dry areas.

El Niño

About every two to seven years, this dry region experiences **El Niño**, an ocean and weather pattern that affects the Pacific coast. During an El Niño year, cool Pacific water near the coast warms. This change may cause extreme ocean and weather events that can have global effects.

As El Niño warms ocean waters, fish leave what is usually a rich fishing area. This change affects fishers. Also, El Niño **causes** heavy rains, and areas along the coast sometimes experience flooding. Some scientists think that air pollutants have made El Niño last longer and have more damaging effects.

READING CHECK **Finding Main Ideas** How does elevation affect climate and vegetation?

ACADEMIC VOCABULARY

cause to make something happen

Natural Resources

The landscapes of Pacific South America provide many valuable natural resources. For example, forests in southern Chile and in eastern Peru and Ecuador provide lumber. Also, as you have read, the coastal waters of the Pacific Ocean are rich in fish.

Satellite View

Salt

Snow

Atacama Desert

The Atacama Desert lies between the Pacific coast and the Andes in northern Chile. In this image you can see two snowcapped volcanoes. The salt in the top right part of the image is formed from minerals carried there by rivers that only appear during certain months of the year. These seasonal rivers also support some limited vegetation.

Drawing Conclusions Why do you think there is snow on the volcanoes even though the desert gets hardly any precipitation?

Bolivia: Resources

Gold | Tin
Lead | Zinc
Silver

0   100   200 Miles
0   100   200 Kilometers

Projection: Lambert
Azimuthal Equal-Area

BRAZIL

Madeira R.

Madre de Dios

Guapore River

Beni River

BOLIVIA

Lake Titicaca

Mamoré River

Lake Poopó

—20°S—

Pilcomayo River

CHILE   ARGENTINA   PARAGUAY

map zone Geography Skills

Place Bolivia has many valuable mineral resources.
1. **Locate** Where are most of Bolivia's gold resources found?
2. **Interpret** What do you notice about the location of the mineral resources and the rivers?

In addition, the region has valuable oil and minerals. Ecuador in particular has large oil and gas reserves, and oil is the country's main export. Bolivia has some deposits of tin, gold, silver, lead, and zinc. Chile has copper deposits. In fact, Chile exports more copper than any other country in the world. Chile is also the site of the world's largest open pit mine.

Although the countries of Pacific South America have many valuable resources, one resource they do not have much of is good farmland. Many people farm, but the region's mostly cool, arid lands make it difficult to produce large crops for export.

READING CHECK **Categorizing** What types of resources do the countries of Pacific South America have?

SUMMARY AND PREVIEW The Andes are the main physical feature of Pacific South America. Next, you will learn how the Andes have affected the region's history and how they continue to affect life there today.

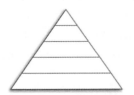

Section 1 Assessment

hmhsocialstudies.com
ONLINE QUIZ

Reviewing Ideas, Terms, and Places

1. **a. Identify** What is the main physical feature of Pacific South America?
   b. Analyze How is Bolivia's location unique in the region?
2. **a. Define** What is **El Niño**, and what are some of its effects?
   b. Draw Conclusions Why are parts of Ecuador, in the tropics, cooler than parts of southern Chile?
3. **a. Identify** What country in this region has large oil reserves?
   b. Make Inferences Why do you think much of the region is not good for farming?
   c. Elaborate What effects do you think copper mining in Chile might have on the environment?

Critical Thinking

4. **Categorizing** Review your notes on climate. Then use a diagram like this one to describe the climate and vegetation in each of the five climate zones.

FOCUS ON SPEAKING

5. **Describing Physical Geography** Note information about the physical features, climate and vegetation, and resources of Pacific South America. Write two questions and answers you can use in your interview.

Interpreting an Elevation Profile

Learn

An elevation profile is a diagram that shows a side view of an area. This kind of diagram shows the physical features that lie along a line from point A to point B. Keep in mind that an elevation profile typically exaggerates vertical distances because vertical and horizontal distances are measured differently on elevation profiles. If they were not, even tall mountains would appear as tiny bumps.

Vertical measurements are given on the sides of the diagram.

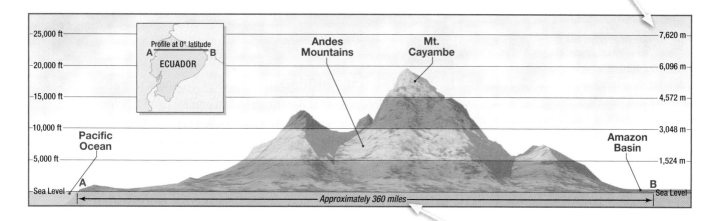

The horizontal measurement is given along the bottom of the diagram.

Practice

Use the elevation profile above to answer the following questions.

1 What place does this elevation profile measure?

2 What is the highest point, and what is its elevation?

3 How can you tell that the vertical distance is exaggerated?

Apply

Look at the physical map of Pacific South America in Section 1 of this chapter. Choose a latitude line and create your own elevation profile for the land at that latitude. Be sure to pay attention to the scale and the legend so that you use correct measurements.

History and Culture

What You Will Learn...

Main Ideas

1. The countries of Pacific South America share a history influenced by the Inca civilization and Spanish colonization.
2. The culture of Pacific South America includes American Indian and Spanish influences.

The Big Idea

Native cultures and Spanish colonization have shaped the history and culture of Pacific South America.

Key Terms

viceroy, *p. 131*
Creoles, *p. 132*

hmhsocialstudies.com
TAKING NOTES

Use the graphic organizer online to take notes on the history and culture of Pacific South America.

If **YOU** lived there...

You live in Cuzco, the capital of the Inca Empire. You are required to contribute labor to the empire, and you have been chosen to work on a construction project. Hauling the huge stones will be difficult, but the work will be rewarding. You can either choose to help build a magnificent temple to the sun god or you can help build a road from Cuzco to the far end of the empire.

Which project will you choose? Why?

BUILDING BACKGROUND Before Spanish conquerors arrived in the early 1500s, a great American Indian empire ruled this region. Cuzco was the Inca capital. The Incas were such skilled engineers and builders that many of their forts and temples still stand today.

History

Thousands of years ago, people in Pacific South America tried to farm on mountainsides as steep as bleachers. Other people tried to farm where there was almost no rain. These early cultures learned how to adapt to and modify their environments.

Early Cultures

Peru's first advanced civilization reached its height in about 900 BC in the Andes. These people built stone terraces into the steep mountainside so they could raise crops. In coastal areas, people created irrigation systems to store water and control flooding.

Agriculture supported large populations, towns, and culture. In the Bolivian highlands one early culture, the Tiahuanaco (tee-uh-wuh-NAH-koh), made huge stone carvings near a lakeshore. In another civilization on the coast, people scratched outlines of animals and other shapes into the surface of the Peruvian desert. These designs, known as the Nazca lines, are so large they can only be recognized from the sky.

An Inca City

The Inca city of Machu Picchu lay undiscovered high in the Andes until 1911.

ANALYZING VISUALS Why do you think Machu Picchu was undiscovered for almost 400 years?

The Inca Empire

Eventually, one group of people came to rule most of the region. By the early 1500s, these people, the Incas, controlled an area that stretched from northern Ecuador to central Chile. The Inca Empire was home to as many as 12 million people.

The huge Inca Empire was highly organized. Irrigation projects turned deserts into rich farmland. Thousands of miles of stone-paved roads connected the empire. Rope suspension bridges helped the Incas cross the steep Andean valleys.

As advanced as their civilization was, the Incas had no wheeled vehicles or horses. Instead, relay teams of runners carried messages from one end of the empire to the other. Working together, a team of runners could carry a message up to 150 miles (240 km) in one day. The runners did not carry any letters, however, because the Incas did not have a written language.

Spanish Rule

In spite of its great organization, however, the Inca Empire did not last long. A new Inca ruler, on his way to be crowned king, met the Spanish explorer Francisco Pizarro. Pizarro captured the Inca king, who ordered his people to bring enough gold and silver to fill a whole room. These riches were supposed to be a ransom for the king's freedom. Instead, Pizarro ordered the Inca king killed. Fighting broke out, and by 1535 the Spaniards had conquered the Inca Empire.

The new Spanish rulers often dealt harshly with the South American Indians of the fallen Inca Empire. Many Indians had to work in gold or silver mines or on the Spaniards' plantations. A Spanish **viceroy**, or governor, was appointed by the king of Spain to make sure the Indians followed the Spanish laws and customs that had replaced native traditions.

VIDEO
Machu Picchu

hmhsocialstudies.com

FOCUS ON READING
How do you think the South American Indians felt about the viceroy?

Independence

By the early 1800s, people in Pacific South America began to want independence. They began to revolt against Spanish rule. **Creoles**, American-born descendants of Europeans, were the main leaders of the revolts. The success of the revolts led to independence for Chile, Ecuador, Peru, and Bolivia by 1825.

READING CHECK **Evaluating** How did Inca civilization influence the history of the region?

Languages in Pacific South America

Legend:
- Spanish
- Aymara
- Guarani
- Quechua
- Mapuche

0   300   600 Miles
0   300   600 Kilometers
Projection: Lambert Azimuthal Equal-Area

Geography Skills

Regions Spanish is an official language throughout the region, but many people speak native languages instead.

1. Interpreting Graphs Where do more people speak native languages than Spanish?

2. Analyze Why do you think many people do not speak Spanish?

Culture

Spanish and native cultures have both left their marks on Pacific South America. Most people in the region speak Spanish, and Spanish is the official language in all of the countries of the region.

However, people in many parts of the region also maintain much of their native culture. Millions of South American Indians speak native languages in addition to or instead of Spanish. In Bolivia, two native languages are official languages in addition to Spanish.

The people and customs of Pacific South America also reflect the region's Spanish and Indian heritage. For example, Bolivia's population has the highest percentage of South American Indians of any country on the continent. Many Bolivian Indians follow customs and lifestyles that have existed for many centuries. They often dress in traditional styles—full skirts and derby hats for the women and colorful, striped ponchos for the men.

Another part of the region's culture that reflects Spanish and Indian influences is religion. Most people in Pacific

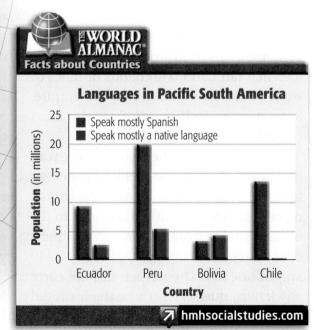

THE WORLD ALMANAC®
Facts about Countries

Languages in Pacific South America

- Speak mostly Spanish
- Speak mostly a native language

Population (in millions) — Country: Ecuador, Peru, Bolivia, Chile

hmhsocialstudies.com

Andean Culture

Every May, high in the Andes, Bolivians gather in Macha, Bolivia for Tinku, a festival honoring *Pachamama*, or mother earth.

ANALYZING VISUALS
What do you think the climate is like in Macha?

Music played on wooden flutes like these is popular in the Andes.

South America practice the religion of the Spanish—Roman Catholicism. Some people in the Andes, however, also still practice ancient religious customs. Every June, for example, people participate in a festival that was celebrated by the Incas to worship the sun. During festivals people wear traditional costumes, sometimes with wooden masks. They also play traditional instruments, such as wooden flutes.

READING CHECK Generalizing What traditional customs do people in the region still practice today?

SUMMARY AND PREVIEW Pacific South America was home to one of the greatest ancient civilizations in the Americas—the Inca. The Spanish conquered the Incas. Today the region's culture still reflects Inca and Spanish influences. Next, you will learn more about the governments and economies of Ecuador, Bolivia, Peru, and Chile today.

Section 2 Assessment

hmhsocialstudies.com
ONLINE QUIZ

Reviewing Ideas, Terms, and Places

1. **a. Recall** What ancient empire built paved roads through the Andes?
   b. Explain What role did **Creoles** play in the history of Pacific South America?
   c. Predict How might the Inca Empire have been different if the Incas had had wheels and horses?
2. **a. Recall** What country has the highest percentage of South American Indians in its population?
   b. Make Generalizations What aspects of culture in Pacific South America reflect Spanish influence, and what aspects reflect Indian heritage?

Critical Thinking

3. **Sequencing** Look over your notes on the region's history. Then draw a graphic organizer like the one here and use it to put major historical events in chronological order.

```
Nazca
lines  →  [    ]  →  [    ]  →  [    ]  →  [    ]
drawn
```

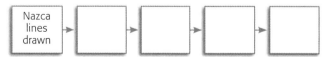
FOCUS ON SPEAKING

4. **Taking Notes on History and Culture** What information about the history and culture is important? Add two more questions, plus answers, to your notes.

Pacific South America Today

What You Will Learn...

Main Ideas

1. Ecuador struggles with poverty and political instability.
2. Bolivia's government is trying to gain stability and improve the economy.
3. Peru has made progress against poverty and violence.
4. Chile has a stable government and a strong economy.

The Big Idea

The countries of Pacific South America are working to overcome challenges of poverty and political instability.

Key Terms and Places

Quito, *p. 135*
La Paz, *p. 135*
Lima, *p. 136*
coup, *p. 137*
Santiago, *p. 138*

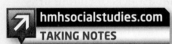
hmhsocialstudies.com
TAKING NOTES

Use the graphic organizer online to take notes on Pacific South America today.

If YOU lived there...

You are at a political rally in Valparaíso, Chile. Your family owns a vineyard nearby, so government policies about the economy affect you personally. You listen carefully to the speakers at the rally. Some politicians are in favor of more free trade with countries in North America. Others speak about different issues, such as housing and education.

What would you like to ask the politicians?

BUILDING BACKGROUND All the countries of Pacific South America have faced similar issues in recent years. These include poverty, unstable governments, economic development, and how to encourage development and still protect the environment. Several of these countries are making progress, while others still have problems.

Ecuador Today

In recent decades, the countries of Pacific South America have all experienced periods of political instability. Ecuador, in particular, has faced recent instability. Widespread poverty is a constant threat to a stable government in this country.

Government

Ecuador has been a democracy since 1979. Still, the country has experienced great political instability and corruption. From 1996–2007, the country had nine different presidents. In 2004, Ecuadorian president Lucio Gutiérrez fired the majority of the nation's supreme court judges because they did not support him. Soon after, to quiet his political opponents, Gutiérrez declared a state of emergency. In response, the Ecuadorian Congress forced Gutiérrez from power in 2005. In 2006, Ecuadorians elected Rafael Correa president. In 2009, Correa was the first Ecuadorian president to be re-elected in more than 30 years.

Economic Regions

Ecuador has three different economic regions. One region, the coastal lowlands, has agriculture and industry. The country's largest city, Guayaquil (gwy-ah-KEEL), is located there. It is Ecuador's major port and commercial center.

The Andean region of Ecuador is poorer. **Quito**, the national capital, is located there. Open-air markets and Spanish colonial buildings attract many tourists to Quito and other towns in the region.

A third region, the Amazon basin, has valuable oil deposits. The oil industry provides jobs that draw people to the region. Oil is also Ecuador's main export. But the oil industry has brought problems as well as benefits. The country's economy suffers if the world oil price drops. In addition, some citizens worry that drilling for oil could harm the rain forest.

READING CHECK **Generalizing** Why has Ecuador's government been unstable?

Bolivia Today

Like Ecuador, Bolivia is a poor country. Poverty has been a cause of political unrest in recent years.

Government

After years of military rule, Bolivia is a democracy. Bolivia's government is divided between two capital cities. The supreme court meets in Sucre (SOO-kray), but the congress meets in **La Paz**. Located at about 12,000 feet (3,660 m), La Paz is the highest capital city in the world. It is also Bolivia's main industrial center.

In the early 2000s, many Bolivians disagreed with their government's plans for fighting poverty. National protests forced several presidents to resign. Then in 2005, Bolivians elected an indigenous leader, Evo

Morales, as president. Re-elected president in 2009, Morales continues to work to improve the lives of Bolivia's poor.

Economy

Bolivia is the poorest country in South America. In the plains of eastern Bolivia there are few roads and little money for investment. However, foreign aid has provided funds for some development. In addition, the country has valuable resources, including metals and natural gas.

READING CHECK **Analyzing** Why might political revolts slow development?

CONNECTING TO Economics

The Informal Economy

Many people in the countries of Pacific South America are part of the informal economy. Street vendors, like the ones shown here in Quito, are common sights in the region's cities. People visit street vendors to buy items like snacks, small electronics, or clothing. The informal economy provides jobs for many people. However, it does not help the national economy because the participants do not pay taxes. Without income from taxes, the government cannot pay for services.

Analyzing How does the informal economy affect taxes?

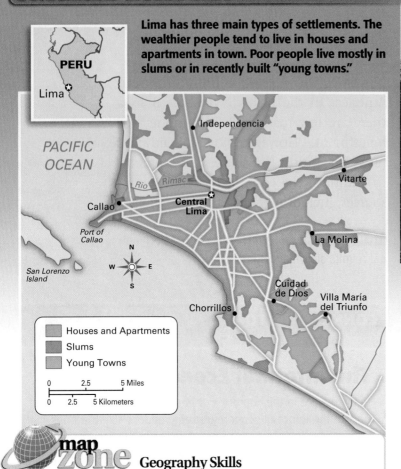

PERU

Lima

PACIFIC OCEAN

Independencia

Rio Rimac

Vitarte

Callao

Central Lima

Port of Callao

La Molina

San Lorenzo Island

N W E S

Cuidad de Dios

Villa María del Triunfo

Chorrillos

Lima has three main types of settlements. The wealthier people tend to live in houses and apartments in town. Poor people live mostly in slums or in recently built "young towns."

Houses and Apartments
Slums
Young Towns

0   2.5   5 Miles
0   2.5   5 Kilometers

map zone Geography Skills

Human-Environment Interaction People have built three different basic types of housing in and around Lima.
1. **Use the Map** What is the most common type of housing?
2. **Draw Conclusions** Why are most young towns built far from central Lima?

Houses and Apartments Most housing in Lima is made up of high-rise apartments and private houses, some of which are from the colonial era.

Peru Today

Peru is the largest and most populous country in Pacific South America. Today it is making some progress against political violence and poverty.

Lima

Peru's capital, **Lima** (LEE-muh), is the largest city in the region. Nearly one-third of all Peruvians live in Lima or the nearby port city of Callao (kah-YAH-oh). Lima has industry, universities, and government jobs, which attract many people from the countryside to Lima.

Lima was the colonial capital of Peru, and the city still contains many beautiful old buildings from the colonial era. It has high-rise apartments and wide, tree-lined boulevards. However, as in many big urban areas, a lot of people there live in poverty.

In spite of the poverty, central Lima has few slum areas. This is because most poor people prefer to claim land on the outskirts of the city and build their own houses. Often they can get only poor building materials. They also have a hard time getting water and electricity from the city.

Settlements of new self-built houses are called "young towns" in Lima. Over time, as people improve and add to their houses, the new settlements develop into large, permanent suburbs. Many of the people in Lima's young towns are migrants from the highlands. Some came to Lima to escape violence in their home villages.

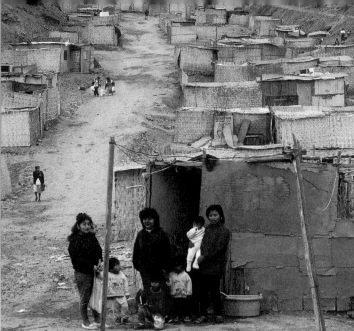

Slums Just outside downtown and near the port area, many people live in slum housing. These buildings are permanent, but run-down.

Young Towns Many poor people in recent years have taken over land on the outskirts of Lima and have built their own shelters.

Government

In the 1980s and 1990s, a terrorist group called the Shining Path was active. This group carried out deadly attacks because it opposed government policies. Some 70,000 people died in violence between the Shining Path and government forces, and Peru's economy suffered. However, after the arrest of the group's leaders, Peru's government began making progress against political violence and poverty. The country has an elected president and congress.

Resources

Peru's resources are key factors in its economic progress. Some mineral deposits are located near the coast, and hydroelectric projects on rivers provide energy. Peru's highlands are less developed than the coastal areas. However, many Peruvian Indians grow potatoes and corn there.

READING CHECK **Identifying Cause and Effect** How did the Shining Path affect Peru?

Chile Today

Like Peru, Chile has ended a long violent period. Chile now has a stable government and a growing economy.

Government

In 1970 Chileans elected a president who had some ideas influenced by communism. A few years later he was overthrown and died in a U.S.-backed military coup (KOO). A **coup** is a sudden overthrow of a government by a small group of people.

In the years after the coup, military rulers tried to crush their political enemies. Chile's military government was harsh and often violent. It imprisoned or killed thousands of people.

In the late 1980s Chile's military dictatorship weakened and Chileans created a new, democratic government. In 2006 Chileans elected their first female president, Michelle Bachelet, and in 2010 they elected business leader Sebastián Piñera president.

FOCUS ON READING

What can you infer about the reason for the end of the military government?

A man in Chile harvests grapes to be made into wine for export.

Resources and Economy

Chile's economy is the strongest in the region. Poverty rates have decreased, and Chile's prospects for the future seem bright. Small businesses and factories are growing quickly. More Chileans are finding work, and wages are rising.

About one-third of all Chileans live in central Chile. This region includes the capital, **Santiago**, and a nearby seaport, Valparaíso (bahl-pah-rah-EE-soh). Its mild Mediterranean climate allows farmers to grow many crops. For example, grapes grow well there, and Chilean fruit and wine are exported around the world.

Farming, fishing, forestry, and mining form the basis of Chile's economy. Copper mining is especially important. It accounts for more than one-third of Chile's exports.

Chile's economic stability was rocked by a massive earthquake that struck on February 27, 2010. The quake killed about 500 Chileans and caused about $30 billion of damage to buildings, homes, and streets. Today, Chile's people and government continue to rebuild their nation.

READING CHECK **Identifying Points of View** Why might Chile want to join a free trade group?

SUMMARY AND PREVIEW In recent years Ecuador, Peru, Bolivia, and Chile have struggled with political violence and poverty. However, Peru and Chile are recovering. Next, you will study the culture and economy of the United States.

Section 3 Assessment

Reviewing Ideas, Terms, and Places

1. **a. Identify** What is Ecuador's largest city?
   b. Make Generalizations Why have Ecuadorians been unhappy with their government in recent years?
2. **a. Identify** What are Bolivia's two capital cities?
   b. Analyze Why might Bolivia's economy improve in the future?
3. **a. Recall** Why did many Peruvians move to Lima from the highlands in the 1980s?
   b. Elaborate What challenges do you think people who move to **Lima** from the highlands face?
4. **a. Define** What is a **coup**?
   b. Make Inferences What might happen to Chile's economy if the world price of copper drops?

Critical Thinking

5. **Solving Problems** Review your notes. Then, in a diagram like the one here, write one sentence about each country, explaining how that country is dealing with poverty or government instability.

Ecuador	
Bolivia	
Peru	
Chile	

FOCUS ON SPEAKING

6. **Thinking about Pacific South America Today** Add questions about each country in Pacific South America to your notes. How might you answer these questions in your interview? Write down the answer to each question.

Chapter Review

Geography's Impact
video series
Review the video to answer the closing question:
Why do descendants of the Incas still live in the difficult high altitudes of the Andes?

Visual Summary

Use the visual summary below to help you review the main ideas of the chapter.

QUICK FACTS

The high Andes affect the climates and landscapes of Pacific South America.

Many South American Indians maintain traditional customs and ways of life in the Andes.

Today the countries of Pacific South America are working toward development and improved economies.

Reviewing Vocabulary, Terms, and Places

Write each word defined below, circling each letter that is marked by a star. Then write the word these letters spell.

1. _ _ * _ _ _ _ _ _ _ _ _ _ _ _—a desert in northern Chile that is one of the cloudiest and driest places on Earth

2. * _ _ _ _ —the capital of Peru

3. _ _ _ _ * _ _—the capital of Ecuador

4. _ * _ _ _ _ _ _ _—a governor appointed by the king of Spain

5. _ _ * _ _ _—one of the capitals of Bolivia

6. _ _ _ _ _ * _—an American-born descendant of Europeans

7. _ _ _ _ * _ _ _—a narrow passageway that connects two large bodies of water

8. _ _ * _ _ _ _—an ocean and weather pattern that affects the Pacific coast

9. _ * _ _ _—a sudden overthrow of a government by a small group of people

Comprehension and Critical Thinking

SECTION 1 *(Pages 124–128)*

10. **a. Describe** What are climate and vegetation like on the altiplano?

   b. Compare and Contrast What are two differences and one similarity between the Atacama Desert and the altiplano?

   c. Evaluate What elevation zone would you choose to live in if you lived in Pacific South America? Why would you choose to live there?

SECTION 2 *(Pages 130–133)*

11. **a. Describe** How did the Incas organize their huge empire?

   b. Analyze How have Spanish and native cultures left their marks on culture in Pacific South America?

   c. Elaborate Why do you think Pizarro killed the Inca king even though he had received riches as ransom?

PACIFIC SOUTH AMERICA **139**

12. **a. Identify** What country in Pacific South America has the healthiest economy?

   b. Analyze What problems in Ecuador and Bolivia cause political unrest?

   c. Evaluate What would be some benefits and drawbacks of moving from the highlands to one of Lima's "young towns"?

Using the Internet

13. **Activity: Analyzing Climate** Chile has steep mountains, volcanoes, a desert, a rich river valley, and thick forests. These diverse areas contain many different climates. Click on the links given in your online textbook to explore the many climates of Chile. Then test your knowledge by taking an online quiz.

   ↗ **hmhsocialstudies.com**

Social Studies Skills

Interpreting an Elevation Profile *Use the elevation profile on the Social Studies Skills page to answer the following questions.*

14. What is the purpose of an elevation profile?

15. Where can you find the vertical measurements on an elevation profile?

16. What horizontal distance does the elevation profile measure?

17. What is the elevation of the Amazon basin?

Map Activity

18. **Pacific South America** On a separate sheet of paper, match the letters on the map with their correct labels.

Strait of Magellan	Santiago, Chile
Quito, Ecuador	Atacama Desert
Andes	La Paz, Bolivia

↗ **hmhsocialstudies.com**   **INTERACTIVE MAP**

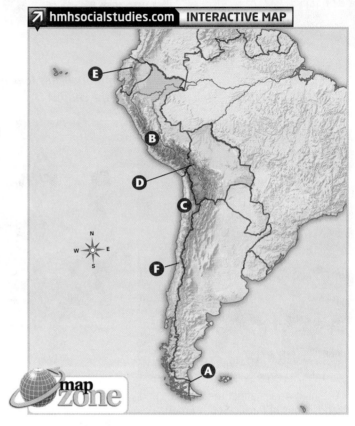

FOCUS ON READING AND SPEAKING

Making Inferences *Use the information in this chapter to answer the following questions.*

19. What is an inference?

20. What can you infer about the size of the population in the Atacama Desert? What clues led you to make this inference?

21. **Presenting an Interview** Now that you have questions and answers, work with a partner to write an interview script. Read through your script several times so that you know it well enough to sound natural during the interview. Remember to use a lively tone as you speak so that your audience will pay attention.

DIRECTIONS: Read questions 1 through 7 and write the letter of the best response. Then read question 8 and write your own well-constructed response.

1 The main mountain range located in Pacific South America is called the

A altiplano.

B Andes.

C Strait of Magellan.

D Pampas.

2 Which of the following conditions is a result of El Niño?

A increased greenhouse gases

B more fish in a usually poor fishing area

C drought on the Pacific coast

D warmer waters near the Pacific coast

3 What early culture had a huge empire in Pacific South America in the early 1500s?

A Inca

B Aztec

C Tiahuanaco

D Nazca

4 Which of the following statements about culture in Pacific South America is false?

A Most people speak Spanish.

B Chile has a higher percentage of Indians than any other country in South America.

C Religion in the region often combines Catholic and ancient native customs.

D Wooden flutes and drums are traditional instruments.

5 Which country's main export is oil?

A Bolivia

B Chile

C Ecuador

D Peru

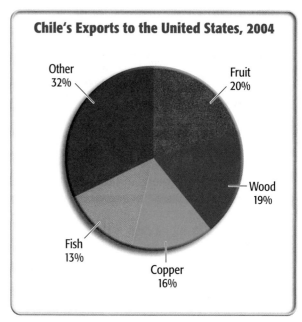

Chile's Exports to the United States, 2004

Other 32%, Fruit 20%, Wood 19%, Copper 16%, Fish 13%

Source: International Trade Administration, TradeStats Express

6 Based on the graph above, what one product is Chile's main export to the United States?

A fish

B wood

C fruit

D copper

7 What has been a major cause of political unrest in the region?

A dissatisfaction with economic policies

B arrest of the leaders of the Shining Path

C development of "young towns" in Peru

D high unemployment in Chile

8 **Extended Response** Using the graph above and your knowledge of Pacific South America today, compare and contrast the economic situations in each of the four countries.

CHAPTER 7

The United States

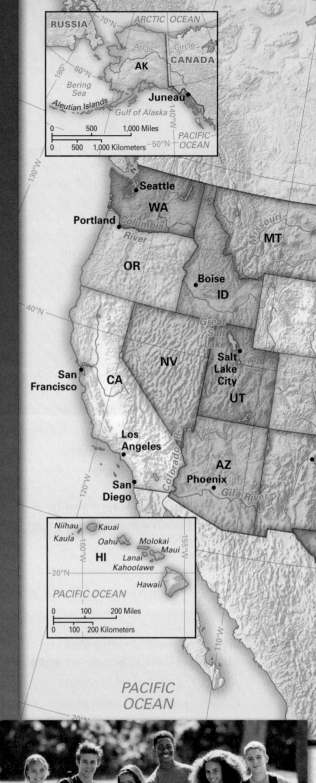

Essential Question What are the unique characteristics of the different regions of the United States?

? What You Will Learn...

In this chapter you will learn about the physical features, climates, and resources of the United States. You will also discover how democratic ideas and immigration have shaped the United States. Finally, you will learn about our country's different regions, diverse population, and the challenges we face as a nation.

FOCUS ON READING AND VIEWING

Categorizing A good way to make sense of what you read is to separate facts and details into groups, called categories. For example, you could sort facts about the United States into categories like natural resources, major cities, or rivers. As you read this chapter, look for ways to categorize details under each topic. **See the lesson, Categorizing, on page 200.**

Creating a Collage Artists create collages by gluing art and photographs onto a flat surface, such as a poster board. As you read this chapter, you will collect ideas for a collage about the United States. After you create your own collage, you will view and evaluate the collages of other students in your class.

Culture People of many different ethnic groups and cultures make up the population of the United States.

The United States: Political

HISTORY Paving America

↗ hmhsocialstudies.com **VIDEO**

CANADA

ND
Fargo
MN
SD
Minneapolis
WI
L. Superior
L. Michigan
L. Huron
MI
Ontario
L. Erie
ME
VT
NH
MA
Boston
CT
RI
NY
New York
40°N

WY
Cheyenne
NE
Lincoln
IA
Des Moines
Milwaukee
Chicago
Detroit
Cleveland
IN
OH
PA
Philadelphia
Baltimore
Washington, D.C.
NJ
DE
MD

CO
Denver
KS
Kansas City
MO
St. Louis
IL
Indianapolis
Ohio R.
KY
Lexington
WV
VA

Santa Fe
NM
OK
Oklahoma City
AR
Little Rock
Missouri R.
Mississippi R.
Memphis
Nashville
TN
NC
Charlotte
SC

TX
Dallas
Houston
Red R.
MS
Montgomery
AL
Atlanta
GA
Charleston
Jacksonville

LA
New Orleans
Rio Grande
Gulf of Mexico
Lake Okeechobee
FL
Miami
80°W

MEXICO
90°W

N W E S

ATLANTIC OCEAN
30°N

National capital ✪
Other cities •

0   200   400 Miles
0 200 400 Kilometers
Projection: Albers Equal Area

map zone

Geography Skills

Place The United States is made up of 50 states.
1. **Locate** What two countries border the United States?
2. **Contrast** How is Maryland's size and location different from California's size and location?

Geography The Grand Canyon in Arizona is one example of the many spectacular landscapes in the United States.

History The Statue of Liberty in New York Harbor symbolizes our freedom and our history as a democratic nation.

143

Physical Geography

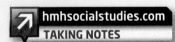
If **YOU** lived there...

You live in St. Louis, Missouri, which is located on the Mississippi River. For the next few days, you will travel down the river on an old-fashioned steamboat. The Mississippi begins in Minnesota and flows south through 10 states in the heart of the United States. On your trip, you bring a video camera to film life along this great river.

What will you show in your video about the Mississippi?

BUILDING BACKGROUND The United States stretches from sea to sea across North America. To the north is Canada and to the south lies Mexico. Because it is so large, the United States has a great variety of landscapes and climates.

Physical Features

The United States is the third largest country in the world behind Russia and Canada. Our country is home to an incredible variety of physical features. All but two of the 50 states—Alaska and Hawaii—make up the main part of the country. Look at the physical map of the United States on the next page. It shows the main physical features of our country. Use the map as you read about America's physical geography in the East and South, the Interior Plains, and the West.

The East and South

If you were traveling across the United States, you might start on the country's eastern coast. This low area, which is flat and close to sea level, is called the Atlantic Coastal Plain. As you go west, the land gradually rises higher to a region called the Piedmont. The **Appalachian Mountains**, which are the main mountain range in the East, rise above the Piedmont. These mountains are very old. For many millions of years, rain, snow, and wind

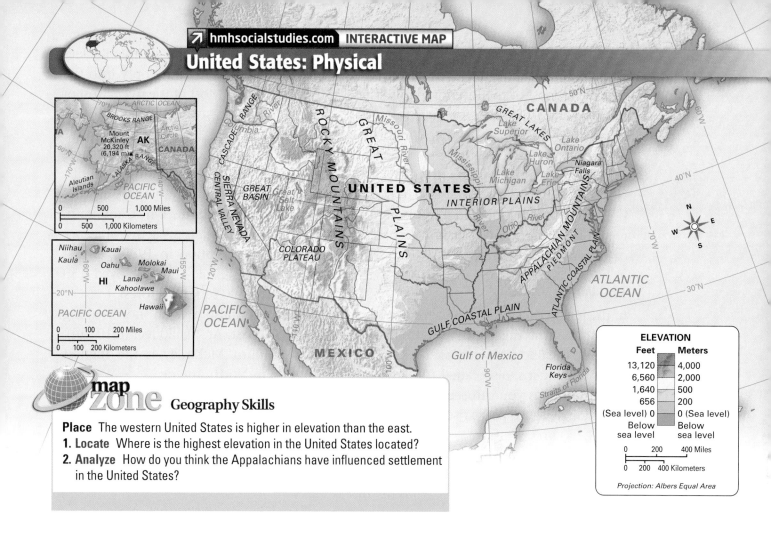

ELEVATION

Feet		Meters
13,120		4,000
6,560		2,000
1,640		500
656		200
(Sea level) 0		0 (Sea level)
Below sea level		Below sea level

Projection: Albers Equal Area

map zone Geography Skills

Place The western United States is higher in elevation than the east.

1. Locate Where is the highest elevation in the United States located?

2. Analyze How do you think the Appalachians have influenced settlement in the United States?

---

have eroded and smoothed their peaks. As a result, the highest mountain in the Appalachians is about 6,700 feet (2,040 m).

The Interior Plains

As you travel west from the Appalachians, you come across the vast Interior Plains that stretch to the Great Plains just east of the Rocky Mountains. The Interior Plains are filled with hills, lakes, and rivers. The first major water feature that you see here is called the **Great Lakes**. These lakes make up the largest group of freshwater lakes in the world. The Great Lakes are also an important waterway for trade between the United States and Canada.

West of the Great Lakes lies North America's largest and most important river, the **Mississippi River**. Tributaries in the interior plains flow to the Mississippi. A **tributary** is a smaller stream or river that flows into a larger stream or river.

Appalachians The smooth peaks of the Appalachian Mountains dominate the landscape of western North Carolina.

Along the way, these rivers deposit rich silt. The silt creates fertile farmlands that cover most of the Interior Plains. The Missouri and Ohio rivers are huge tributaries of the Mississippi. They help drain the entire Interior Plains.

Look at the map on the previous page. Notice the land begins to increase in elevation west of the Interior Plains. This higher region is called the Great Plains. Vast areas of grasslands cover these plains.

The West

In the region called the West, several of the country's most rugged mountain ranges make up the **Rocky Mountains**. These enormous mountains, also called the Rockies, stretch as far as you can see. Many of the mountains' jagged peaks rise above 14,000 feet (4,270 m).

FOCUS ON READING

Into what two categories might you group the details on rivers?

In the Rocky Mountains is a line of high peaks called the Continental Divide. A **continental divide** is an area of high ground that divides the flow of rivers towards opposite ends of a continent.

Rivers east of the divide in the Rockies mostly flow eastward and empty into the Mississippi River. Most of the rivers west of the divide flow westward and empty into the Pacific Ocean.

Farther west, mountain ranges include the Cascade Range and the Sierra Nevada. Most of the mountains in the Cascades are dormant volcanoes. One mountain, Mount Saint Helens, is an active volcano. A tremendous eruption in 1980 blew off the mountain's peak and destroyed 150 square miles (390 sq km) of forest.

Mountains also stretch north along the Pacific coast. At 20,320 feet (6,194 m), Alaska's Mount McKinley is the highest mountain in North America.

Far out in the Pacific Ocean are the islands that make up the state of Hawaii. Volcanoes formed these islands millions of years ago. Today, hot lava and ash continue to erupt from the islands' volcanoes.

READING CHECK **Summarizing** What are the major physical features of the United States?

Satellite View

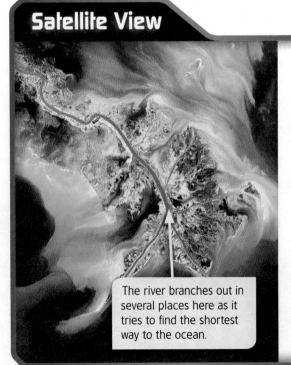

The river branches out in several places here as it tries to find the shortest way to the ocean.

The Mississippi River Delta

From its source in Minnesota, the Mississippi River flows south across the central United States. It ends at the tip of Louisiana, which is shown here. This satellite image shows the area where the Mississippi River meets the Gulf of Mexico. This area is called a delta. A river's delta is formed from sediment that a river carries downstream to the ocean. Sediment is usually made up of rocks, soil, sand, and dead plants. Each year, the Mississippi dumps more than 400 million tons of sediment into the Gulf of Mexico.

The light blue and green areas in this image are shallow areas of sediment. The deeper water of the Gulf of Mexico is dark blue. Also, notice that much of the delta land looks fragile. This is new land that the river has built up by depositing sediment.

Making Inferences What natural hazards might people living in the Mississippi Delta experience?

United States: Climate

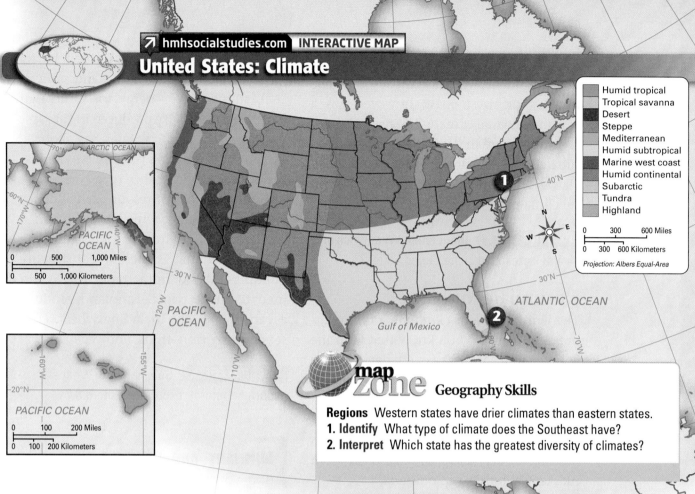

Humid tropical
Tropical savanna
Desert
Steppe
Mediterranean
Humid subtropical
Marine west coast
Humid continental
Subarctic
Tundra
Highland

0   300   600 Miles
0   300   600 Kilometers

Projection: Albers Equal-Area

ARCTIC OCEAN

PACIFIC OCEAN

PACIFIC OCEAN

PACIFIC OCEAN

Gulf of Mexico

ATLANTIC OCEAN

map zone Geography Skills

Regions Western states have drier climates than eastern states.
1. **Identify** What type of climate does the Southeast have?
2. **Interpret** Which state has the greatest diversity of climates?

Climate

Did you know that the United States has a greater variety of climates than any other country? Look at the map above to see the different climates of the United States.

The East and South

The eastern United States has three climate regions. In the Northeast, people live in a humid continental climate with snowy winters and warm, humid summers. Southerners, on the other hand, experience milder winters and the warm, humid summers of a humid subtropical climate. Most of Florida is warm all year.

The Interior Plains

Temperatures throughout the year can vary greatly in the Interior Plains. Summers are hot and dry in the Great Plains. However, most of the region has a humid continental climate with long, cold winters.

1 With a humid continental climate, New York City experiences cold winters with snowfall. In this climate people can ice skate during the winter.

2 With a humid subtropical climate, most of Florida has warm sunny days during most of the year. In this climate people can enjoy the region's beaches.

The West

Climates in the West are mostly dry. The Pacific Northwest coast, however, has a wet, mild coastal climate. The region's coldest climates are in Alaska, which has both subarctic and tundra climates. In contrast, Hawaii is the only state with a warm, tropical climate.

READING CHECK **Identifying** What types of climates are found in the United States?

Natural Resources

The United States is extremely rich in natural resources. Do you know that your life is affected in some way every day by these natural resources? For example, if you ate bread today, it was probably made with wheat grown in the fertile soils of the Interior Plains. If you rode in a car or on a bus recently, it may have used gasoline from Alaska, California, or Louisiana.

The United States is a major oil producer but uses more oil than it produces. In fact, we import more than one half of the oil we need.

Valuable minerals are mined in the Appalachians and Rockies. One mineral, coal, supplies the energy for more than half of the electricity produced in the United States. The United States has about 25 percent of the world's coal reserves and is a major coal exporter.

Other important resources include forests and farmland, which cover much of the country. The trees in our forests provide lumber that is used in constructing buildings. Wood from these trees is also used to make paper. Farmland produces a variety of crops including wheat, corn, soybeans, cotton, fruits, and vegetables.

READING CHECK **Summarizing** What are important natural resources in the U.S.?

SUMMARY AND PREVIEW In this section you learned about the geography, climates, and natural resources of the United States. In the next section, you will learn about the history and culture of the United States.

Section 1 Assessment

hmhsocialstudies.com
ONLINE QUIZ

Reviewing Ideas, Terms, and Places

1. a. **Define** What is a **tributary**?
   b. **Contrast** How are the **Appalachian Mountains** different from the **Rocky Mountains**?
   c. **Elaborate** Why are the **Great Lakes** an important waterway?
2. a. **Describe** What is the climate like in the Northeast?
   b. **Draw Conclusions** What would winter be like in Alaska?
3. a. **Recall** What kinds of crops are grown in the United States?
   b. **Explain** Why is coal an important resource?
   c. **Predict** What natural resources might not be as important to your daily life in the future?

Critical Thinking

4. **Categorizing** Copy the graphic organizer below. Use it to organize your notes on physical features, climate, and resources by region of the country.

East and South	Interior Plains	West

FOCUS ON VIEWING

5. **Thinking about Physical Geography** Jot down key words that describe the physical features and climate of the United States. Think of at least three objects or images you might use to illustrate physical features and climate.

Social Studies Skills

Using a Political Map

Learn

Many types of maps are useful in studying geography. Political maps are one of the most frequently used types of maps. These maps show human cultural features such as cities, states, and countries. Look at the map's legend to figure out how these features are represented on the map.

Most political maps show national boundaries and state boundaries. The countries on political maps are sometimes shaded different colors to help you tell where the borders of each country are located.

Practice

Use the political map here to answer the following questions.

• What countries does this map show?

• How does the map show the difference between state boundaries and national boundaries?

• What is the capital of Canada?

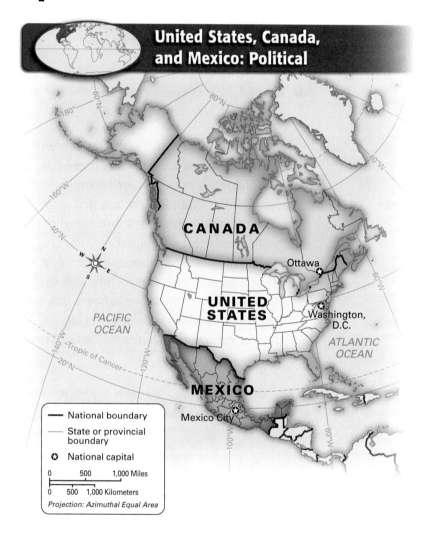

United States, Canada, and Mexico: Political

CANADA

Ottawa

UNITED STATES

PACIFIC OCEAN

Washington, D.C.

ATLANTIC OCEAN

MEXICO

Mexico City

— National boundary
— State or provincial boundary
✪ National capital

0   500   1,000 Miles
0 500 1,000 Kilometers
Projection: Azimuthal Equal Area

Apply

Using an atlas or the Internet, find a political map of your state. Use that map to answer the following questions.

1. What is the state capital and where is it located?

2. What other states or countries border your state?

3. What are two other cities in your state besides the capital and the city you live in?

Natural Hazards
in the United States

Essential Elements

The World in Spatial Terms
Places and Regions
Physical Systems
Human Systems
Environment and Society
The Uses of Geography

Background Earth's physical systems create patterns around us, and these patterns influence our lives. For example, every region of the United States has distinctive natural hazards. Volcanoes threaten the Pacific Northwest. Earthquakes rattle California. Wildfires strike forests in the West. Hurricanes endanger the Atlantic and Gulf of Mexico coasts, and major rivers are prone to flooding. Tornadoes regularly rip across flat areas of central and southeast United States.

In fact, the United States lies in danger of getting hit by an average of six hurricanes a year. Formed by the warm waters of the Atlantic Ocean and Caribbean Sea and the collision of strong winds, hurricanes are the most powerful storms on Earth. Most hurricanes look like large doughnuts with a hole, or eye, in the middle of the storm. Around the eye, high winds and rain bands rotate counterclockwise. Once the hurricane moves over land or cold water it weakens.

Natural Hazards in the United States

Tornado Alley

Earthquakes
Wildfires
Hurricanes
Flood areas
Volcanoes
Tornadoes
Tornado Risk
  Moderate
  High

After Hurricane Katrina hit New Orleans, people escaped the floodwaters by fleeing to rooftops and high-rise apartment buildings like this one.

Using satellite images like this one of Hurricane Katrina, scientists saw how large the storm was and warned people along the Gulf coast to evacuate.

Hurricane Katrina

On August 29, 2005, one of the most destructive hurricanes ever hit the United States. Hurricane Katrina devastated coastal regions of Louisiana, the city of New Orleans, and the entire coast of Mississippi.

With winds as high as 145 mph (235 km), Katrina destroyed hundreds of thousands of homes and businesses. In addition, the force of Katrina's storm surge pushed water from the Gulf of Mexico onto land to a height of about two stories tall. As a result, low-lying areas along the Gulf coast experienced massive flooding.

The storm surge also caused several levees that protected New Orleans from the waters of Lake Pontchartrain to break. The loss of these levees caused the lake's waters to flood most of the city. About 150,000 people who did not evacuate before the storm were left stranded in shelters, high-rise buildings, and on rooftops. Using boats and helicopters, emergency workers rescued thousands of the city's people. Total damages from the storm along the Gulf coast was estimated to be nearly $130 billion. More than 1,300 people died and over a million were displaced.

What It Means

Natural hazards can influence where we live, how we build our homes, and how we prepare for storms. In addition to hurricanes, other hazards affect the United States. For example, Tornado Alley is a region of the Great Plains that experiences a high number of tornadoes, or "twisters"—rapidly spinning columns of air that stay in contact with the ground. In Tornado Alley, special warning sirens go off when storms develop that might form a dangerous tornado.

Geography for Life Activity

1. How are hurricanes formed?

2. Many people train and volunteer as storm chasers. They may follow storms for hundreds of miles to gather scientific data, take photographs, or file news reports. What might be the risks and rewards of such activity? Would it interest you?

3. **Comparing Windstorms** Do some research to find out how tornadoes and hurricanes differ. Summarize the differences in a chart that includes information about how these storms start, where and when they tend to occur in the United States, and their wind strength.

History and Culture

Main Ideas

1. The United States is the world's first modern democracy.
2. The people and culture of the United States are very diverse.

The Big Idea

Democratic ideas and immigration have shaped the history and culture of the United States.

Key Terms and Places

colony, *p. 152*
Boston, *p. 152*
New York, *p. 152*
plantation, *p. 153*
pioneers, *p. 154*
bilingual, *p. 156*

hmhsocialstudies.com
TAKING NOTES

Use the graphic organizer online to take notes on the history and culture of the United States.

If **YOU** lived there...

It is 1803, and President Jefferson just arranged the purchase of a huge area of land west of the Mississippi River. It almost doubles the size of the United States. Living on the frontier in Ohio, you are a skillful hunter and trapper. One day, you see a poster calling for volunteers to explore the new Louisiana Territory. An expedition is heading west soon. You think it would be exciting but dangerous.

Will you join the expedition to the West? Why or why not?

BUILDING BACKGROUND From 13 colonies on the Atlantic coast, the territory of the United States expanded all the way to the Pacific Ocean in about 75 years. Since then, America's democracy has attracted immigrants from almost every country in the world. Looking for new opportunities, these immigrants have made the country very diverse.

First Modern Democracy

Long before Italian explorer Christopher Columbus sailed to the Americas in 1492, native people lived on the land that is now the United States. These Native Americans developed many distinct cultures. Soon after Columbus and his crew explored the Americas, other Europeans began to set up colonies there.

The American Colonies

Europeans began settling in North America and setting up colonies in the 1500s. A **colony** is a territory inhabited and controlled by people from a foreign land. By the mid-1700s the British Empire included more than a dozen colonies along the Atlantic coast. New cities in the colonies such as **Boston** and **New York** became major seaports.

Some people living in the British colonies lived on plantations. A **plantation** is a large farm that grows mainly one crop. Many of the colonial plantations produced tobacco, rice, or cotton. Thousands of enslaved Africans were brought to the colonies and forced to work on plantations.

By the 1770s many colonists in America were unhappy with British rule. They wanted independence from Britain. In July 1776, the colonial representatives adopted the Declaration of Independence. The document stated that "all men are created equal" and have the right to "life, liberty, and the pursuit of happiness." Although not everyone in the colonies was considered equal, the Declaration was a great step toward equality and justice.

To win their independence, the American colonists fought the British in the Revolutionary War. First, colonists from Massachusetts fought in the early battles of the war in and around Boston. As the war spread west and south, soldiers from all the American colonies joined the fight against Britain.

In 1781 the American forces under General George Washington defeated the British army at the Battle of Yorktown in Virginia. With this defeat, Britain recognized the independence of the United States. As a consequence, Britain granted all its land east of the Mississippi River to the new nation.

Expansion and Industrial Growth

After independence, the United States gradually expanded west. Despite the challenges of crossing swift-moving rivers and traveling across rugged terrain and huge mountains, people moved west for land and plentiful resources.

BIOGRAPHY

George Washington
(1732–1799)

As the first president of the United States, George Washington is known as the Father of His Country. Washington was admired for his heroism and leadership as the commanding general during the Revolutionary War. Delegates to the Constitutional Convention chose him to preside over their meetings. Washington was then elected president in 1789 and served two terms.

Drawing Inferences Why do you think Washington was elected president?

Fight for Independence

This painting shows General George Washington leading American troops across the Delaware River to attack British forces.

These first settlers that traveled west were called **pioneers**. Many followed the 2,000-mile Oregon Trail west from Missouri to the Oregon Territory. Groups of families traveled together in wagons pulled by oxen or mules. The trip was harsh. Food, supplies, and water were scarce.

While many pioneers headed west seeking land, others went in search of gold. The discovery of gold in California in the late 1840s had a major impact on the country. Tens of thousands of people moved to California.

By 1850 the population of the United States exceeded 23 million and the country stretched all the way to the Pacific Ocean. As the United States expanded, the nation's economy also grew. By the late 1800s, the country was a major producer of goods like steel, oil, and textiles, or cloth products. The steel industry grew around cities that were located near coal and iron ore deposits. Most of those new industrial cities were in the Northeast and Midwest. The country's economy also benefited from the **development** of waterways and railroads. This development helped industry and people move farther into the interior.

Attracted by a strong economy, millions of people immigrated, or came to, the United States for better jobs and land. Immigration from European countries was especially heavy in the late 1800s and early 1900s. As a result of this historical pattern of immigration, the United States is a culturally diverse nation today.

ACADEMIC VOCABULARY
development the process of growing or improving

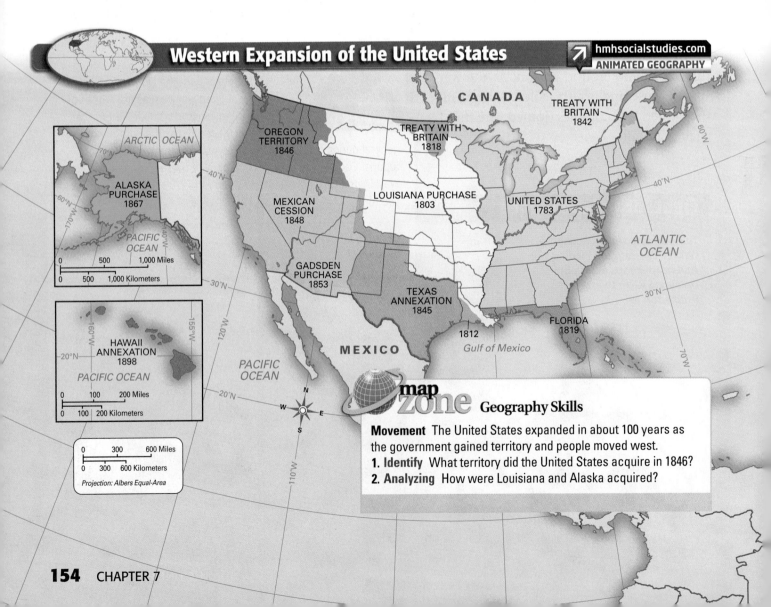

Western Expansion of the United States

hmhsocialstudies.com
ANIMATED GEOGRAPHY

map zone Geography Skills

Movement The United States expanded in about 100 years as the government gained territory and people moved west.
1. **Identify** What territory did the United States acquire in 1846?
2. **Analyzing** How were Louisiana and Alaska acquired?

Wars and Peace

The United States fought in several wars during the 1900s. Many Americans died in two major wars, World Wars I and II. After World War II, the United States and the Soviet Union became rivals in what was known as the Cold War. The Cold War lasted until the early 1990s, when the Soviet Union collapsed. U.S. troops also served in long wars in Korea in the 1950s and in Vietnam in the 1960s and 1970s. In 1991, the U.S. fought Iraq in the Persian Gulf War. More recently, the U.S. invaded Iraq in 2003 and is helping Iraqis rebuild their country today.

Today the United States is a member of many international organizations. The headquarters of one such organization, the United Nations (UN), is located in New York City. About 190 countries are UN members. The United States is one of the most powerful members.

Government and Citizenship

The United States has a limited, democratic government based on the U.S. Constitution. This document spells out the powers and functions of the branches of the federal government. The federal government includes an elected president and Congress. In general, the federal government handles issues affecting the whole country, but many powers are left to the 50 state governments. Counties and cities also have their own local governments. Many of these local governments provide services to the community such as trash collection, road building, electricity, and public transportation.

Rights and Responsibilities

American citizens have many rights and responsibilities, including the right to vote. Starting at age 18, U.S. citizens are allowed to vote. They are also encouraged

to play an active role in government. For example, Americans can call or write their public officials to ask them to help solve problems in their communities. Without people participating in their government, the democratic process suffers.

READING CHECK **Sequencing** What were some major events in the history of the United States?

Primary Source

HISTORIC DOCUMENT
The Constitution

On September 17, 1787, state delegates gathered in Philadelphia to create a constitution, a written statement of the powers and functions of the new government of the United States. The Preamble, or introduction, to the U.S. Constitution is shown below. It states the document's general purpose.

" *We the People* of the United States, in order to form a more perfect Union, establish justice, insure domestic tranquillity, provide for the common defense, promote the general welfare, and secure the blessings of liberty to ourselves and our posterity, do ordain and establish this Constitution for the United States of America. "

Americans wanted peace within the United States and a national military force.

They wanted to ensure freedoms for themselves and for future generations.

ANALYSIS SKILL **ANALYZING PRIMARY SOURCES**

How do you think the ideas that appear in the Preamble affect your daily life?

THE UNITED STATES **155**

People and Culture

About 7 out of 10 Americans are descended from European immigrants. However, the United States is also home to people of many other cultures and ethnic groups. As a result, the United States is a diverse nation where many languages are spoken and different religions and customs are practiced. The blending of these different cultures has helped produce a unique American culture.

Ethnic Groups in the United States

FOCUS ON READING
What details would be included under a category called *ethnic groups*?

Some ethnic groups in the United States include Native Americans, African Americans, Hispanic Americans, and Asian Americans. As you can see on the maps on the next page, higher percentages of these ethnic groups are concentrated in different areas of the United States.

For thousands of years, Native Americans were the only people living in the Americas. Today, most Native Americans live in the western United States. Many Native Americans are concentrated in Arizona and New Mexico.

Even though African Americans live in every region of the country, some areas of the United States have a higher percentage of African Americans. For example, a higher percentage of African Americans live in southern states. Many large cities also have a high percentage of African Americans. On the other hand, descendants of people who came from Asian countries, or Asian Americans, are mostly concentrated in California.

Many Hispanic Americans originally migrated to the United States from Mexico, Cuba, and other Latin American countries. As you can see on the map of Hispanic Americans, a higher percentage of Hispanic Americans live in the southwestern states. These states border Mexico.

Language

What language or languages do you hear as you walk through the hall of your school? Since most people in the United States speak English, you probably hear English spoken every day. However, in many parts of the country, English is just one of many languages you might hear. Are you or is someone you know bilingual? People who speak two languages are **bilingual**.

Today more than 55 million U.S. residents speak a language in addition to English. These languages include Spanish, French, Chinese, Russian, Arabic, Navajo, and many others.

After English, Spanish is the most widely spoken language in the United States. About 34 million Americans speak Spanish at home. Many of these people live near the border between the United States and Mexico and in Florida.

Religion

Americans also practice many religious faiths. Most people are Christians. However, some are Jewish or Muslim. A small percentage of Americans are Hindu or Buddhist. What religions are practiced in your community? Your community might have Christian churches, Jewish synagogues, and Islamic mosques, as well as other places of worship. Religious variety adds to our country's cultural diversity.

With so many different religions, many religious holidays are celebrated in the United States. These holidays include the Christian celebrations of Christmas and Easter and the Jewish holidays of Hanukkah, Yom Kippur, and Rosh Hashanah. Some African Americans also celebrate Kwanzaa, a holiday that is based on a traditional African festival. Muslims celebrate the end of the month of Ramadan with a large feast called 'Id al-Fitr.

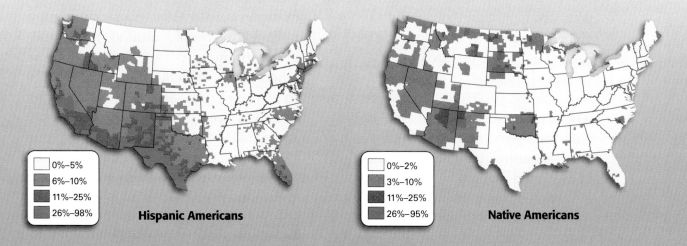

Hispanic Americans

0%–5%
6%–10%
11%–25%
26%–98%

Native Americans

0%–2%
3%–10%
11%–25%
26%–95%

Diverse America

People of different ethnic groups enjoy a concert in Miami, Florida. Like most large American cities, Miami has a very diverse population. More than half of all Hispanic Americans of Cuban descent live in Miami.

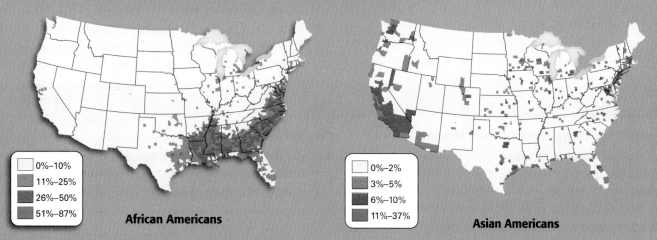

African Americans

0%–10%
11%–25%
26%–50%
51%–87%

Asian Americans

0%–2%
3%–5%
6%–10%
11%–37%

Source: U.S. Census Bureau, 2000

map zone
Geography Skills

Regions These maps show population information from the U.S. Census. Every 10 years, Americans answer census questions about their race or ethnic group.

1. Locate In what region of the United States does the highest percentage of African Americans live?

2. Analyze Why do you think many Hispanic Americans live in the southwestern United States?

Foods and Music

Diversity shows itself through cultural practices. In addition to language and religion, cultural practices include the food we eat and the music we listen to.

America's food is as diverse as the American people. Think about some of the foods you have eaten this week. You may have eaten Mexican tacos, Italian pasta, or Japanese sushi. These dishes are now part of the American diet.

Different types of music from around the world have also influenced American culture. For example, salsa music from Latin America is popular in the United States today. Many American musicians now combine elements of salsa into their pop songs. However, music that originated in the United States is also popular in other countries. American musical styles include blues, jazz, rock, and hip hop.

American Popular Culture

As the most powerful country in the world, the United States has tremendous influence around the world. American popular culture, such as movies, television programs, and sports, is popular elsewhere. For example, the *Star Wars* movies are seen by millions of people around the world. Other examples of American culture in other places include the popularity of baseball in Japan, Starbucks coffee shops in almost every major city in the world, and an MTV channel available throughout Asia. As you can see, Americans influence the rest of the world in many ways through their culture.

READING CHECK **Generalizing** How has cultural diversity enriched life in the United States?

SUMMARY AND PREVIEW The history of the United States has helped shape the democratic nation it is today. Drawn to the United States because of its democracy, immigrants from around the world have shaped American culture. In the next section, you will learn about the different regions of the United States and the issues the country is facing today.

Section 2 Assessment

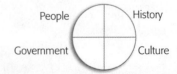
hmhsocialstudies.com
ONLINE QUIZ

Reviewing Ideas, Terms, and Places

1. **a. Define** What is a **colony**?
   b. Make Inferences Why did the pioneers move west?
   c. Elaborate What is an example of the rights and responsibilities that American citizens have?
2. **a. Recall** What language other than English is widely spoken in the United States?
   b. Summarize What are some religions practiced in the United States?
   c. Predict How do you think American culture will be different in the future, and what influences do you think will bring about the changes?

Critical Thinking

3. **Summarizing** Using your notes, write one descriptive sentence about the history, government, people, and culture of the United States.

People | History

Government | Culture

FOCUS ON VIEWING

4. **Thinking about History and Culture** How would you describe the history and culture of the United States? Identify two images for your collage.

from
Bearstone

by Will Hobbs

About the Reading *In* Bearstone, *writer Will Hobbs tells about an orphaned Native American boy named Cloyd who lives on a Colorado farm. While roaming the nearby canyons, Cloyd finds a relic from his ancestors. The relic is a stone in the shape of a turquoise bear, which becomes his Bearstone, the title of this story.*

AS YOU READ Identify what the mountains mean to Cloyd.

. . . This was a shining new world. To the north and east, peaks still covered with snow shone in the cloudless blue sky. He'd never seen mountains so sharp and rugged, so fierce and splendid. Below him, an eagle soared high above the old man's field. It was a good sign.

Then he remembered his grandmother's parting words as he left for Colorado. She told him something he'd never heard before: their band of Weminuche Utes ❶ hadn't always lived at White Mesa. ❷ Colorado, especially the mountains above Durango, had been their home until gold was discovered there and the white men wanted them out of the way. Summers the people used to hunt and fish in the high mountains, she'd said; they knew every stream, places so out of the way that white men still hadn't seen them. 'So don't feel bad about going to Durango,' she told him.

Cloyd regarded the distant peaks with new strength, a fierce kind of pride he'd never felt before. These were the mountains where his people used to live.

In this book, a Native American boy named Cloyd learns more about his ancestors.

GUIDED READING

WORD HELP

band a group of Native American families

❶ Weminuche Utes are a band of Utes, a Native American cultural group.

❷ White Mesa is a Ute community in Utah where Cloyd lived before he moved to Colorado.

Connecting Literature to Geography

1. **Describing** What details in the first paragraph show us that Cloyd feels happy and at home in these mountains? Which details describe the physical features of these mountains?

2. **Making Inferences** Why did Cloyd's grandmother think he shouldn't feel bad about going to Durango? How does this fact affect his feelings about the mountains of Colorado?

The United States Today

What You Will Learn...

Main Ideas

1. The United States has four regions—the Northeast, South, Midwest, and West.
2. The United States has a strong economy and a powerful military but is facing the challenge of world terrorism.

The Big Idea

The United States has four main regions and faces opportunities and challenges.

Key Terms and Places

megalopolis, *p. 161*
Washington, D.C., *p. 161*
Detroit, *p. 163*
Chicago, *p. 163*
Seattle, *p. 164*
terrorism, *p. 166*

hmhsocialstudies.com
TAKING NOTES

Use the graphic organizer online to take notes on the United States today.

If **YOU** lived there...

You and your family run a small resort hotel in Fort Lauderdale, on the east coast of Florida. You love the sunny weather and the beaches there. Now your family is thinking about moving the business to another region where the tourist industry is important. They have looked at ski lodges in Colorado, lake cottages in Michigan, and hotels on the coast of Maine.

How will you decide among these different regions?

BUILDING BACKGROUND Geography, history, climate, and population give each region of the United States its own style. Some differences between the regions are more visible than others. For example, people in each region speak with different accents and have their favorite foods. Even with some differences, however, Americans are linked by a sense of unity in confronting important issues.

Regions of the United States

Because the United States is such a large country, geographers often divide it into four main regions. These are the Northeast, South, Midwest, and the West. You can see the four regions on the map on the next page. Find the region where you live. You probably know more about your own region than you do the three others. The population, resources, and economies of the four regions are similar in some ways and unique in others.

The Northeast

The Northeast shares a border with Canada. The economy in this region is heavily dependent on banks, investment firms, and insurance companies. Education also contributes to the economy. The area's respected universities include Harvard and Yale.

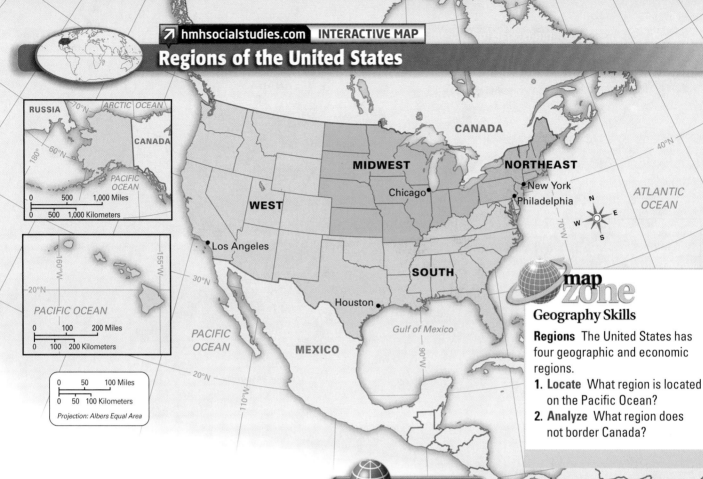

RUSSIA

ARCTIC OCEAN

CANADA

PACIFIC OCEAN

0   500   1,000 Miles
0   500   1,000 Kilometers

PACIFIC OCEAN

0   100   200 Miles
0   100   200 Kilometers

0   50   100 Miles
0   50   100 Kilometers

Projection: Albers Equal Area

CANADA

MIDWEST

NORTHEAST

•New York

Chicago•

•Philadelphia

ATLANTIC OCEAN

WEST

•Los Angeles

SOUTH

Houston•

PACIFIC OCEAN

MEXICO

Gulf of Mexico

map zone

Geography Skills

Regions The United States has four geographic and economic regions.
1. **Locate** What region is located on the Pacific Ocean?
2. **Analyze** What region does not border Canada?

Some natural resources of the Northeast states include rich farmland and huge pockets of coal. Used in the steelmaking process, coal remains very important to the region's economy. The steel industry helped make Pittsburgh, in western Pennsylvania, the largest industrial city in the Appalachians.

Today fishing remains an important industry in the Northeast. Major seaports allow companies to ship their products to markets around the world. Cool, shallow waters off the Atlantic coast are good fishing areas. Cod and shellfish such as lobster are the most valuable seafood.

The Northeast is the most densely populated region of the United States. Much of the Northeast is a **megalopolis**, a string of large cities that have grown together. This area stretches along the Atlantic coast from Boston to **Washington, D.C.** The three other major cities in the megalopolis are New York, Philadelphia, and Baltimore.

THE WORLD ALMANAC Facts about Countries **Population of Major U.S. Cities**

	City	Population
1	New York	8,363,710
2	Los Angeles	3,833,995
3	Chicago	2,853,114
4	Houston	2,242,193
5	Phoenix	1,567,924

New York, New York

↗ hmhsocialstudies.com

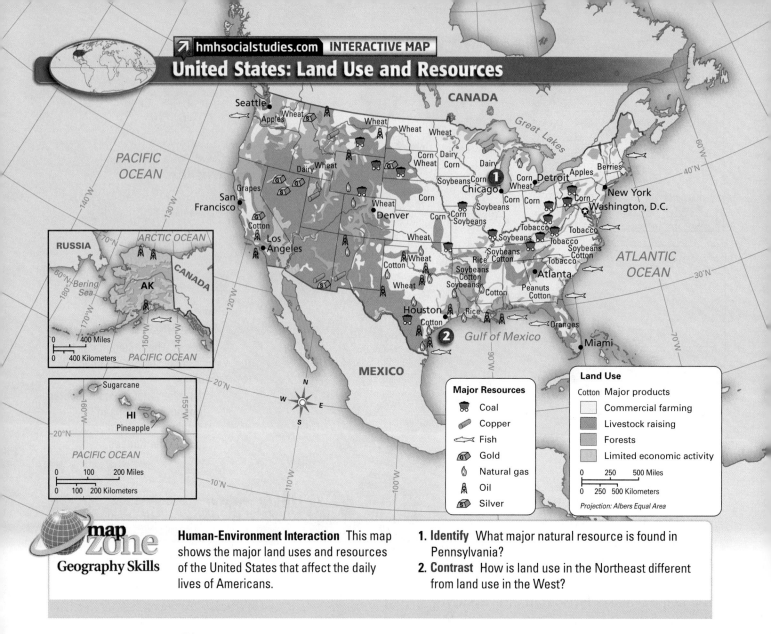

United States: Land Use and Resources

hmhsocialstudies.com **INTERACTIVE MAP**

CANADA

Great Lakes

PACIFIC OCEAN

Seattle
Apples Wheat
Wheat
Wheat Wheat Wheat
Corn Dairy
Corn Wheat Corn Dairy
Dairy Wheat Soybeans Corn
Grapes Corn Chicago Corn Corn
San Francisco Wheat Corn Soybeans
Denver Corn Soybeans
Cotton Los Angeles Corn Soybeans
Wheat

Detroit Apples Berries
Corn Wheat New York
Washington, D.C.
Soybeans
Tobacco
Soybeans Tobacco Tobacco
Rice Cotton Soybeans Cotton
Cotton Soybeans Tobacco
Soybeans Cotton Atlanta
Wheat Soybeans Peanuts
Cotton Cotton

ATLANTIC OCEAN

Houston
Cotton
Rice
Gulf of Mexico
Oranges
Miami

MEXICO

RUSSIA

ARCTIC OCEAN
Bering Sea
AK
CANADA
0 400 Miles
0 400 Kilometers
PACIFIC OCEAN

Sugarcane
HI
Pineapple
PACIFIC OCEAN
0 100 200 Miles
0 100 200 Kilometers

Major Resources

Coal	
Copper	
Fish	
Gold	
Natural gas	
Oil	
Silver	

Land Use

Cotton Major products
Commercial farming
Livestock raising
Forests
Limited economic activity

0 250 500 Miles
0 250 500 Kilometers
Projection: Albers Equal Area

map zone
Geography Skills

Human-Environment Interaction This map shows the major land uses and resources of the United States that affect the daily lives of Americans.

1. **Identify** What major natural resource is found in Pennsylvania?
2. **Contrast** How is land use in the Northeast different from land use in the West?

At least 40 million people live in this urban area. All of these cities were founded during the colonial era. They grew because they were important seaports. Today these cities are industrial and financial centers.

The South

The South is a region that includes long coastlines along the Atlantic Ocean and the Gulf of Mexico. Along the coastal plains rich soils provide farmers with abundant crops of cotton, tobacco, and citrus fruit.

In recent years, the South has become more urban and industrial and is one of the country's fastest-growing regions. The South's cities, such as Atlanta, have grown along with the economy. The Atlanta metropolitan area has grown from a population of only about 1 million in 1960 to more than 5 million today.

Other places in the South have also experienced growth in population and industry. The Research Triangle in North Carolina is an area of high-tech companies and several large universities. The Texas Gulf Coast and the lower Mississippi River area have huge oil refineries and petrochemical plants. Their products, which include gasoline, are mostly shipped from the ports of Houston and New Orleans.

1 Farms with fertile soils like this one in Wisconsin cover much of the rural Midwest.

2 Large white containers, shown here at the Port of Houston, store oil from the Gulf Coast.

Millions of Americans vacation in the South, which makes the travel industry profitable in the region. Warm weather and beautiful beaches draw many vacationers to resorts in the South. You may not think of weather and beaches when you think about industry, but you should. Resort areas are an industry because they provide jobs and help local economies grow.

Many cities in the South trade goods and services with Mexico and countries in Central and South America. This trade is possible because several of the southern states are located near these countries. For example, Miami is an important trading port and travel connection with Caribbean countries, Mexico, and South America. Atlanta, Houston, and Dallas are also major transportation centers.

The Midwest

The Midwest is one of the most productive farming regions in the world. The Mississippi River and many of its tributaries carry materials that help create the region's rich soils, which are good for farming. Midwestern farmers grow mostly corn, wheat, and soybeans. Farmers in the region also raise livestock such as dairy cows.

The core of the Midwest's corn-growing region stretches from Ohio to Nebraska. Much of the corn is used to feed livestock, such as beef cattle and hogs.

To the north of the corn-growing region is an area of dairy farms. States with dairy farms are major producers of milk, cheese, and other dairy products. This area includes Wisconsin and most of Michigan and Minnesota. Much of the dairy farm region is pasture, but farmers also grow crops to feed dairy cows.

Many of the Midwest's farm and factory products are shipped to markets by water routes, such as those along the Ohio and Mississippi rivers. The other is through the Great Lakes and the Saint Lawrence Seaway to the Atlantic Ocean.

Most major cities in the Midwest are located on rivers or the Great Lakes. As a result, they are important transportation centers. Farm products, coal, and iron ore are easily shipped to these cities from nearby farms and mines. These natural resources support industries such as automobile manufacturing. For example, **Detroit**, Michigan, is the country's leading automobile producer.

One of the busiest shipping ports on the Great Lakes is **Chicago**, Illinois. The city also has one of the world's busiest airports. Chicago's industries attracted many immigrants in the late 1800s. People moved here to work in the city's steel mills. Today Chicago is the nation's third-largest city.

FOCUS ON READING

As you read about the Midwest, sort the details into three categories.

The West

The West is the largest region in the United States. Many western states have large open spaces with few people. The West is not all open spaces, however. Many large cities are on the Pacific coast.

One state on the coast, California, is home to more than 10 percent of the U.S. population. California's mild climate and wealth of resources attract people to the state. Most Californians live in Los Angeles, San Diego, and the San Francisco Bay area. The center of the country's entertainment industry, Hollywood, is in Los Angeles. Farming and the technology industry are also important to California's economy.

The economy of other states in the West is dependent on ranching and growing wheat. Wheat is grown mostly in Montana, Idaho, and Washington.

Much of the farmland in the West must be irrigated, or watered. One method of irrigation uses long sprinkler systems mounted on huge wheels. The wheels rotate slowly. This sprinkler system waters the area within a circle. From the air, parts of the irrigated Great Plains resemble a series of green circles.

The West also has rich deposits of coal, oil, gold, silver, copper, and other minerals. However, mining these minerals can cause problems. For example, coal miners in parts of the Great Plains use a **process** called strip mining, which strips away soil and rock. This kind of mining leads to soil erosion and other problems. Today laws require miners to restore mined areas.

In Oregon and Washington, forestry and fishing are two of the most important economic activities. **Seattle** is Washington's largest city. The Seattle area is home to many important industries, including a major computer software company. More than half of the people in Oregon live in and around Portland.

Alaska's economy is largely based on oil, forests, and fish. As in Washington and Oregon, people debate over developing

ACADEMIC VOCABULARY

process a series of steps by which a task is accomplished

Olympic National Park

One of the largest sections of coastal wilderness in the United States, shown here, stretches along the Pacific coast in Washington's Olympic National Park.

these resources. For example, some people want to limit oil drilling in wild areas of Alaska. Others want to expand drilling to produce more oil.

Hawaii's natural beauty, mild climate, and fertile soils are its most important resources. The islands' major crops are sugarcane and pineapples. Millions of tourists visit the islands each year.

READING CHECK **Comparing** How is the economy of the West different from the economy of the South?

Changes in the Nation

Because of its economic and military strength, the United States is often called the world's only superpower. In recent years, however, the United States has faced many challenges and changes.

Economy

An abundance of natural resources, technology, and plentiful jobs have helped make the U.S. economy strong. The United States also benefits by trading with other countries. The three largest trading partners of the United States are Canada, China, and Mexico. In 1992 the United States, Mexico, and Canada signed the North American Free Trade Agreement, or NAFTA. This agreement made trade easier and cheaper between the three neighboring nations.

Still, the U.S. economy has experienced significant ups and downs since the 1990s. In the 1990s the nation experienced the longest period of economic growth in its history. By the end of 2007, the United States faced a recession, or a sharp decrease in economic activity. In this recession, the housing market collapsed, major banks and businesses failed, and an estimated 8.4 million jobs were lost in the United States.

The War on Terror

In the 1990s the United States began to experience acts of terrorism against its people. Terrorism is the threat or use of violence to intimidate or cause fear for political or social reasons. Some terrorists have been from foreign countries, whereas others have been U.S. citizens.

On September 11, 2001, the United States suffered the deadliest terrorist attack in the country's history. Wanting to disrupt the U.S. economy, 19 Islamic extremist terrorists hijacked four American jets. They crashed two into the World Trade Center and one into the Pentagon.

In response, U.S. President George W. Bush declared a "war on terrorism." He sent military forces to Afghanistan, to kill or capture members of a terrorist group called al-Qaeda, which had planned the September 11 attacks. The United States then turned its attention to Iraq. President Bush believed that Iraqi leader Saddam Hussein was another threat to Americans. In March 2003 Bush sent U.S. troops into Iraq to remove Hussein from power.

Today world leaders are working with the United States to combat terrorism. In the United States, the Department of Homeland Security was established to prevent terrorist attacks on American soil. Many other countries have also increased security within their borders, especially at international airports.

Government

The 2008 presidential election pitted Republican senator John McCain and his running mate Governor Sarah Palin against Democratic senator Barack Obama and his running mate Joe Biden, a fellow senator. The two presidential candidates differed in many ways. For example, McCain was 25 years older than Obama and he held opposing views on the war in Iraq.

The 2008 presidential campaign of Barack Obama captured the imagination of many Americans

On election day, about 128 million people voted, the highest voter turnout for any election in U.S. history. Barack Obama won the election, winning 365 electoral votes to McCain's 173. Obama became the nation's first African American president.

READING CHECK **Summarizing** What issues shaped the 2008 presidential election?

McCain, a distinguished military veteran, thought that U.S. forces should stay in Iraq indefinitely. Obama supported plans to withdraw U.S. troops as soon as possible. The two also differed over how best to address the economy, taxes, and health care.

SUMMARY AND PREVIEW In this section, you learned about the geographic features, resources, and economic activities found in different regions of the United States. You also learned that the economy and terrorism are two important issues facing the country today. In the next chapter, you will learn about Canada, our neighbor to the north of the United States.

Section 3 Assessment

hmhsocialstudies.com
ONLINE QUIZ

Reviewing Ideas, Terms, and Places

1. **a. Define** What is a **megalopolis**? What major cities are part of the largest megalopolis in the United States?
   b. Compare and Contrast How is land use in the Midwest similar to and different from land use in the South?
   c. Elaborate How are the regions of the United States different from one another?
2. **a. Define** What is **terrorism**? What terrorist attack occurred in September 2001?
   b. Explain How did a recession affect the U.S. economy in 2007?
   c. Elaborate What steps are the United States and other countries taking in an attempt to combat world terrorism?

Critical Thinking

3. **Finding Main Ideas** Use your notes to help you list at least one main idea about the population, resources, and economy of each region.

	Northeast	South	Midwest	West
Population				
Resources				
Economy				

FOCUS ON VIEWING

4. **Thinking about the United States Today** You have read about the regions of the United States, as well as issues facing the country today. What key words, images, and objects might represent what you have learned?

Chapter Review

Geography's Impact
video series
Review the video to answer the closing question:
What do you think it would be like to live in a country that had no cultural diversity?

Visual Summary

Use the visual summary below to help you review the main ideas of the chapter.

QUICK FACTS

The physical geography of the United States includes mountains, rivers, and plains.

After gaining independence from the British, Americans created the first modern democracy.

The United States has four geographic and economic regions—the Northeast, South, Midwest, and the West.

Reviewing Vocabulary, Terms, and Places

Match the terms or places with their definitions or descriptions.

a. Boston
b. Great Lakes
c. tributary
d. Rocky Mountains
e. colony
f. Appalachian Mountains
g. pioneers
h. bilingual
i. megalopolis
j. Washington, D.C.
k. Chicago
l. terrorism

1. a string of cities that have grown together
2. major seaport in the British colonies
3. stream or river that flows into a larger stream or river
4. violent attacks that cause fear
5. first settlers
6. largest freshwater lake system in the world
7. major mountain range in the West
8. capital of the United States
9. third-largest city in the United States
10. major mountain range in the East
11. having the ability to speak two languages
12. territory controlled by people from a foreign land

Comprehension and Critical Thinking

SECTION 1 *(Pages 144–148)*

13. a. **Identify** What river drains the entire Interior Plains and is the longest river in North America?

SECTION 1 *(continued)*

    b. Contrast How are the Appalachians different from the Rocky Mountains?

    c. Elaborate What natural resources affect your daily life?

SECTION 2 *(Pages 152–158)*

14. a. Define Who were the pioneers?

    b. Draw Conclusions Why do you think people immigrate to the United States?

    c. Elaborate How has American culture influenced cultures around the world?

SECTION 3 *(Pages 160–166)*

15. a. Recall What are the four regions of the United States?

    b. Compare Is corn grown mostly in the Midwest or the South?

    c. Elaborate How should the United States protect itself from terrorism?

Using the Internet

16. Activity: Making a Brochure The United States is a country with a diverse population. This diversity is seen in many of the holidays Americans celebrate. Through your online textbook, research holidays celebrated in the United States. Take notes on what you find. Then use your notes to create an illustrated brochure about three holidays. Be sure to tell about the history, background, and traditions of each holiday.

hmhsocialstudies.com

Social Studies Skills

Reading a Political Map Look at the political map of the United States at the beginning of this chapter. Then answer the following questions.

17. What four states border Mexico?

18. What river forms the boundary between Illinois and Missouri?

Map Activity

19. The United States On a sheet of paper, match the letters on the map with their correct labels.

Great Lakes	Rocky Mountains
Mississippi River	Pacific Ocean
Atlantic Ocean	Alaska

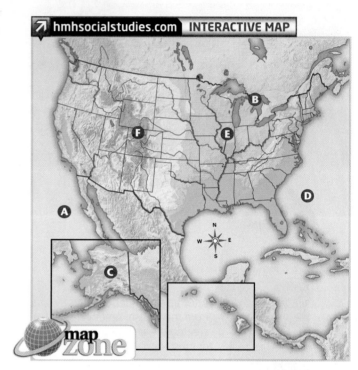

hmhsocialstudies.com INTERACTIVE MAP

FOCUS ON READING AND VIEWING

20. Categorizing For each category below, list details from the chapter.

Geography	People	Regions

21. Creating a Collage Gather the information and images you need to create a collage about the United States. Next, decide how to organize your collage. You might, for example, organize it by region or by time period. After you have attached your images to the poster board, create a label for each grouping. Finally, write a title for the entire collage. Be prepared to display your work and evaluate your classmates' collages for organization and clarity.

Standardized Test Prep

DIRECTIONS: Read questions 1 through 7 and write the letter of the best response. Question 8 will require a brief essay.

1 **What physical feature does the Mississippi River and its tributaries drain?**

   A Piedmont

   B Rocky Mountains

   C Interior Plains

   D Great Lakes

2 **What country did the United States gain independence from?**

   A Britain

   B France

   C Canada

   D Mexico

3 **Many pioneers moved west hoping to find**

   A silver.

   B diamonds.

   C coal.

   D gold.

4 **People who are bilingual speak how many languages?**

   A one

   B five

   C two

   D three

5 **NAFTA is a trade agreement among the United States, Mexico, and**

   A Brazil.

   B Canada.

   C Britain.

   D Australia.

Regions of the United States

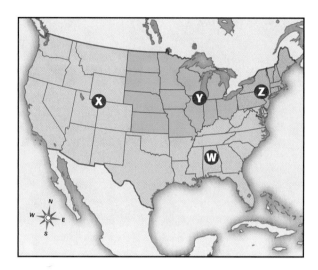

6 **Based on the map above, which region is the Midwest?**

   A X

   B W

   C Z

   D Y

7 **Which region is known for its dense population?**

   A Z

   B W

   C Y

   D X

8 **Extended Response** Look at the map of U.S. regions and the chart of major U.S. cities in Section 3. Write a short essay describing the population, resources, and economies of each region of the United States.

THE *American* REVOLUTION

The American Revolution led to the formation of the United States of America in 1776. Beginning in the 1760s, tensions grew between American colonists and their British rulers when Britain started passing a series of new laws and taxes for the colonies. With no representation in the British government, however, colonists had no say in these laws, which led to growing discontent. After fighting broke out in 1775, colonial leaders met to decide what to do. They approved the Declaration of Independence, announcing that the American colonies were free from British rule. In reality, however, freedom would not come until after years of fighting.

Explore some of the people and events of the American Revolution online. You can find a wealth of information, video clips, primary sources, activities, and more at ⓐ hmhsocialstudies.com.

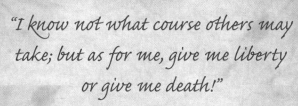

> "I know not what course others may take; but as for me, give me liberty or give me death!"
>
> — Patrick Henry

 "Give Me Liberty or Give Me Death"
Read an excerpt from Patrick Henry's famous speech, which urged the colonists to fight against the British.

Seeds of Revolution
Watch the video to learn about colonial discontent in the years before the Revolutionary War.

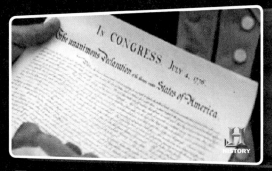

Independence!
Watch the video to learn about the origins of the Declaration of Independence.

Victory!
Watch the video to learn how the American colonists won the Revolutionary War.

Canada

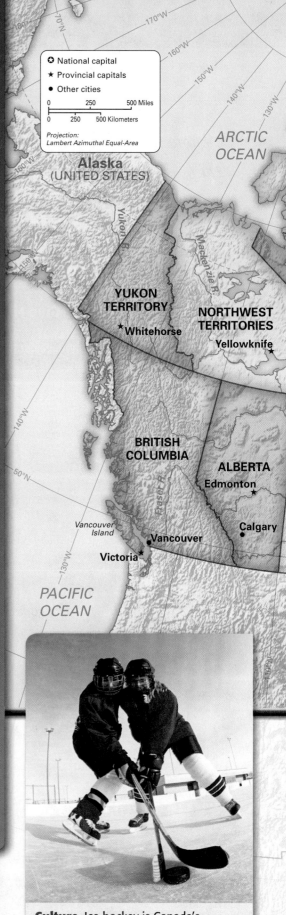

Essential Question How has geography and climate shaped the development of Canada's provinces?

? What You Will Learn...

In this chapter you will learn about the physical features, climates, and resources of Canada. You will study the history of Canada and the country's different cultures. Finally, you will learn about Canada's government, regions, and economy.

FOCUS ON READING AND SPEAKING

Understanding Lists Identifying a list of the interesting facts that you read about may help you understand the topic you are studying. For example, you could identify facts about Canada's physical features, regions, government, or economy. As you read this chapter, look for lists of facts. **See the lesson, Understanding Lists, on page 201.**

Creating a Radio Ad You are a member of the Canadian tourism board and your job is to develop a radio ad to attract visitors to Canada. Read about Canada in this chapter. Then, write a script for a one-minute radio ad. Be ready to present your ad to the class.

Culture Ice hockey is Canada's national sport. Many Canadians grow up playing on frozen lakes.

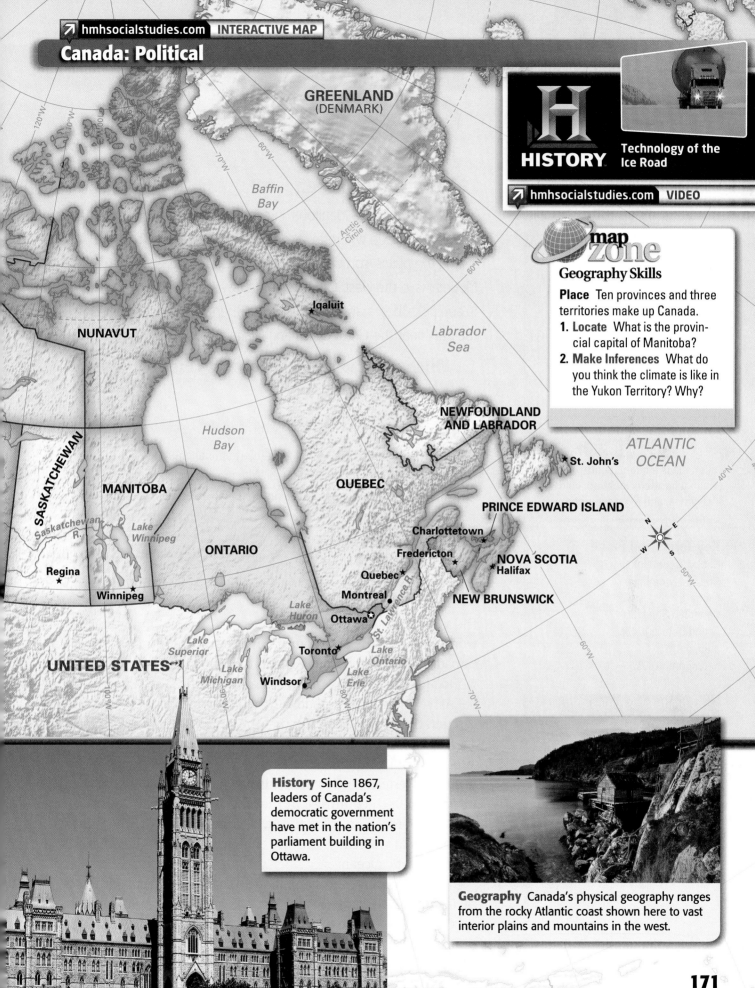

GREENLAND
(DENMARK)

HISTORY   Technology of the Ice Road

↗ hmhsocialstudies.com   VIDEO

Baffin Bay

Arctic Circle

Iqaluit

NUNAVUT

Labrador Sea

map Zone

Geography Skills

Place Ten provinces and three territories make up Canada.

1. **Locate** What is the provincial capital of Manitoba?
2. **Make Inferences** What do you think the climate is like in the Yukon Territory? Why?

NEWFOUNDLAND AND LABRADOR

ATLANTIC OCEAN

★ St. John's

Hudson Bay

SASKATCHEWAN

MANITOBA

Saskatchewan R.

Lake Winnipeg

QUEBEC

PRINCE EDWARD ISLAND

Charlottetown ★

ONTARIO

Fredericton ★

NOVA SCOTIA
★ Halifax

Regina ★

Quebec ★

Winnipeg ★

Montreal ●

NEW BRUNSWICK

Lake Huron

Ottawa ✪

St. Lawrence R.

Lake Superior

Toronto ★

Lake Ontario

UNITED STATES ↗

Lake Michigan

Windsor ●

Lake Erie

History Since 1867, leaders of Canada's democratic government have met in the nation's parliament building in Ottawa.

Geography Canada's physical geography ranges from the rocky Atlantic coast shown here to vast interior plains and mountains in the west.

Physical Geography

What You Will Learn...

Main Ideas

1. A huge country, Canada has a wide variety of physical features, including rugged mountains, plains, and swamps.
2. Because of its northerly location, Canada is dominated by cold climates.
3. Canada is rich in natural resources like fish, minerals, fertile soil, and forests.

The Big Idea

Canada is a huge country with a northerly location, cold climates, and rich resources.

Key Terms and Places

Rocky Mountains, *p. 172*
St. Lawrence River, *p. 172*
Niagara Falls, *p. 172*
Canadian Shield, *p. 173*
Grand Banks, *p. 174*
pulp, *p. 175*
newsprint, *p. 175*

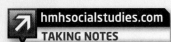
hmhsocialstudies.com
TAKING NOTES

Use the graphic organizer online to take notes on the physical geography of Canada.

If YOU lived there...

You live in Winnipeg, Manitoba, in central Canada. Your hiking club is trying to decide where to go on a trip this summer. Since you live on the plains, some people want to visit the rugged Rocky Mountains in the west. Others want to travel north to Hudson Bay to see polar bears and other wildlife. Others would rather hike in the east near the Great Lakes and Niagara Falls.

Which place will you choose for this year's trip?

BUILDING BACKGROUND A long international boundary separates Canada and the United States. With the exception of the St. Lawrence River and the Great Lakes, there is no actual physical boundary between the two countries. Rivers, lakes, prairies, and mountain ranges cross the border.

Physical Features

Did you know that Canada is the second-largest country in the world? Russia is the only country in the world that is larger than Canada. The United States is the third-largest country in the world and shares many physical features with Canada.

As you look at the map on the following page, see if you can find the physical features that the United States and Canada share. You may notice that mountains along the Pacific coast and the **Rocky Mountains** extend north into western Canada from the western United States. Broad plains stretch across the interiors of both countries. In the east, the two countries share a natural border formed by the **St. Lawrence River**. An important international waterway, the St. Lawrence links the Great Lakes to the Atlantic Ocean.

The United States and Canada also share a spectacular physical feature called **Niagara Falls**. The falls are located on the Niagara River between the province of Ontario and New York State.

Created by the waters of the Niagara River, the falls flow between two of the Great Lakes—Lake Erie and Lake Ontario. The falls here plunge an average of 162 feet (50 m) down a huge ledge. That is higher than many 15-story buildings!

Canada has a region of rocky uplands, lakes, and swamps called the **Canadian Shield**. See on the map how this feature curves around Hudson Bay. The Shield covers about half the country.

Farther north, Canada stretches all the way up to the Arctic Ocean. The land here is covered with ice year-round. Ellesmere Island is very rugged with snow-covered mountains and jagged coastlines. Very few people live this far north, but wildlife such as the polar bear and the Arctic wolf have adapted to the harsh environment.

READING CHECK **Summarizing** What are the major physical features of Canada?

hmhsocialstudies.com **INTERACTIVE MAP**

Canada: Physical

map zone

Geography Skills

Place Canada is located between the United States and the Arctic Ocean.
1. **Locate** What mountain range has the highest elevation?
2. **Draw Conclusions** How does Canada's northerly location affect its climate?

ARCTIC OCEAN
Ellesmere Island
Greenland (DENMARK)
Arctic Circle
Beaufort Sea
Baffin Bay
Baffin Island
Victoria Island
Mt. Logan 19,524 ft (5,951 m)
Great Bear Lake
Hudson Strait
Labrador Sea
Great Slave Lake
COAST MOUNTAINS
ROCKY MOUNTAINS
INTERIOR PLAINS
CANADIAN SHIELD
Hudson Bay
James Bay
LABRADOR
Newfoundland Island
Grand Banks
Gulf of St. Lawrence
Vancouver Island
Saskatchewan River
Lake Winnipeg
Laurentian Plateau
PACIFIC OCEAN
Lake Superior
Lake Huron
Ottawa
Lake Michigan
Lake Ontario
Niagara Falls
Lake Erie
Bay of Fundy
ATLANTIC OCEAN
UNITED STATES
Mackenzie Mts.
Mackenzie R.
Yukon R.
Fraser R.
St. Lawrence R.

ELEVATION

Feet	Meters
13,120	4,000
6,560	2,000
1,640	500
656	200
(Sea level) 0	0 (Sea level)
Below sea level	Below sea level

0   500   1,000 Miles
0   500   1,000 Kilometers

Projection: Lambert Azimuthal Equal-Area

Mist rises over Niagara Falls where the Niagara River forms a natural boundary between the United States and Canada.

Climate

FOCUS ON READING
What climates would you include in a list of the climates of Canada?

Canada's location greatly influences the country's climate. Canada is located far from the equator at much higher latitudes than the United States. This more northerly location gives Canada cool to freezing temperatures year-round.

The farther north you go in Canada, the colder it gets. The coldest areas of Canada are located close to the Arctic Circle. Much of central and northern Canada has a subarctic climate. The far north has tundra and ice cap climates. About half of Canada lies in these extremely cold climates.

The central and eastern parts of southern Canada have a much different climate. It is humid and relatively mild. However, the mildest area of Canada is along the coast of British Columbia. This location on the Pacific coast brings rainy winters and mild temperatures. Inland areas of southern Canada are colder and drier.

READING CHECK **Categorizing** What are Canada's climates?

Resources

Canada is incredibly rich in natural resources such as fish, minerals, and forests. Canada's Atlantic and Pacific coastal waters are among the world's richest fishing areas. Off the Atlantic coast lies a large fishing ground near Newfoundland and Labrador called the **Grand Banks**. Here, cold waters from the Labrador Sea meet the warm waters of the Gulf Stream. These conditions are ideal for the growth of tiny organisms, or plankton, that fish like to eat. As a result, large schools of fish gather at the Grand Banks. However, recent overfishing of this region has left many fishers in Canada unemployed.

Minerals are also valuable resources in Canada. The Canadian Shield contains many mineral deposits. Canada is a main source of the world's nickel, zinc, and uranium. Lead, copper, gold, and silver are also important resources. Saskatchewan has large deposits of potash, a mineral used to make fertilizer. Alberta produces most of Canada's oil and natural gas.

Banff National Park

Some of Canada's most spectacular scenery is found here in the Rockies at Banff National Park.

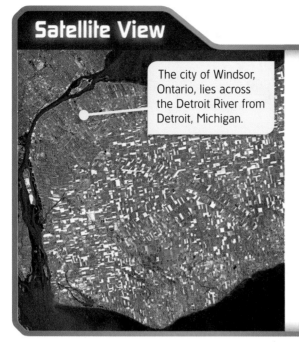

The city of Windsor, Ontario, lies across the Detroit River from Detroit, Michigan.

Agriculture in Ontario

In this satellite image, crop fields in different stages of growth appear scattered throughout the province of Ontario. These rectangular fields of vegetation appear red at their height of growth and white after the crops are harvested. Rich soils and a mild climate in this region, which lies north of Lake Erie, make it one of Canada's most fertile regions. Crops grown here include wheat, soybeans, corn, and a variety of vegetables. Some of these crops are exported to the United States through the Canadian port of Windsor to Detroit, Michigan, just across the Detroit River. Both cities appear in this image as shades of blue and brown.

Drawing Conclusions What is the economy of southern Ontario based on?

Vast areas of forests stretch across most of Canada from Labrador to the Pacific coast. These trees provide lumber and pulp. **Pulp**—softened wood fibers—is used to make paper. The United States, the United Kingdom, and Japan get much of their newsprint from Canada. **Newsprint** is cheap paper used mainly for newspapers.

READING CHECK Drawing Conclusions How do Canada's major resources affect its economy?

SUMMARY AND PREVIEW In this section, you learned that Canada shares many physical features with the United States. However, Canada's geography is also different. Due to its northerly location, Canada has a cold climate. Fish, minerals, fertile soil, and forests are all important natural resources. In the next section, you will learn about the history and culture of Canada.

Section 1 Assessment

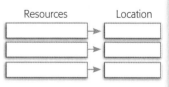

hmhsocialstudies.com
ONLINE QUIZ

Reviewing Ideas, Terms, and Places

1. **a. Recall** What river links the Great Lakes to the Atlantic Ocean?
   b. Explain What physical features does **Niagara Falls** flow between?
   c. Develop If you were to live in Canada, where would you not want to live?
2. **a. Describe** How is Canada's climate related to its northerly location?
   b. Draw Conclusions Where would you expect to find Canada's coldest climate? Why?
3. **a. Define** What is the **Grand Banks**?
   b. Interpret How are Canada's forests a valuable resource?

Critical Thinking

4. **Generalizing** Using your notes on Canada's resources, identify the location of each type of resource.

Resources		Location
	→	
	→	
	→	

FOCUS ON SPEAKING

5. **Writing about Physical Geography** What information about Canada's physical features, climate, and resources might visitors find appealing? Jot down what descriptions you want to include in your radio ad.

History and Culture

What You Will Learn...

Main Ideas

1. Beginning in the 1600s, Europeans settled the region that would later become Canada.
2. Immigration and migration to cities have shaped Canadian culture.

The Big Idea

Canada's history and culture reflect Native Canadian and European settlement, immigration, and migration to cities.

Key Terms and Places

provinces, *p. 178*
Quebec, *p. 178*
British Columbia, *p. 178*
Toronto, *p. 180*

hmhsocialstudies.com
TAKING NOTES

Use the graphic organizer online to take notes on the history and culture of Canada.

If **YOU** lived there...

You own a general store in Calgary, Alberta, in the early 1880s. Your town is a center for agriculture and ranching on the prairies around you. Still, it sometimes feels very isolated. You miss your family in Ontario. Now the news comes that the Canadian Pacific Railway will soon reach Calgary. It will connect the town with all of central and eastern Canada.

How will the railroad change your life?

BUILDING BACKGROUND Canada is a close neighbor with the United States. The two countries are linked by a common language and a history of British colonial rule. But the two countries developed in different ways. Canada's diverse population developed its own culture and way of life.

History

As the ice sheets of the ice ages melted, people moved into all areas of what is now Canada. As they did elsewhere in the Americas, these ancient settlers adapted to the physical environment.

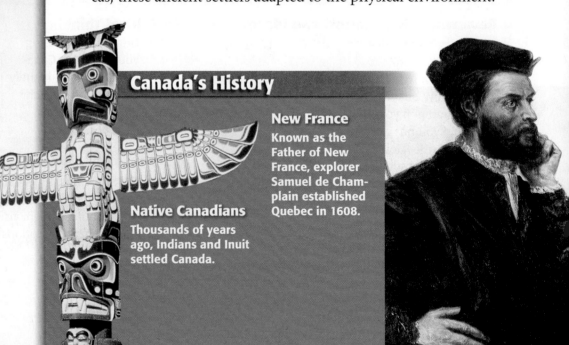

Canada's History

New France
Known as the Father of New France, explorer Samuel de Champlain established Quebec in 1608.

Native Canadians
Thousands of years ago, Indians and Inuit settled Canada.

Native Canadians

Indians and the Inuit (IH-nu-wuht) people were the first Canadians. Over the years, some of these native peoples divided into groups that became known as the First Nations. One group living on Canada's vast interior plains, the Cree, were skilled bison hunters. In the far north the Inuit adapted to the region's extreme cold, where farming was impossible. By hunting seals, whales, walruses, and other animals, the Inuit could feed, clothe, and house themselves. Today about 400,000 Indians and Inuit live in Canada.

European Settlement

Other people migrated to Canada from Europe. The first Europeans in Canada were the Vikings, or Norse. They settled on Newfoundland Island in about AD 1000, but later abandoned their settlements. In the late 1400s other Europeans arrived and explored Canada. Soon more explorers and fishermen from western Europe began crossing the Atlantic.

Trade quickly developed between the Europeans and Native Canadians. Europeans valued the furs that Native Canadians supplied. The Canadians wanted European metal goods like axes and guns. Through trading, they began to also exchange foods, clothing, and methods of travel.

New France

France was the first European country to successfully settle parts of what would become Canada. The French **established** Quebec City in 1608. They called their new territories New France. At its height, New France included much of eastern Canada and the central United States.

New France was important for several reasons. It was part of the French Empire, which provided money and goods to French settlers. It also served as a base to spread French culture.

France had to compete with Britain, another European colonial power, for control of Canada. To defend their interests against the British, the French built trade and diplomatic relationships with Native Canadians. They exported furs, fish, and other products from New France to other parts of their empire. In addition, the French sent manufactured goods from France to New France. French missionaries also went to New France to convert people to Christianity.

All of these efforts protected French interests in New France for 150 years, until the British finally defeated the French. Although it did not last, New France shaped Canada's cultural makeup. The descendants of French settlers form one of Canada's major ethnic groups today.

ACADEMIC VOCABULARY

establish to set up or create

British Settlement
The British built forts throughout Canada like this one in Halifax, Nova Scotia.

Dominion of Canada
After 1867, Canadians created their own government and a mounted police force patrolled the border with the United States.

British Conquest

In the mid-1700s, the rivalry between France and England turned to war. The conflict was called the French and Indian War. This was the war that resulted in the British taking control of New France away from the French. A small number of French went back to France. However, the great majority stayed. For most of them, few changes occurred in their daily activities. They farmed the same land, prayed in the same churches, and continued to speak French. Few English-speaking settlers came to what is now called **Quebec**.

Canadian Pacific Railroad

Since 1885, the Canadian Pacific Railway has snaked through the Canadian Rockies on its way to the Pacific coast.

The British divided Quebec into two colonies. Lower Canada was mostly French-speaking, and Upper Canada was mostly English-speaking. The boundary between Upper and Lower Canada forms part of the border between the provinces of Quebec and Ontario today. **Provinces** are administrative divisions of a country. To the east, the colony of Nova Scotia (noh-vuh SKOH-shuh) was also divided. A new colony called New Brunswick was created where many of the British settlers lived.

Creation of Canada

For several decades these new colonies developed separately from each other. The colonists viewed themselves as different from other parts of the British Empire. Therefore, the British Parliament created the Dominion of Canada in 1867. A dominion is a territory or area of influence. For Canadians, the creation of the Dominion was a step toward independence from Britain. The motto of the new Dominion was "from sea to sea."

How would Canadians create a nation from sea to sea? With railroads. When the Dominion was established, Ontario and Quebec were already well served by railroads. **British Columbia**, on the Pacific coast, was not. To connect British Columbia with the provinces in the east, the Canadians built a transcontinental railroad. Completed in 1885, the Canadian Pacific Railway was Canada's first transcontinental railroad.

After the Canadian Pacific Railway linked the original Canadian provinces to British Columbia, Canada acquired vast lands in the north. Much of this land was bought from the Hudson's Bay Company, a large British fur-trading business. Most of the people living in the north were Native Canadians and people of mixed European and native ancestry. With the building

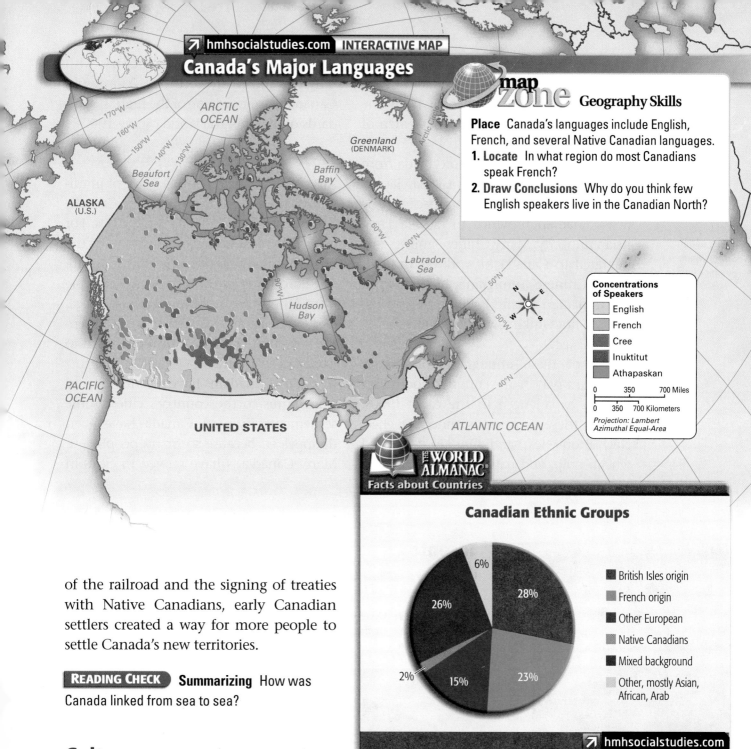

Canada's Major Languages

ARCTIC OCEAN

170°W
160°W
150°W
140°W
130°W

ALASKA (U.S.)

Beaufort Sea

Greenland (DENMARK)

Arctic Circle

Baffin Bay

60°W

60°N

Labrador Sea

90°W

Hudson Bay

50°N

50°N

40°N

PACIFIC OCEAN

UNITED STATES

ATLANTIC OCEAN

map zone Geography Skills

Place Canada's languages include English, French, and several Native Canadian languages.
1. **Locate** In what region do most Canadians speak French?
2. **Draw Conclusions** Why do you think few English speakers live in the Canadian North?

Concentrations of Speakers
- English
- French
- Cree
- Inuktitut
- Athapaskan

0   350   700 Miles
0   350   700 Kilometers
Projection: Lambert Azimuthal Equal-Area

THE WORLD ALMANAC
Facts about Countries

Canadian Ethnic Groups

6%
28%
26%
2%
15%
23%

- British Isles origin
- French origin
- Other European
- Native Canadians
- Mixed background
- Other, mostly Asian, African, Arab

hmhsocialstudies.com

of the railroad and the signing of treaties with Native Canadians, early Canadian settlers created a way for more people to settle Canada's new territories.

READING CHECK **Summarizing** How was Canada linked from sea to sea?

Culture

Canada's people reflect a history of British and French colonial rule. In addition, the country has experienced waves of immigration. The country is home to a great variety of people who belong to different ethnic groups and cultures. Although individual groups still keep their own cultural ways, many Canadians have tried to create a single national identity.

Immigration

During the late 1800s and early 1900s, many immigrants came to Canada from Europe. Most were from Britain, Russia, and Germany. Some people also came from the United States. While most of these immigrants farmed, others worked in mines, forests, and factories.

Other immigrants were lured to Canada in 1897 by the discovery of gold in the Yukon Territory. Many people from the United States migrated north in search of Canada's gold.

FOCUS ON READING
What details of this paragraph could you add to a list of countries from which immigrants came?

Immigrants also came to Canada from Asian countries, especially China, Japan, and India. British Columbia became the first Canadian province to have a large Asian minority. Many Chinese immigrants migrated to Canada to work on the railroads. Chinese immigrants built most of the Canadian Pacific Railway, one of the railroad lines linking eastern Canada to the Pacific coast.

All of these immigrants played an important part in an economic boom that Canada experienced in the early 1900s. During these prosperous times, Quebec, New Brunswick, and Ontario produced wheat, pulp, and paper. British Columbia and Ontario supplied the country with minerals and hydroelectricity. As a result, Canadians enjoyed one of the highest standards of living in the world by the 1940s.

Movement to Cities

After World War II, another wave of immigrants from Europe arrived in Canada. Many settled in Canada's large cities. For example, **Toronto** has become one of the most culturally diverse cities in the world. The Europeans were joined by other people from Africa, the Caribbean, Latin America, and particularly Asia. Asian businesspeople have brought a great deal of wealth to Canada's economy.

Many Canadians have recently moved from farms to the country's cities. Some settlements in rural Canada have even disappeared because so many people left. Many Canadians have moved to cities in

Toronto

With about 5 million people, Toronto is Canada's largest city.

ANALYZING VISUALS How is Toronto's history reflected in this city square?

Vancouver's Chinatown

If you walked around Vancouver, British Columbia, you would quickly realize when you entered the neighborhood of Chinatown. First you would notice that most signs are in Chinese and you would hear some people speaking Chinese. Then you would realize most restaurants serve Chinese food, and shops sell colorful silk clothing, herbs, and art imported from China. If you were in the city for the Chinese New Year, you would probably see a parade of people in traditional Chinese dress. Vancouver's Chinatown is a unique place where Chinese culture is kept alive in Canada today.

Drawing Conclusions How is Vancouver's Chinatown a unique neighborhood?

Ontario to find jobs. Others moved to Vancouver, British Columbia, for its good job opportunities, mild climate, and location near plentiful resources. Resources such as oil, gas, potash, and uranium have provided wealth to many cities in the Western Provinces. However, the political and economic center of power remains in the cities of Ottawa, Toronto, and Montreal.

READING CHECK Analyzing How has immigration changed Canada?

SUMMARY AND PREVIEW In this section, you learned that Canada was greatly influenced by British and French settlement, the building of the railroad to the Pacific coast, immigration, and movement to cities. In the next section you will learn about Canada's regions and economy today.

Section 2 Assessment

hmhsocialstudies.com
ONLINE QUIZ

Reviewing Ideas, Terms, and Places

1. **a. Recall** What is a **province**?
   b. Summarize How did Britain gain control of New France from the French?
   c. Elaborate How do you think the Canadian Pacific Railway changed Canada?
2. **a. Identify** What immigrant group helped build the railroads?
   b. Draw Conclusions Why did people migrate to Canada?
   c. Elaborate Why do you think many Canadians moved from farms to the cities?

Critical Thinking

3. **Analyzing** Draw a diagram like the one below. Using your notes, write a sentence in each box about how each topic influenced the next topic.

Railroad	Immigration	Cities

FOCUS ON SPEAKING

4. **Adding Details** Add information about the history and culture of Canada to your notes. Which details would most interest potential visitors?

Canada Today

If YOU lived there...

You and your family live in Toronto, Ontario. Your parents, who are architects, have been offered an important project in Montreal. If they accept it, you would live there for two years. Montreal is a major city in French-speaking Quebec. You would have to learn a new language. In Montreal, most street signs and advertisements are written in French.

How do you feel about moving to a city with a different language and culture?

What You Will Learn...

Main Ideas

1. Canada has a democratic government with a prime minister and a parliament.
2. Canada has four distinct geographic and cultural regions.
3. Canada's economy is largely based on trade with the United States.

The Big Idea

Canada's democratic government oversees the country's regions and economy.

Key Terms and Places

regionalism, *p. 183*
maritime, *p. 183*
Montreal, *p. 184*
Ottawa, *p. 185*
Vancouver, *p. 186*

hmhsocialstudies.com
TAKING NOTES

Use the graphic organizer online to take notes on present-day Canada.

BUILDING BACKGROUND Canada today has been shaped by both history and geography. Canada's first European settlers were French, but the British eventually controlled the territory. Differences in culture still remain, however. In addition, the four regions of Canada are separated by vast distances, economic activities, and culture.

Canada's Government

"Peace, order, and good government" is a statement from Canada's constitution that Canadians greatly value. Canadians are proud of their democratic government, which is led by a prime minister. Similar to a president, a prime minister is the head of a country's government.

Canada's prime minister oversees the country's parliament, Canada's governing body. Parliament consists of the House of Commons and the Senate. Canadians elect members of the House of Commons. However, senators are appointed by the prime minister.

Canada's 10 provincial governments are each led by a premier. These provincial governments are much like our state governments. Canada's central government is similar to our federal government. The Canadian federal system lets people keep their feelings of loyalty to their own province.

READING CHECK **Comparing** How is Canada's government similar to that of the United States?

Canada's Regions

Canada's physical geography separates the country into different regions. For example, people living on the Pacific coast in British Columbia are isolated from Canadians living in the eastern provinces on the Atlantic coast. Just as geographic distance separates much of Canada, differences in culture also define regions.

Regionalism

The cultural differences between English-speaking and French-speaking Canadians have led to problems. English is the main language in most of Canada. In Quebec, however, French is the main language. When Canadians from different regions discuss important issues, they are often influenced by regionalism. **Regionalism** refers to the strong connection that people feel toward the region in which they live.

In some places, this connection is stronger than people's connection to their country as a whole. To better understand regionalism in Canada, we will now explore each region of the country. As you read, refer to the map below to locate each region.

The Eastern Provinces

The region called the Eastern Provinces is a region that lies on the Atlantic coast of Canada. The provinces of New Brunswick, Nova Scotia, and Prince Edward Island are often called the Maritime Provinces. **Maritime** means on or near the sea. The province of Newfoundland and Labrador is usually not considered one of the Maritime Provinces. It includes the island of Newfoundland and a large region of the mainland called Labrador.

A short growing season limits farming in the Eastern Provinces. However, farmers in Prince Edward Island grow potatoes.

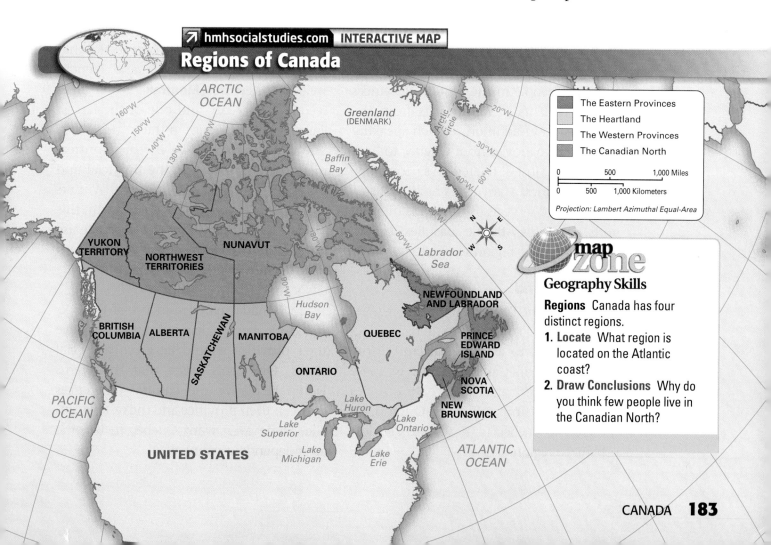

hmhsocialstudies.com **INTERACTIVE MAP**

Regions of Canada

Map legend:
- The Eastern Provinces
- The Heartland
- The Western Provinces
- The Canadian North

0   500   1,000 Miles
0   500   1,000 Kilometers
Projection: Lambert Azimuthal Equal-Area

map zone

Geography Skills

Regions Canada has four distinct regions.
1. **Locate** What region is located on the Atlantic coast?
2. **Draw Conclusions** Why do you think few people live in the Canadian North?

Quebec's Winter Carnival

At the annual Winter Carnival in the city of Quebec, millions of Canadians and visitors from around the world brave below-freezing temperatures to celebrate French Canadian culture.

The Inuit people traditionally used dogsleds as a means of transportation. Today dogsledding is a popular sport in Canada and a highlight of the carnival.

Most of the economy in Canada's Eastern Provinces is related to the forestry and fishing industries.

Many people in the Eastern Provinces are descendants of immigrants from the British Isles. In addition, French-speaking families have moved from Quebec to New Brunswick. Most of the region's people live in coastal cities. Many cities have industrial plants and serve as fishing and shipping ports. Along the Atlantic coast lies Halifax, Nova Scotia, the region's largest city.

The Heartland

FOCUS ON READING

In the paragraphs under The Heartland sort the facts into different lists.

Inland from the Eastern Provinces are Quebec and Ontario, which together are sometimes referred to as the Heartland. More than half of all Canadians live in these two provinces. In fact, the chain of cities that extends from Windsor, Ontario, to the city of Quebec is the country's most urbanized region.

The provincial capital of Quebec is also called Quebec. The city's older section has narrow streets, stone walls, and French-style architecture. **Montreal** is Canada's second-largest city and one of the largest French-speaking cities in the world. About 3.5 million people live in the Montreal metropolitan area. It is the financial and industrial center of the province. Winters in Montreal are very cold. To deal with this harsh environment, Montreal's people use underground passages and overhead tunnels to move between buildings in the city's downtown.

In Canada many residents of Quebec, called Quebecois (kay-buh-KWAH), believe their province should be given a special status. Quebecois argue that this status would recognize the cultural differences between their province and the rest of Canada. Some even want Quebec to become an independent country.

Many of the city's buildings reflect French architecture.

ANALYSIS SKILL ANALYZING VISUALS

From the clues you see in this scene, what do you think is unique about French Canadian culture?

Ice sculptures created by Canadian and international artists line the carnival's grounds.

The carnival's mascot is a snowman who wears a traditional Canadian sash and hat.

On the other hand, many English-speaking Canadians think Quebec already has too many privileges. Most Canadians, however, still support a united Canada. Strong feelings of regionalism will continue to be an important issue.

With an even larger population than Quebec, the province of Ontario is Canada's leading manufacturing province. Hamilton, Ontario, is the center of Canada's steel industry. Canada exports much of its steel to the United States.

Ontario's capital, Toronto, is a major center for industry, finance, education, and culture. Toronto's residents come from many different parts of the world, including China, Europe, and India.

Canada's national capital, **Ottawa**, is also in Ontario. In Ottawa many people speak both English and French. The city is known for its grand government buildings, parks, and several universities.

The Western Provinces

West of Ontario are the prairie provinces of Manitoba, Saskatchewan, and Alberta. On the Pacific coast is the province of British Columbia. Together, these four provinces make up Canada's Western Provinces.

More people live in Quebec than in all of the prairie provinces combined. The southern grasslands of these provinces are part of a rich wheat belt. Farms here produce far more wheat than Canadians need. The extra wheat is exported. Oil and natural gas production is a very important economic activity in Alberta. The beauty of the Canadian Rockies attracts many visitors to national parks in western Alberta and eastern British Columbia.

British Columbia is Canada's westernmost province and home to almost 4 million people. This mountainous province has rich natural resources, including forests, salmon, and valuable minerals.

Even in June, snow covers the small town of Pond Inlet, Nunavut. The Inuit here travel by snowmobile and enjoy ice fishing.

Nearly half of British Columbia's population lives in and around the coastal city of **Vancouver**. The city's location on the Pacific coast helps it to trade with countries in Asia.

The Canadian North

Northern Canada is extremely cold due to its location close to the Arctic Circle. The region called the Canadian North includes the Yukon Territory, the Northwest Territories, and Nunavut (NOO-nuh-voot). These three territories cover more than a third of Canada but are home to only about 100,000 people.

Nunavut is a new territory created for the native Inuit people who live there. Nunavut means "Our Land" in the Inuit language. Even though Nunavut is part of Canada, the people there have their own **distinct** culture and government. About 30,000 people live in Nunavut.

The physical geography of the Canadian North includes forests and tundra. The frozen waters of the Arctic Ocean separate

ACADEMIC VOCABULARY

distinct separate

isolated towns and villages. During some parts of the winter, sunlight is limited to only a few hours.

READING CHECK **Drawing Conclusions** How does geography affect the location of economic activities in the Western Provinces?

Canada's Economy

As you learned in Section 1, Canada has many valuable natural resources. Canada's economy is based on the industries associated with these resources. In addition, Canada's economy also benefits from trade.

Industries

Canada is one of the world's leading mineral producers. Canadians mine valuable titanium, zinc, iron ore, gold, and coal. Canada's iron and steel industry uses iron ore to manufacture products like planes, automobiles and household appliances. However, most Canadians work in the services industry. For example, tourism is

Canada's fastest-growing services industry. Canada's economy also benefits from the millions of dollars visitors spend in the country each year.

Trade

Canada's economy depends on trade. Many of Canada's natural resources that you have learned about are exported to countries around the world. Canada's leading trading partner is the United States.

As the world's largest trading relationship, Canada and the United States rely heavily on each other. About 60 percent of Canada's imported goods are from the United States. About 85 percent of Canada's exports, such as lumber, goes to the United States.

However, the United States placed tariffs, or added fees, on Canadian timber. American lumber companies accused Canada of selling their lumber at unfairly low prices. Canada argued that the tariffs were unfair according to the North American Free Trade Agreement (NAFTA).

The export of cattle to the United States is another area of dispute between the two countries. When a Canadian cow was discovered with mad cow disease in 2003, the United States banned the import of all cattle from Canada. Canadian ranchers now claim that all their cows are free of the disease. After a two-year ban, the United States imports Canadian cattle and beef again.

READING CHECK **Summarizing** What goods does Canada export?

SUMMARY In this section you learned that Canada has distinct regions that are separated by both geography and culture. The U.S. and Canada are trading partners that share a common colonial history, a border, and the English language.

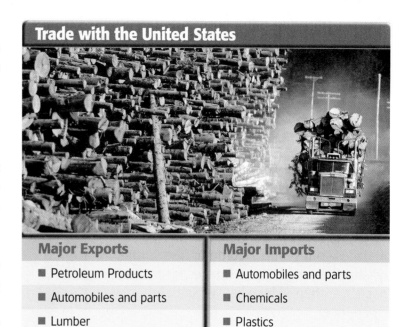

Trade with the United States

Major Exports	Major Imports
■ Petroleum Products	■ Automobiles and parts
■ Automobiles and parts	■ Chemicals
■ Lumber	■ Plastics

Section 3 Assessment

hmhsocialstudies.com
ONLINE QUIZ

Reviewing Ideas, Terms, and Places

1. **a. Recall** What office heads Canada's government?
   b. Summarize How is Canada's parliament structured?
2. **a. Define** What is **regionalism**?
   b. Contrast How are Canada's Western Provinces different from the Canadian North?
   c. Evaluate Why do you think the Quebecois want to break away from Canada?
3. **a. Describe** How are Canada's natural resources important to the country's economy?
   b. Draw Conclusions Why do Canada and the United States rely on each other as trading partners?

Critical Thinking

4. **Comparing and Contrasting** Use your notes to complete this chart. List the similarities and differences between the Eastern Provinces and Western Provinces.

Similarities	Differences
1.	1.
2.	

FOCUS ON SPEAKING

5. **Presenting Canada Today** Add details about present-day Canada to your notes. Consider which images you will use to persuade your audience to visit Canada after they listen to your ad.

Using Mental Maps and Sketch Maps

Learn

We create maps in our heads of all kinds of places—our schools, communities, country, and the world. These images, or mental maps, are shaped by what we see and experience.

We use mental maps of places when we draw sketch maps. A sketch map uses very simple shapes to show the relationship between places and the relative size of places. Notice the sketch map of the world shown here. It may not look like any other map in your book, but it does give you an idea of what the world looks like.

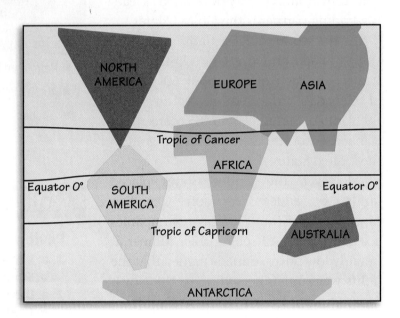

Practice

Does your mental map of the world look like the sketch map here? It is alright if they do not look exactly alike. Now think about the places in your own neighborhood. Use your mental map to draw a sketch map of your neighborhood. Then use your sketch map to answer the following questions.

- What are the most important features of your map?
- What is the largest building in your neighborhood?
- What labels did you use on your map?

Apply

Draw a sketch map of Canada. Make sure to include the cities and physical features you learned about in this chapter. Then exchange your map with another student. Ask your partner to make corrections to your map if he or she does not understand it.

Chapter Review

Geography's Impact
video series
Review the video to answer the closing question:
Why did the people of Nunavut want their own territory?

Visual Summary

Use the visual summary below to help you review the main ideas of the chapter.

QUICK FACTS

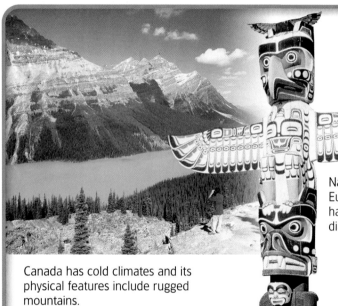

Canada has cold climates and its physical features include rugged mountains.

Native Canadian and European settlement has influenced Canadian culture.

Canada has distinctive cultural regions today.

Reviewing Vocabulary, Terms, and Places

Choose the letter of the answer that best completes each statement below.

1. A physical feature of rocky uplands, lakes, and swamps in Canada is called the
   a. Niagara Falls.   **c.** Grand Banks.
   b. Great Lakes.   **d.** Canadian Shield.

2. Which part of Canada did the French settle?
   a. Ontario   **c.** Quebec
   b. New Brunswick   **d.** British Colombia

3. What province was the first to have a large Asian population?
   a. Manitoba   **c.** Quebec
   b. British Columbia   **d.** Saskatchewan

4. A strong connection that people feel toward their region is called
   a. maritime.   **c.** heartland.
   b. province.   **d.** regionalism.

Comprehension and Critical Thinking

SECTION 1 *(Pages 172–175)*

5. **a. Define** What is pulp?

   b. Make Inferences What is the coldest area in Canada?

   c. Evaluate What makes the Grand Banks an ideal fishing ground?

SECTION 2 *(Pages 176–181)*

6. **a. Identify** Who were the first Canadians?

   b. Draw Conclusions Why did Canadians build a rail line across Canada?

   c. Predict Do you think Canada's cities will increase or decrease in population in the future? Explain your answers.

SECTION 3 *(Pages 182–187)*

7. **a. Recall** What kind of government does Canada have?

SECTION 3 (continued)

b. Compare and Contrast How are the Eastern Provinces different than the Western Provinces?

c. Evaluate Why do the Quebecois see themselves as different from other Canadians?

Using the Internet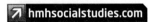

8. **Activity: Writing Newspaper Articles** You are a reporter for The Quebec Chronicle assigned to write articles for the next issue of the newspaper. Through your online textbook, explore the people of Quebec and find background information for your articles covering Quebec. Use the links provided to conduct your research and then write three short articles. Go to press using the interactive template and publish your Canadian newspaper.

⏋ **hmhsocialstudies.com**

Social Studies Skills

9. **Using Mental Maps and Sketch Maps** Without looking at a map of Canada think about what the Eastern Provinces look like. Then create a sketch map of the Eastern Provinces. Make sure to include a compass rose and important physical features.

Map Activity

10. **Canada** On a separate sheet of paper, match the letters on the map with their correct labels.

Rocky Mountains	Manitoba
Nunavut	St. Lawrence River
Vancouver	

FOCUS ON READING AND SPEAKING

11. **Understanding Lists** Use your notes about Canada to create a list of important facts for each section. Organize your lists using this chart.

Physical Geography	History and Culture	Canada Today

12. **Creating a Tourism Ad** Now that you have collected notes on Canada's geography, history, and culture, choose the information you think will most appeal to visitors. Write a one-minute radio script, using descriptive and persuasive language to convince your audience to visit Canada. Describe Canada in a way that will capture your audience's imagination. Ask the class to listen carefully as you read your radio ad to them. Then ask the class to evaluate your ad on how persuasive it was or was not.

Standardized Test Prep

DIRECTIONS: Read questions 1 through 7 and write the letter of the best response. Then read question 8 and write your own well-constructed response.

1 The United States and Canada share which physical feature?

  A Canadian Shield

  B Rocky Mountains

  C Hudson Bay

  D Saskatchewan River

2 What resource in Canada provides pulp and newsprint?

  A forests

  B nickel

  C potash

  D fish

3 Many Canadians moved from farms to cities to find

  A gold.

  B good schools.

  C jobs.

  D better weather.

4 Canada's prime minister oversees the country's

  A railroads.

  B parliament.

  C provincial governments.

  D city governments.

5 Canada's capital, Ottawa, is located in

  A Northwest Territories.

  B Nova Scotia.

  C Ontario.

  D British Columbia.

Climate of British Columbia

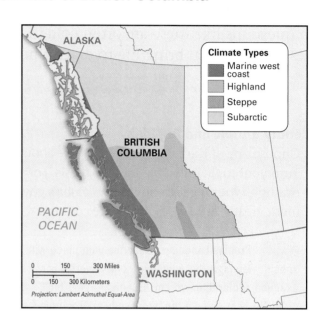

6 Based on the map above, which climate type does the Pacific coast of British Columbia experience?

  A subarctic

  B marine west coast

  C highland

  D steppe

7 About 60 percent of Canada's imported goods come from which country?

  A Mexico

  B Greenland

  C Russia

  D United States

8 **Extended Response** Look at the political map of Canada at the beginning of this chapter. Using information from the map, explain why the United States and Canada are major trading partners.

Describing a Place

What are the physical features of a country? What is the weather like? What drives the economy? The answers to questions like these are often cold, hard facts and statistics. But they can bring life to a description of a place.

Assignment
Write a paper describing one of these places in the Americas:
- a city
- a country

1. Prewrite
Identify a Topic and Big Idea
- Choose one of the topics above to write about.
- Turn your topic into a big idea, or thesis. For example, your big idea might be, "Cuba's government greatly influences life in the country."

> **TIP** **Precise Language** Describe your place with specific nouns, verbs, adjectives, and adverbs. For example, rather than writing "Buenos Aires is big," write "Buenos Aires is the largest city in Argentina."

Gather and Organize Information
- Look for information about your place in the library or on the Internet. Organize your notes in groupings such as physical features, economy, or culture. Decide which facts about the place you are describing are most important or unique.

2. Write
Use a Writer's Framework

A Writer's Framework

Introduction
- Start with an interesting fact or question.
- Identify your big idea and provide any necessary background information.

Body
- Write at least one paragraph for each category. Include facts that help explain each detail.
- Write about each detail in order of importance.

Conclusion
- Summarize your description in your final paragraph.

3. Evaluate and Revise
Review and Improve Your Paper
- Re-read your paper and use the questions below to identify ways to revise your paper.
- Make the changes needed to improve your paper.

Evaluation Questions for a Description of a Place
1. Do you begin with an interesting fact or question?
2. Does your introduction identify your big idea? Do you provide background information to help your readers better understand your idea?
3. Do you have at least one paragraph for each category?
4. Do you use order of importance to organize the details of your description?
5. Are there more details you would like to know about your place? If so, what are they?

4. Proofread and Publish
Give Your Description the Finishing Touch
- Make sure you used commas correctly when listing more than two details in a sentence.
- Check your spelling of the names of places.
- Share your description with classmates or with students in another social studies class.

5. Practice and Apply
Use the steps and strategies outlined in this workshop to write your description of a place. Share your description with classmates. With your classmates, group the descriptions by country and then identify the places you would like to visit.

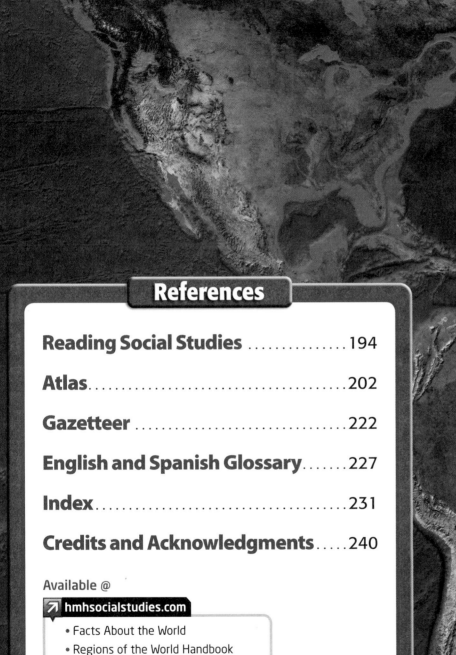

References

Available @

⇗ hmhsocialstudies.com

- Facts About the World
- Regions of the World Handbook
- Standardized Test-Taking Strategies
- Economics Handbook

Setting a Purpose

FOCUS ON READING

When you go on a trip, you have a purpose or a destination in mind before you start. Maps can help you get to your destination. When you read, you should also have a purpose in mind before you start. This purpose keeps you focused and moving toward your goal of understanding. Textbooks often provide "maps" to help you set a purpose for your reading. A textbook's "map" includes a chapter's headings, pictures, and study tips. To determine a purpose for your reading, look over the headings, pictures, and study tips. Then ask yourself a question that can guide you. See how looking over the chapter's first page can help you set a purpose.

What You Will Learn...

From Early History of the Americas

In this chapter you will learn about the location, growth, and decline of the Maya, Aztec, and Inca civilizations in the Americas.

SECTION 1
The Maya 14

SECTION 2
The Aztecs 20

SECTION 3
The Incas 25

Notice Headings, Pictures or Tips
Here's a tip on what I should learn about in this chapter.

Ask Questions
What do I want to learn about these three civilizations?

Set a Purpose
I've never heard of these civilizations. I wonder what they were like and why they declined. I'll read to find out.

YOU TRY IT!

You can also use the method described above to set a purpose for reading the main text in your book. Look at the heading for the following caption. Then write down one or two questions about what you will read. Finally, develop a purpose for reading about Tenochtitlán. State this purpose in one to two sentences.

Tenochtitlán

The Aztecs turned a swampy, uninhabited island into one of the largest and grandest cities in the world. The first Europeans to visit Tenochtitlán were amazed. At the time, the Aztec capital was about five times bigger than London.

From Section 2, The Aztecs

Chapter 2 Mexico

Predicting

FOCUS ON READING

Predicting is guessing what will happen next based on what you already know. In reading about geography, you can use what you know about the place you live to help you make predictions about other countries. Predicting helps you stay involved with your reading as you see whether your prediction was right. Your mind follows these four steps when you make predictions as you read:

Takes what you already know → Adds new information from your reading → Forms a prediction that makes sense → Confirms or adjusts your prediction based on what you just read

See how you might make a prediction from the following text:

> From snowcapped mountain peaks to warm, sunny beaches, Mexico has many different climates.
>
> *From Section 1, Physical Geography*

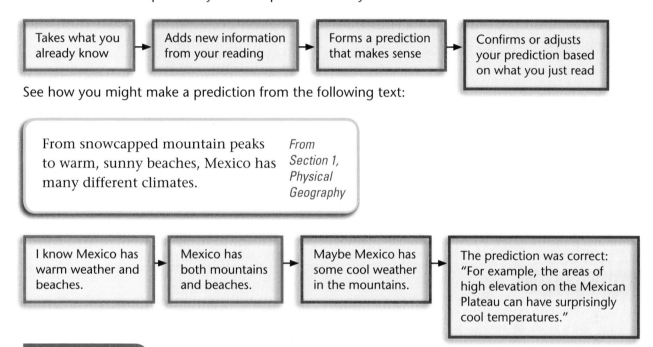

I know Mexico has warm weather and beaches. → Mexico has both mountains and beaches. → Maybe Mexico has some cool weather in the mountains. → The prediction was correct: "For example, the areas of high elevation on the Mexican Plateau can have surprisingly cool temperatures."

YOU TRY IT!

Read the following sentences. Then use a graphic organizer like the one below to help you predict what you will learn in your reading. Check the text in Section 3 to see if your prediction was correct.

> Mexico has a democratic government. However, Mexico is not like the United States where different political parties have always competed for power.
>
> *From Section 3, Mexico Today*

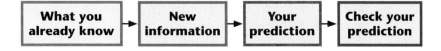

What you already know → New information → Your prediction → Check your prediction

READING SOCIAL STUDIES

READING SOCIAL STUDIES

195

Understanding Comparison-Contrast

FOCUS ON READING

Comparing shows how things are alike. Contrasting shows how things are different. You can understand comparison-contrast by learning to recognize clue words and points of comparison. Clue words let you know whether to look for similarities or differences. Points of comparison are the main topics that are being compared or contrasted.

> Many Caribbean islands share a similar history and culture. However, today the islands' different economies, governments, and cultural landscapes encourage many different ways of life in the Caribbean.
>
> *From Section 3, The Caribbean Islands*

Underlined words are clue words.

Highlighted words are points of comparison.

Clue Words	
Comparison	**Contrast**
share, similar, like, also, both, in addition, besides	however, while, unlike, different, but, although

YOU TRY IT!

Read the following passage to see how Haiti and the Dominican Republic are alike and different. Use a diagram like the one here to compare and contrast the two countries.

> Haiti occupies the western part of the island of Hispaniola. Haiti's capital, Port-au-Prince, is the center of the nation's limited industry. Most Haitians farm small plots. Coffee and sugarcane are among Haiti's main exports.
>
> The Dominican Republic occupies the eastern part of Hispaniola. The Dominican Republic is not a rich country. However, its economy, health care, education, and housing are more developed than Haiti's. Agriculture is the basis of the economy
>
> *From Section 3, The Caribbean Islands*

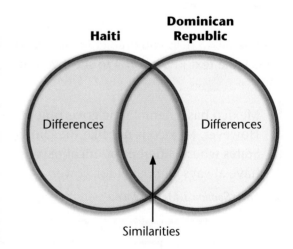

Haiti | Dominican Republic

Differences | Differences

Similarities

Identifying Supporting Details

FOCUS ON READING

Why believe what you read? One reason is because of details that support or prove the main idea. These details might be facts, statistics, examples, or definitions. In the example below, notice what kind of proof or supporting details help you believe the main idea.

> Colombia's economy relies on several valuable resources. Rich soil, steep slopes, and tall shade trees produce world-famous Colombian coffee. Other major export crops include bananas, sugarcane, and cotton. Many farms in Colombia produce flowers that are exported around the world. In fact, 80 percent of the country's flowers are shipped to the United States.
>
> *From Section 2, Colombia*

Main Idea
Colombia's economy relies on several valuable resources.

Supporting Details			
Example	**Fact**	**Fact**	**Statistic**
Colombian coffee	Other export crops	Export flowers	80 percent shipped to U.S.

YOU TRY IT!

Read the following sentences. Then identify the supporting details in a graphic organizer like the one above.

> Caribbean South America is home to some remarkable wildlife. For example, hundreds of bird species, meat-eating fish called piranhas, and crocodiles live in or around the Orinoco River. Colombia has one of the world's highest concentrations of plant and animal species. The country's wildlife includes jaguars, ocelots, and several species of monkeys.
>
> *From Section 1, Physical Geography*

Using Context Clues

FOCUS ON READING

One practical way to tackle unfamiliar words you encounter is to look at the context. Reading the words and sentences surrounding the word will often help you because they give definitions, examples, or synonyms. For example, maybe you're not sure what the word *context* means. Just from reading the previous sentences, however, you probably understood that it means the "the part of a text surrounding a word or passage that makes its meaning clear." You have relied on the context to help you define the word. In reading geography, you may forget what some of the geographical terms mean. You can use context clues to figure them out. See how this process works in the example below with the word *tributary*.

> The Amazon River is about 4,000 miles long. It extends from the Andes Mountains in Peru to the Atlantic Ocean. Hundreds of tributaries flow into it, draining an area that includes parts of most South American countries.
>
> *From Section 1, Physical Geography*

1. Look at the surrounding words or sentences.
The passage talks about the Amazon River and what flows into it.

2. Make a guess at the word's meaning.
A tributary must be a smaller river or stream that flows into a bigger river.

3. Check your guess by inserting it into the passage.
Hundreds of smaller rivers flow into it.

YOU TRY IT!

Read the following sentences, and then use the three steps described above to help you define *hydroelectric*.

> Atlantic South America also has good mineral and energy resources such as gold, silver, copper, iron, and oil. Dams on some of the region's large rivers also provide hydroelectric power.
>
> *From Section 1, Physical Geography*

Making Inferences

FOCUS ON READING

Sometimes reading effectively means understanding both what the writer tells you directly and what the writer doesn't tell you. When you fill in the gaps, you are making inferences, or educated guesses. Why worry about what the writer doesn't tell you? Making inferences can help you make connections with the text. It can also give you a fuller picture of the information. To make an inference, think about the text and what you know or can guess from the information. The example below shows you the process.

> At the southern tip of the continent, the Strait of Magellan links the Atlantic and Pacific oceans. A strait is a narrow body of water connecting two larger bodies of water. The large island south of the strait is Tierra del Fuego, or "land of fire."
>
> *From Section 1, Physical Geography*

1. Determine what the passage says:
The Strait of Magellan connects the Atlantic and Pacific oceans. There is an island south of it.

2. Determine what you know about the topic or what you can connect to your experience.
This sounds like a shortcut to me. It would keep boats from having to sail all the way around the island.

3. Make an inference.
Many ships probably use the Strait of Magellan because it is a shortcut.

YOU TRY IT!

Read the following sentences. Then use the three steps described above to make an inference about the Galápagos Islands.

> Chile and Ecuador both control large islands in the Pacific Ocean. Ecuador's volcanic Galápagos Islands have wildlife not found anywhere else in the world.
>
> *From Section 1, Physical Geography*

Categorizing

FOCUS ON READING

When you sort things into groups of similar items, you are categorizing. When you read, categorizing helps you to identify the main groups of information. Then you can find and see the individual facts in each group. Notice how the information in the paragraph below has been sorted into three main groups, with details listed under each group.

> If you were traveling across the United States, you might start on the country's eastern coast. This low area, which is flat and close to sea level, is called the Atlantic Coastal Plain. As you go west, the land gradually rises higher to a region called the Piedmont. The Appalachian Mountains, which are the main mountain range in the East, rise above the Piedmont.
>
> *From Section 1, Physical Geography*

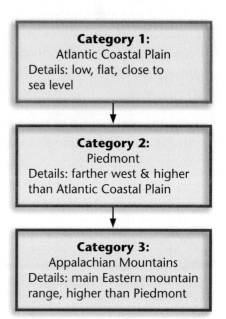

Category 1:
Atlantic Coastal Plain
Details: low, flat, close to sea level

Category 2:
Piedmont
Details: farther west & higher than Atlantic Coastal Plain

Category 3:
Appalachian Mountains
Details: main Eastern mountain range, higher than Piedmont

YOU TRY IT!

Read the following paragraph, and then use a graphic organizer like the one above to categorize the group and details in the paragraph. Create as many boxes as you need to list the main groups.

> The eastern United States has three climate regions. In the Northeast, people live in a humid continental climate with snowy winters and warm, humid summers. Southerners, on the other hand, experience milder winters and the warm, humid summers of a humid subtropical climate. Most of Florida is warm all year.
>
> *From Section 1, Physical Geography*

Understanding Lists

FOCUS ON READING

A to-do list can keep you focused on what you need to get done. Keeping lists while you read can keep you focused on understanding the main points of a text. In the example below, a list helps the reader identify and focus on the types of cold climates found in central and northern Canada.

The farther north you go in Canada, the colder it gets. The coldest areas of Canada are located close to the Arctic Circle. Much of central and northern Canada has a sub-arctic climate. The far north has tundra and ice cap climates. About half of Canada lies in these extremely cold climates.

From Section 1, Physical Geography

List of cold climates
1. subarctic
2. tundra
3. ice cap

YOU TRY IT!

Read the sentences and then list the territories that make up the Canadian North region.

Northern Canada is extremely cold due to its location close to the Arctic Circle. The region called the Canadian North includes the Yukon Territory, the Northwest Territories, and Nunavut. These three territories cover more than a third of Canada but are home to only about 100,000 people.

From Section 3, Canada Today

ATLAS

Strait of Juan de Fuca

Puget Sound

Mount Rainier
14,410 ft
(4,392 m)

Franklin D. Roosevelt Lake

COAST RANGES

CASCADE RANGE

Columbia River

Columbia Plateau

Bitterroot Range

Salmon River Mts.

Sawtooth Mts.

Snake River

Pend Oreille River

Clearwater River

Flathead Lake

Milk River

Missouri River

Lake Sakakawea

ROCKY

CONTINENTAL

Grand Tetons

Gannett Peak
13,804 ft
(4,207 m)

Wind River Range

Yellowstone River

Bighorn Mts.

Bighorn River

Powder River

Fort Peck Lake

Lake Oahe

Black Hills

Cheyenne River

White River

James River

G R E A T

Cape Mendocino

Klamath River

Goose Lake

Shasta Lake

Pyramid Lake

GREAT

BASIN

Great Salt Lake

Utah Lake

Uinta Mts.

Wasatch Range

MOUNTAINS

Green River

DIVIDE

Front Range

South Platte River

North Platte River

Platte River

Niobrara River

Republican River

Smoky Hill River

I N T E R

P L A I N S

Sacramento River

Central Valley

SIERRA NEVADA

Lake Tahoe

San Joaquin River

Coast Ranges

San Francisco Bay

Monterey Bay

Mount Whitney
14,494 ft
(4,419 m)

Death Valley

Mojave Desert

COLORADO

PLATEAU

Colorado River

Lake Powell

San Juan River

Mount Elbert
14,433 ft
(4,400 m)

Pikes Peak
14,110 ft
(4,301 m)

San Luis Valley

Sangre De Cristo Mts.

DIVIDE

Painted Desert

Rio Grande

Canadian River

PACIFIC

OCEAN

Channel Islands

Salton Sea

Imperial Valley

Lake Mead

Grand Canyon

Colorado River

Gila River

Sonoran Desert

CONTINENTAL

Gulf of California

Pecos River

Colorado River

Amistad Reservoir

Rio Grande

Nueces River

MEXICO

Padre Island

To understand the relative locations of Alaska and Hawaii, as well as the vast distances separating them from the rest of the United States, see the world map.

HAWAII

Kauai

Niihau

Oahu

PACIFIC OCEAN

Molokai

Lanai

Maui

Kahoolawe

Mauna Kea
13,796 ft
(4,206 m)

Hawaii

0   75   150 Miles
0   75   150 Kilometers
Projection: Mercator

RUSSIA

ARCTIC OCEAN

Arctic Circle

BROOKS RANGE

Bering Strait

St. Lawrence Island

St. Matthew Island

Nunivak Island

Yukon River

Kuskokwim River

Tanana River

ALASKA RANGE

Mount McKinley
20,320 ft
(6,194 m)

CANADA

Bering Sea

Gulf of Alaska

Kodiak Island

Alexander Archipelago

PACIFIC OCEAN

ALEUTIAN ISLANDS

Attu Island

0   250   500 Miles
0   250   500 Kilometers
Projection: Albers Equal Area

CANADA

Red River

Mesabi Range

Isle Royale

Lake Superior

Minnesota River

Mississippi River

Wisconsin River

Lake Michigan

Lake Huron

Lake Ontario

Lake Erie

St. Lawrence River

St. Lawrence Seaway

Lake Champlain

Adirondack Mts.

Catskill Mts.

Green Mts.

White Mts.

Hudson River

Connecticut River

Longfellow Mts.

Penobscot River

St. John River

Cape Cod

Long Island Sound

Long Island

40°N

Des Moines River

Missouri River

Kansas R.

P L A I N S

Illinois River

Wabash River

Scioto River

Ohio River

Allegheny R.

PLATEAU

Susquehanna River

ALLEGHENY

APPALACHIAN MOUNTAINS

Monongahela R.

Potomac River

Kanawha River

James River

Delaware River

Delaware Bay

Chesapeake Bay

ATLANTIC OCEAN

70°W

Lake of the Ozarks

OZARK PLATEAU

Keystone Lake

White River

Arkansas River

Eufaula Lake

Lake Barkley

Cumberland River

Kentucky Lake

Lake Texoma

Ouachita Mts.

Tennessee River

Cumberland Plateau

Great Smoky Mts.

BLUE RIDGE MOUNTAINS

P I E D M O N T

Roanoke River

Pamlico Sound

Cape Hatteras

35°N

Trinity River

Brazos River

Saline River

Red River

Toledo Bend Reservoir

Mississippi River

Pearl River

Tombigbee River

Alabama R.

Coosa River

Chattahoochee River

Oconee River

Savannah River

Altamaha River

Sea Islands

COASTAL PLAIN

GULF

Chandeleur Islands

Mississippi Delta

Okefenokee Swamp

FLORIDA PENINSULA

Cape Canaveral

80°W

N
W   E
S

Gulf of Mexico

Lake Okeechobee

The Everglades

Cape Sable

Florida Keys

Straits of Florida

BAHAMAS

25°N

75°W

85°W

90°W

95°W

ELEVATION

Feet		Meters
13,120		4,000
6,560		2,000
1,640		500
656		200
(Sea level) 0		0 (Sea level)
Below sea level		Below sea level

0   100   200 Miles

0   100   200 Kilometers

Projection: Albers Equal Area

United States: Political

WASHINGTON
Strait of Juan de Fuca
Puget Sound
Seattle
Tacoma
Olympia
Spokane
Portland
Columbia River
★ Salem
Eugene
OREGON
Cape Mendocino
Goose Lake
Shasta Lake
Sacramento River
Pyramid Lake
Berkeley
Oakland
San Francisco
San Francisco Bay
San Jose
San Joaquin River
Monterey Bay
Sacramento ★
Reno
★ Carson City
Lake Tahoe
NEVADA
Fresno
CALIFORNIA
Santa Barbara
Ventura
Los Angeles
Long Beach
Anaheim
Santa Ana
Channel Islands
San Diego
Riverside
Palm Springs
Salton Sea
Las Vegas
Lake Mead
Colorado River
PACIFIC OCEAN

IDAHO
★ Boise
Sun Valley
Snake River
Pocatello
Great Salt Lake
Ogden
★ Salt Lake City
Provo
Utah Lake
UTAH
Green River
Lake Powell

MONTANA
Great Falls
Helena
Fort Peck Lake
Missouri River
Yellowstone River
Billings

Yellowstone Lake
WYOMING
Cheyenne ★

NORTH DAKOTA
Lake Sakakawea
Bismarck ★

SOUTH DAKOTA
Lake Oahe
Pierre ★
Rapid City

NEBRASKA
Platte River

COLORADO
Aspen
Vail
Boulder
★ Denver
Colorado Springs
Pueblo
Arkansas River

KANSAS

ARIZONA
Flagstaff
Phoenix ★
Casa Grande
Tucson
Gila River

NEW MEXICO
Taos
Santa Fe ★
Albuquerque
Las Cruces
El Paso

Gulf of California

OKLAHOMA
Canadian River
Oklahoma City
Amarillo
Lawton
Lubbock
Brazos River
Abilene
Fort Worth
Midland
Odessa
TEXAS
Colorado River
Pecos River
Austin ★
Amistad Reservoir
Rio Grande
San Antonio
Corpus Christi
Laredo
Padre Island

MEXICO

To understand the relative locations of Alaska and Hawaii, as well as the vast distances separating them from the rest of the United States, see the world map.

Kauai
Niihau
Oahu
Honolulu ★
Molokai
Lanai
Maui
Kahoolawe
HAWAII
PACIFIC OCEAN
Hilo
Hawaii
22°N
19°N
0   75   150 Miles
0   75   150 Kilometers
Projection: Mercator

ARCTIC OCEAN
Arctic Circle
RUSSIA
Bering Strait
Nome
Yukon River
St. Lawrence Island
St. Matthew Island
Nunivak Island
Fairbanks
ALASKA
CANADA
Anchorage
Valdez
Skagway
Gulf of Alaska
Juneau ★
Kodiak Island
Alexander Archipelago
Bering Sea
Attu Island
ALEUTIAN ISLANDS
PACIFIC OCEAN
0   250   500 Miles
0   250   500 Kilometers
Projection: Albers Equal Area
55°N
55°N
50°N

45°N
40°N
35°N
30°N
125°W
120°W
160°W
155°W
170°E
180°
170°W
160°W
150°W
140°W

CANADA

Grand Forks

MINNESOTA

Fargo

Duluth

Superior

Marquette

Sault Ste. Marie

Lake Superior

MICHIGAN

WISCONSIN

Minneapolis

St. Paul

Green Bay

Lake Huron

Lake Michigan

MAINE

Augusta

Burlington

Montpelier

Portland

VT

NH

Concord

Manchester

Lake Champlain

Rochester

Syracuse

MA

Boston

Worcester

Providence

Cape Cod

Albany

Springfield

Hartford

CT

RI

Buffalo

NEW YORK

Bridgeport

New Haven

Long Island Sound

Yonkers

Long Island

Jersey City

Newark

New York City

Sioux Falls

Madison

Milwaukee

Grand Rapids

Saginaw

Lansing

Detroit

Ann Arbor

Toledo

Cleveland

Youngstown

Akron

Erie

PENNSYLVANIA

Allentown

Trenton

Sioux City

IOWA

Cedar Rapids

Rockford

Chicago

South Bend

Gary

Fort Wayne

OHIO

Harrisburg

Pittsburgh

Philadelphia

Camden

NJ

Atlantic City

Omaha

Lincoln

Davenport

Des Moines

Peoria

INDIANA

Columbus

Dayton

Cincinnati

Baltimore

DE

Dover

MISSOURI

Springfield

Indianapolis

WEST VIRGINIA

Charleston

Washington, D.C.

Annapolis

MD

Delaware Bay

Kansas City

Kansas City

St. Louis

East St. Louis

Louisville

Evansville

Frankfort

Lexington

VIRGINIA

Richmond

Newport News

Norfolk

Virginia Beach

Chesapeake Bay

ATLANTIC OCEAN

Topeka

Jefferson City

ILLINOIS

Wichita

Lake of the Ozarks

Ohio River

KENTUCKY

Lake Barkley

Cape Hatteras

Keystone Lake

Tulsa

Springfield

Fayetteville

Nashville

TENNESSEE

Knoxville

Asheville

Greensboro

Winston-Salem

Durham

Raleigh

Charlotte

NORTH CAROLINA

Eufaula Lake

ARKANSAS

Little Rock

Pine Bluff

Memphis

Chattanooga

Huntsville

Greenville

SOUTH CAROLINA

Columbia

Lake Texoma

Dallas

Shreveport

MISSISSIPPI

Vicksburg

Jackson

Meridian

ALABAMA

Birmingham

Montgomery

GEORGIA

Atlanta

Macon

Columbus

Savannah River

Charleston

Savannah

Sea Islands

Waco

Toledo Bend Reservoir

Red River

LOUISIANA

Beaumont

Houston

Baton Rouge

New Orleans

Biloxi

Chandeleur Islands

Mobile

Pensacola

Tallahassee

Jacksonville

Chattahoochee River

Gulf of Mexico

Gainesville

FLORIDA

Cape Canaveral

Orlando

Tampa

St. Petersburg

Lake Okeechobee

Fort Myers

Fort Lauderdale

Miami

BAHAMAS

Cape Sable

Florida Keys

Straits of Florida

National capital

State capitals

Other cities

100   200 Miles

100   200 Kilometers

Projection: Albers Equal Area

Galveston

N S E W

St. Lawrence River

Hudson R.

Connecticut R.

Lake Ontario

Lake Erie

Susquehanna River

Mississippi River

Minnesota River

Red River

Missouri River

Illinois River

Kentucky Lake

40°N

35°N

30°N

25°N

70°W

75°W

80°W

85°W

90°W

95°W

ATLAS

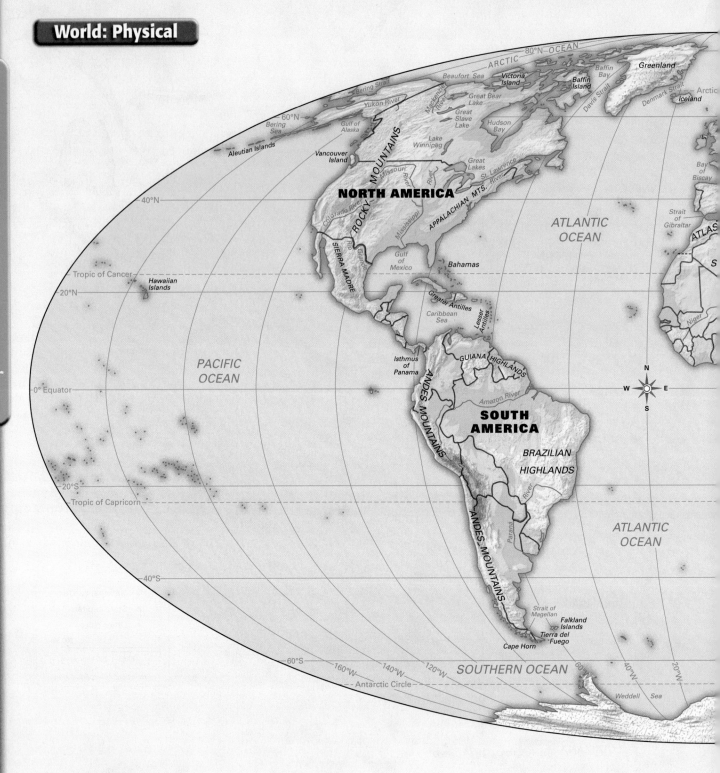

ATLAS

ARCTIC 80°N **OCEAN**

Greenland

Beaufort Sea
Victoria Island
Baffin Bay
Baffin Island
Davis Strait
Denmark Strait
Arctic
Iceland

Bering Strait
Yukon River
Gulf of Alaska
Great Bear Lake
Great Slave Lake
Hudson Bay

60°N

Bering Sea

Aleutian Islands

Vancouver Island

ROCKY MOUNTAINS
Missouri River
Lake Winnipeg
Great Lakes
St. Lawrence River

APPALACHIAN MTS.

Bay of Biscay

NORTH AMERICA

40°N

Colorado River

Mississippi

ATLANTIC OCEAN

Strait of Gibraltar
ATLAS
S

SIERRA MADRE
Rio Grande

Gulf of Mexico

Bahamas

Tropic of Cancer

Hawaiian Islands

20°N

Greater Antilles
Caribbean Sea
Lesser Antilles

Niger

PACIFIC OCEAN

Isthmus of Panama

GUIANA HIGHLANDS

ANDES MOUNTAINS
Amazon River

N
W E
S

0° Equator

SOUTH AMERICA

BRAZILIAN HIGHLANDS

20°S

Tropic of Capricorn

ANDES MOUNTAINS
Paraná
River

ATLANTIC OCEAN

40°S

Strait of Magellan
Falkland Islands
Tierra del Fuego
Cape Horn

60°S
160°W 140°W 120°W

SOUTHERN OCEAN

60°

40°W 20°W

Antarctic Circle

Weddell Sea

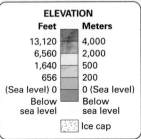

ELEVATION

Feet		Meters
13,120		4,000
6,560		2,000
1,640		500
656		200
(Sea level) 0		0 (Sea level)
Below sea level		Below sea level

Ice cap

0 500 1,000 1,500 2,000 Miles
0 1,000 2,000 Kilometers

Projection: Mollweide

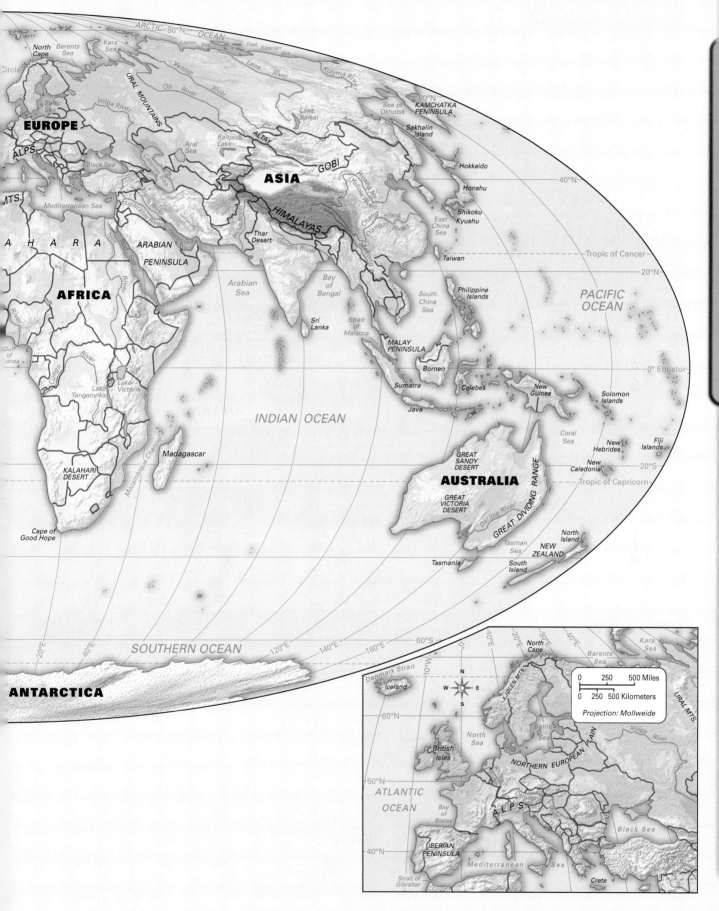

ARCTIC—80°N OCEAN

North Cape
Barents Sea
Kara Sea
Laptev Sea
East Siberian Sea
Circle
Baltic Sea
URAL MOUNTAINS
Ob River
Yenisei River
Lena River
Kolyma River
Volga River
60°N
Sea of Okhotsk
KAMCHATKA PENINSULA
EUROPE
ALPS
Black Sea
Aral Sea
Balqash Lake
Caspian Sea
Lake Baikal
ALTAY
Amur River
Sakhalin Island
MTS.
Mediterranean Sea
ASIA
GOBI
Huang He/Yellow River
Hokkaido
40°N
Honshu
SAHARA
Tigris River
Euphrates River
ARABIAN PENINSULA
Nile River
HIMALAYAS
Indus River
Thar Desert
Ganges River
Chang Jiang (Yangzi) River
Mekong River
Shikoku
Kyushu
East China Sea
AFRICA
Gulf of Guinea
Congo River
River
Arabian Sea
Bay of Bengal
Sri Lanka
Strait of Malacca
MALAY PENINSULA
South China Sea
Taiwan
Philippine Islands
Tropic of Cancer
20°N
PACIFIC OCEAN
Lake Tanganyika
Lake Victoria
Borneo
Celebes
New Guinea
Solomon Islands
0° Equator
Sumatra
Java
INDIAN OCEAN
Madagascar
Mozambique Channel
Coral Sea
New Hebrides
New Caledonia
Fiji Islands
KALAHARI DESERT
GREAT SANDY DESERT
AUSTRALIA
GREAT VICTORIA DESERT
Darling River
GREAT DIVIDING RANGE
20°S
Tropic of Capricorn
Cape of Good Hope
North Island
Tasman Sea
NEW ZEALAND
South Island
Tasmania
20°E
40°E
SOUTHERN OCEAN
120°E
140°E
160°E
60°S

ANTARCTICA

Denmark Strait
Iceland
North Cape
Barents Sea
Kara Sea
KJØLEN MTS.
10°E
20°E
30°E
40°E
URAL MTS.
Volga River
0   250   500 Miles
0   250   500 Kilometers
Projection: Mollweide
60°N
British Isles
North Sea
Baltic Sea
NORTHERN EUROPEAN PLAIN
ATLANTIC OCEAN
50°N
Bay of Biscay
Rhine
Danube
A L P S
Black Sea
40°N
IBERIAN PENINSULA
Mediterranean   Sea
Strait of Gibraltar
Crete

ATLAS

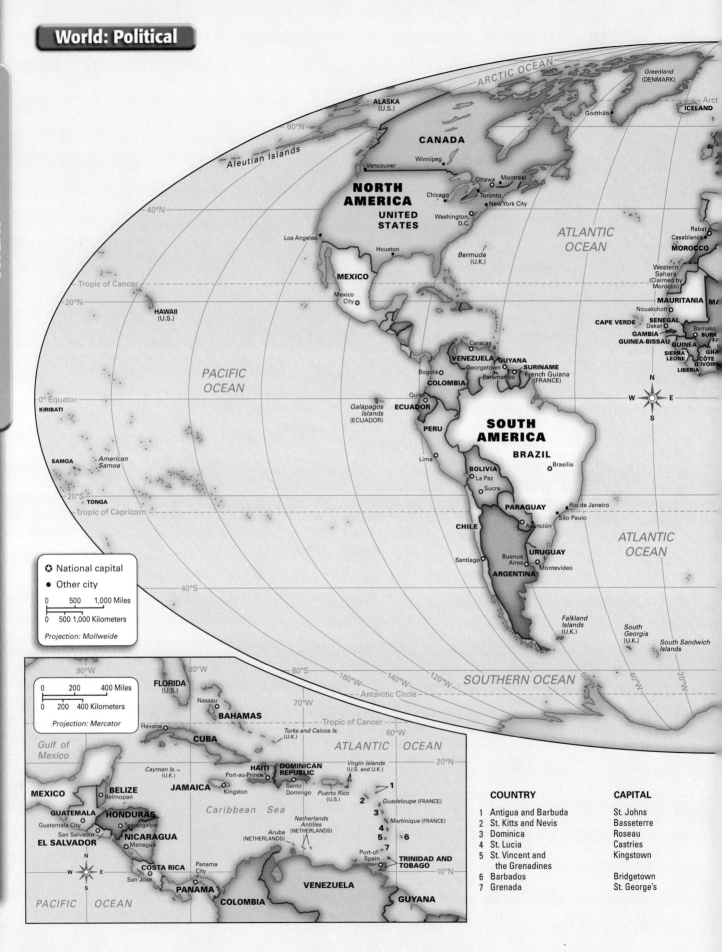

ARCTIC OCEAN

Greenland
(DENMARK)

ALASKA
(U.S.)

60°N

Godthåb

Arct

ICELAND

CANADA

Aleutian Islands

Winnipeg

Vancouver

40°N

Ottawa Montreal

NORTH
AMERICA

Chicago

Toronto

ATLANTIC
OCEAN

UNITED
STATES

New York City

Washington,
D.C.

Rabat
Casablanca
MOROCCO

Los Angeles

Houston

Bermuda
(U.K.)

Western
Sahara
(Claimed by
Morocco)

Tropic of Cancer

MEXICO

20°N

MAURITANIA   MA

HAWAII
(U.S.)

Mexico
City

Nouakchott

CAPE VERDE   SENEGAL
Dakar

GAMBIA   Bamako   BURK
GUINEA-BISSAU   GUINEA   FA

Caracas

VENEZUELA   GUYANA   SURINAME

SIERRA   GHA
LEONE   CÔTE
D'IVOIR
LIBERIA

PACIFIC
OCEAN

0° Equator

Bogotá

Georgetown   French Guiana
Paramaribo   (FRANCE)

COLOMBIA

N

Quito

W   E

KIRIBATI

ECUADOR

Galápagos
Islands
(ECUADOR)

S

SOUTH
AMERICA

SAMOA

American
Samoa

PERU

BRAZIL

Lima

Brasília

BOLIVIA
La Paz

20°S

TONGA

Sucre

Tropic of Capricorn

PARAGUAY

Rio de Janeiro
São Paulo

CHILE

Asunción

ATLANTIC
OCEAN

URUGUAY

40°S

Buenos
Aires

Santiago

Montevideo

ARGENTINA

Falkland
Islands
(U.K.)

South
Georgia
(U.K.)

South Sandwich
Islands

60°S   160°W   140°W   120°W   SOUTHERN OCEAN   60°   40°   20°

Antarctic Circle

⊗ National capital

● Other city

0   500   1,000 Miles

0   500 1,000 Kilometers

Projection: Mollweide

90°W   80°W

0   200   400 Miles

0   200   400 Kilometers

Projection: Mercator

FLORIDA
(U.S.)

70°W

Tropic of Cancer

Nassau

Havana

BAHAMAS

60°W

Turks and Caicos Is.
(U.K.)

ATLANTIC   OCEAN

CUBA

Virgin Islands
(U.S. and U.K.)

20°N

Gulf of
Mexico

Cayman Is.
(U.K.)

HAITI   DOMINICAN
REPUBLIC

Port-au-Prince

1

MEXICO

BELIZE
Belmopan

JAMAICA

Caribbean Sea

Kingston

Santo
Domingo

Puerto Rico
(U.S.)

2

Guadeloupe (FRANCE)

3

Martinique (FRANCE)

GUATEMALA   HONDURAS
Guatemala City   Tegucigalpa

Netherlands
Antilles
(NETHERLANDS)

4

6

San Salvador

NICARAGUA

Aruba
(NETHERLANDS)

7

EL SALVADOR   Managua

Port-of-
Spain

COSTA RICA

TRINIDAD AND
TOBAGO

N

Panama
City

10°N

W   E

San Jose

S

PANAMA

PACIFIC   OCEAN

VENEZUELA

GUYANA

COLOMBIA

	COUNTRY	CAPITAL
1	Antigua and Barbuda	St. Johns
2	St. Kitts and Nevis	Basseterre
3	Dominica	Roseau
4	St. Lucia	Castries
5	St. Vincent and the Grenadines	Kingstown
6	Barbados	Bridgetown
7	Grenada	St. George's

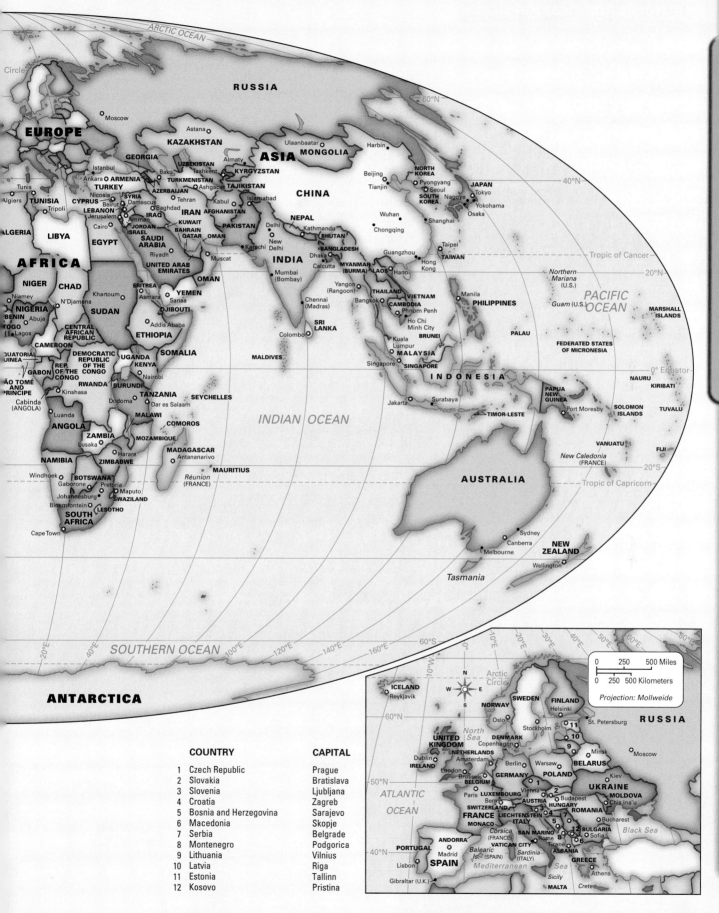

ARCTIC OCEAN

RUSSIA

EUROPE

Moscow

KAZAKHSTAN

Astana

Ulaanbaatar

ASIA

MONGOLIA

Harbin

GEORGIA

Istanbul

ARMENIA

Ankara

Almaty

Baku

UZBEKISTAN

Tashkent

KYRGYZSTAN

Beijing

NORTH KOREA

Pyongyang

JAPAN

Tokyo

TURKEY

Nicosia

CYPRUS

AZERBAIJAN

Ashgabat

TURKMENISTAN

TAJIKISTAN

CHINA

Tianjin

SOUTH KOREA

Seoul

Nagoya

Yokohama

TUNISIA

Algiers

Tunis

Tripoli

LEBANON

Beirut

SYRIA

Damascus

IRAN

Tehran

Kabul

Islamabad

Wuhan

Shanghai

Osaka

Jerusalem

ISRAEL

Amman

IRAQ

Baghdad

JORDAN

KUWAIT

AFGHANISTAN

Delhi

Kathmandu

NEPAL

Chongqing

LIBYA

ALGERIA

Cairo

SAUDI ARABIA

BAHRAIN

QATAR

OMAN

PAKISTAN

New Delhi

Karachi

BHUTAN

BANGLADESH

Dhaka

Taipei

Guangzhou

Hong Kong

TAIWAN

Tropic of Cancer

EGYPT

Riyadh

UNITED ARAB EMIRATES

Muscat

INDIA

Calcutta

MYANMAR (BURMA)

LAOS

Hanoi

Northern Mariana (U.S.)

20°N

AFRICA

NIGER

CHAD

Khartoum

ERITREA

Asmara

YEMEN

Sanaa

OMAN

Mumbai (Bombay)

Chennai (Madras)

Yangon (Rangoon)

THAILAND

Bangkok

VIETNAM

Manila

Guam (U.S.)

PACIFIC OCEAN

MARSHALL ISLANDS

Niamey

NIGERIA

Abuja

N'Djamena

DJIBOUTI

SUDAN

Addis Ababa

ETHIOPIA

SRI LANKA

Colombo

CAMBODIA

Phnom Penh

Ho Chi Minh City

PHILIPPINES

PALAU

FEDERATED STATES OF MICRONESIA

BENIN

TOGO

Lagos

CAMEROON

CENTRAL AFRICAN REPUBLIC

EQUATORIAL GUINEA

GABON

ÃO TOMÉ AND PRINCIPE

DEMOCRATIC REPUBLIC OF THE CONGO

REP. OF THE CONGO

Kinshasa

UGANDA

KENYA

RWANDA

BURUNDI

SOMALIA

MALDIVES

Kuala Lumpur

BRUNEI

MALAYSIA

Singapore

SINGAPORE

INDONESIA

NAURU

KIRIBATI

0° Equator

Cabinda (ANGOLA)

Luanda

TANZANIA

Dodoma

Dar es Salaam

SEYCHELLES

Jakarta

Surabaya

PAPUA NEW GUINEA

Port Moresby

SOLOMON ISLANDS

TUVALU

ANGOLA

ZAMBIA

Lusaka

MALAWI

COMOROS

MOZAMBIQUE

MADAGASCAR

Antananarivo

INDIAN OCEAN

TIMOR-LESTE

VANUATU

New Caledonia (FRANCE)

FIJI

NAMIBIA

Windhoek

ZIMBABWE

Harare

BOTSWANA

Gaborone

Pretoria

Johannesburg

SWAZILAND

Maputo

Réunion (FRANCE)

MAURITIUS

AUSTRALIA

20°S

Tropic of Capricorn

SOUTH AFRICA

Bloemfontein

LESOTHO

Cape Town

Sydney

Canberra

Melbourne

NEW ZEALAND

Wellington

SOUTHERN OCEAN

20°E

40°E

100°E

120°E

140°E

160°E

60°S

Tasmania

ANTARCTICA

	COUNTRY	CAPITAL
1	Czech Republic	Prague
2	Slovakia	Bratislava
3	Slovenia	Ljubljana
4	Croatia	Zagreb
5	Bosnia and Herzegovina	Sarajevo
6	Macedonia	Skopje
7	Serbia	Belgrade
8	Montenegro	Podgorica
9	Lithuania	Vilnius
10	Latvia	Riga
11	Estonia	Tallinn
12	Kosovo	Pristina

0 250 500 Miles
0 250 500 Kilometers

Projection: Mollweide

ICELAND

Reykjavik

Arctic Circle

SWEDEN

FINLAND

Helsinki

St. Petersburg

RUSSIA

NORWAY

Oslo

Stockholm

11

10

60°N

North Sea

DENMARK

Copenhagen

9

Minsk

Moscow

UNITED KINGDOM

Dublin

IRELAND

London

NETHERLANDS

Amsterdam

Berlin

Warsaw

BELARUS

Kiev

Brussels

BELGIUM

GERMANY

POLAND

UKRAINE

50°N

ATLANTIC OCEAN

Paris

LUXEMBOURG

Bern

Vienna

1

2

Budapest

MOLDOVA

Chisinau

SWITZERLAND

AUSTRIA

HUNGARY

ROMANIA

FRANCE

LIECHTENSTEIN

3

4

5

7

Bucharest

MONACO

SAN MARINO

ITALY

Rome

12

BULGARIA

Sofia

Black Sea

Corsica (FRANCE)

VATICAN CITY

8

6

ANDORRA

Balearic Is. (SPAIN)

Sardinia (ITALY)

Tirane

ALBANIA

PORTUGAL

Madrid

SPAIN

Lisbon

Mediterranean Sea

GREECE

Athens

40°N

Gibraltar (U.K.)

Sicily

MALTA

Crete

10°W

10°E

20°E

30°E

40°E

50°E

60°E

ATLAS

ATLAS 209

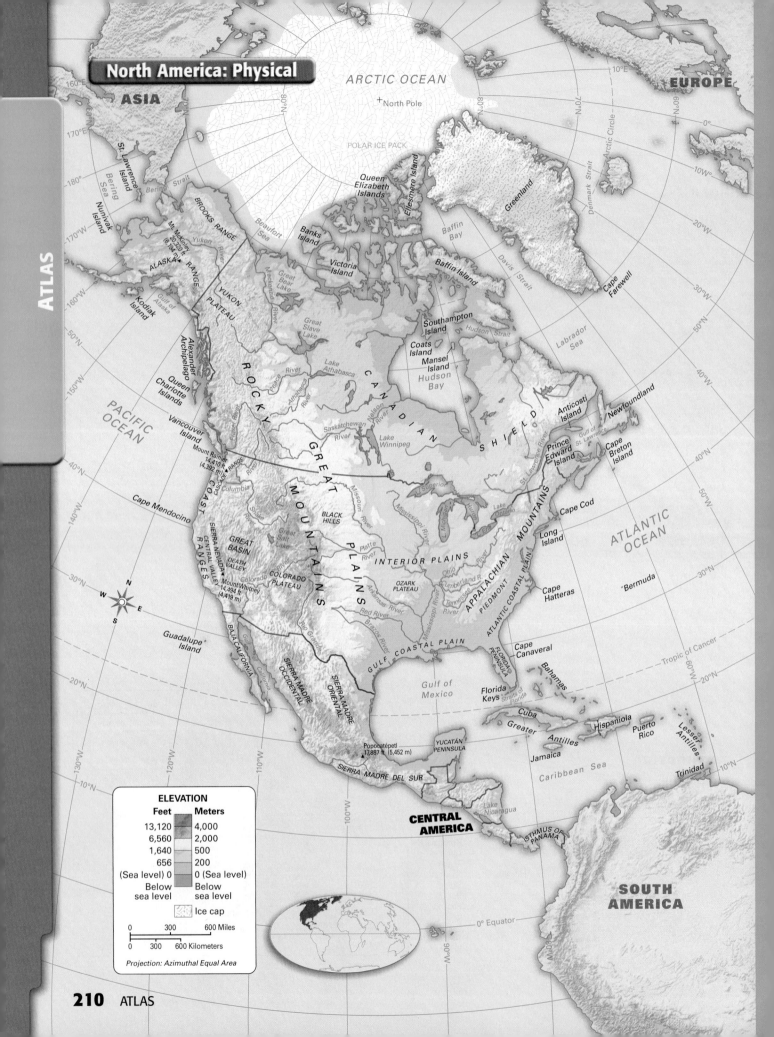

North America: Physical

ARCTIC OCEAN

ASIA

EUROPE

North Pole

POLAR ICE PACK

Queen Elizabeth Islands

Ellesmere Island

Greenland

Beaufort Sea

Banks Island

Baffin Bay

Cape Farewell

BROOKS RANGE

St. Lawrence Island

Bering Sea

Nunivak Island

Mt. McKinley 20,320 ft (6,194 m)▲

ALASKA RANGE

Yukon River

Victoria Island

Great Bear Lake

Mackenzie River

Baffin Island

Davis Strait

Denmark Strait

Kodiak Island

Gulf of Alaska

YUKON PLATEAU

Southampton Island

Hudson Strait

Labrador Sea

Alexander Archipelago

Great Slave Lake

Coats Island

Queen Charlotte Islands

Peace River

Lake Athabasca

Mansel Island

Hudson Bay

Anticosti Island

Newfoundland

Vancouver Island

Athabasca River

C A N A D I A N   S H I E L D

Fraser River

Nelson River

Mount Rainier 14,410 ft (4,392 m)▲

CASCADE RANGE

Saskatchewan River

Lake Winnipeg

Prince Edward Island

Gulf of St. Lawrence

Cape Breton Island

Columbia River

L. Superior

St. Lawrence River

PACIFIC OCEAN

Cape Mendocino

Snake River

BLACK HILLS

Missouri River

Lake Michigan

Lake Huron

Lake Ontario

Lake Erie

Cape Cod

Long Island

ATLANTIC OCEAN

SIERRA NEVADA

GREAT BASIN

Great Salt Lake

Platte River

Mississippi River

APPALACHIAN MOUNTAINS

Bermuda

COAST RANGES

CENTRAL VALLEY

DEATH VALLEY

COLORADO PLATEAU

INTERIOR PLAINS

Ohio River

Cumberland R.

PIEDMONT

ATLANTIC COASTAL PLAIN

Cape Hatteras

Mount Whitney 14,494 ft (4,419 m)▲

Colorado River

OZARK PLATEAU

Arkansas River

Tennessee River

Guadalupe Island

Gulf of California

Rio Grande

Red River

Brazos River

GULF COASTAL PLAIN

FLORIDA PENINSULA

Cape Canaveral

Tropic of Cancer

BAJA CALIFORNIA

SIERRA MADRE OCCIDENTAL

Gulf of Mexico

Florida Keys

Bahamas

SIERRA MADRE ORIENTAL

Straits of Florida

Cuba

Greater Antilles

Hispaniola

Puerto Rico

Lesser Antilles

Popocatépetl 17,887 ft (5,452 m)▲

YUCATÁN PENINSULA

Jamaica

Caribbean Sea

Trinidad

SIERRA MADRE DEL SUR

CENTRAL AMERICA

Lake Nicaragua

ISTHMUS OF PANAMA

SOUTH AMERICA

Equator

ELEVATION

Feet	Meters
13,120	4,000
6,560	2,000
1,640	500
656	200
(Sea level) 0	0 (Sea level)
Below sea level	Below sea level

Ice cap

0   300   600 Miles

0   300   600 Kilometers

Projection: Azimuthal Equal Area

ASIA

ARCTIC OCEAN

+ North Pole

EUROPE

160°E
170°E
180°
170°W
160°W
150°W
140°W
130°W
120°W
110°W
100°W
90°W
80°N
70°N
60°N
50°N
40°N
30°N
20°N
10°N

0°E
10°E
10°W
20°W
30°W
40°W
50°W
60°W

Arctic Circle

ICELAND

St. Lawrence Island

Bering Sea

Nunivak Island

Bering Strait

Point Barrow

Beaufort Sea

Banks Island

Queen Elizabeth Islands

Ellesmere Island

Greenland (DENMARK)

Denmark Strait

ALASKA (U.S.)

Victoria Island

Baffin Bay

Anchorage

Great Bear Lake

Baffin Island

Davis Strait

Cape Farewell

Kodiak Island

Gulf of Alaska

Alexander Archipelago

Juneau

Great Slave Lake

Southampton Island

Hudson Strait

Labrador Sea

Queen Charlotte Islands

Coats Island

Mansel Island

Hudson Bay

PACIFIC OCEAN

Vancouver Island

Edmonton

CANADA

Anticosti Island

Newfoundland

Lake Winnipeg

Calgary

Prince Edward Island

Cape Breton Island

St. Pierre and Miquelon (FRANCE)

Vancouver

Gulf of St. Lawrence

Seattle

Winnipeg

Portland

Quebec

Lake Superior

Montreal

Lake Huron

Ottawa

Minneapolis

Lake Michigan

Toronto

Lake Ontario

Boston

Cape Cod

Lake Erie

Milwaukee

Detroit

Cleveland

New York City

San Francisco

Chicago

Columbus

Philadelphia

San Jose

Salt Lake City

Baltimore

ATLANTIC OCEAN

Great Salt Lake

Denver

Indianapolis

Washington, D.C.

Kansas City

St. Louis

Norfolk

UNITED STATES

Bermuda (U.K.)

Los Angeles

Memphis

Atlanta

San Diego

Tijuana

Phoenix

Birmingham

Dallas

Jacksonville

Austin

San Antonio

Houston

New Orleans

Tropic of Cancer

Monterrey

Gulf of Mexico

Florida Keys

Miami

BAHAMAS

Nassau

Turks and Caicos Islands (U.K.)

DOMINICAN REPUBLIC

Puerto Rico (U.S.)

ST. KITTS & NEVIS

MEXICO

Havana

CUBA

San Juan

ANTIGUA & BARBUDA

Guadeloupe (FRANCE)

Guadalajara

Mexico City

Mérida

HAITI

Santo Domingo

Virgin Is. (U.S., U.K.)

DOMINICA

Puebla

Cayman Is. (U.K.)

Kingston

Port-au-Prince

Martinique (FRANCE)

BARBADOS

ST. LUCIA

Belmopan

JAMAICA

ST. VINCENT AND THE GRENADINES

BELIZE

Caribbean Sea

Netherlands Antilles (NETHERLANDS)

GRENADA

GUATEMALA

HONDURAS

Guatemala City

Tegucigalpa

Aruba (NETHERLANDS)

TRINIDAD AND TOBAGO

San Salvador

NICARAGUA

Managua

Panama Canal

EL SALVADOR

San José

Panama City

COSTA RICA

PANAMA

SOUTH AMERICA

Gulf of California

Straits of Florida

Equator

CENTRAL AMERICA

Caribbean Sea

Panama Canal

Gulf of Panama

Malpelo Island

Lake Maracaibo

LLANOS

Margarita Island

Tobago

Trinidad

Orinoco River Delta

Orinoco River

Meta River

Angel Falls

GUIANA HIGHLANDS

Devil's Island
Cape Orange

ATLANTIC OCEAN

Cauca River

Magdalena

Mount Tolima
18,425 ft
(5,616 m)

Orinoco River

Rio Negro

Amazon River Delta

Caqueta River

Japurá River

AMAZON BASIN

Amazon River

Mount Chimborazo
20,561 ft
(6,267 m)

Galápagos Islands

Gulf of Guayaquil

ANDES

Marañón River

Amazon River

River

Tapajós River

River

Tocantins River

River

0° Equator

Juruá River

Ucayali River

Madeira

Xingu River

Araguaia

Parnaíba

Juruá River

Purus

BRAZILIAN HIGHLANDS

Mount Huascarán
22,205 ft
(6,768 m)

Beni River

Mamoré

MATO GROSSO PLATEAU

São Francisco

PACIFIC OCEAN

Ancohuma Peak
20,958 ft
(6,388 m)

Titicaca

Lake Poopó

Pilcomayo River

ATACAMA DESERT

ANDES

CHACO

Paraguay River

BRAZILIAN PLATEAU

San Ambrosio Island

San Félix Island

Tropic of Capricorn

Salado River

Paraná River

Uruguay River

Tropic of Capricorn

Juan Fernández Islands

Mount Aconcagua
22,834 ft
(6,960 m)

Salado River

Río de la Plata

ATLANTIC OCEAN

PAMPAS

Colorado River

ELEVATION

Feet	Meters
13,120	4,000
6,560	2,000
1,640	500
656	200
(Sea level) 0	0 (Sea level)
Below sea level	Below sea level

0   250   500 Miles
0   250   500 Kilometers

Projection: Azimuthal Equal Area

Chiloé Island

Chonos Archipelago

Gulf of San Matías

Gulf of San Jorge

Cape Tres Puntas

PATAGONIA

Bahía Grande

Strait of Magellan

Tierra del Fuego

Falkland Islands

South Georgia Islands

Cape Horn

South America: Political

CENTRAL AMERICA

Caribbean Sea

Barranquilla
Cartagena
Caracas
Lake Maracaibo
VENEZUELA
Georgetown
Paramaribo
GUYANA
Cayenne
SURINAME
French Guiana (FRANCE)
Medellín
Bogotá
COLOMBIA
Cali
Malpelo Island (COLOMBIA)
Quito
ECUADOR
Guayaquil
Galápagos Islands (ECUADOR)
0° Equator
Belém
PERU
BRAZIL
Recife
Trujillo
10°S
Callao Lima
Arequipa
Lake Titicaca
La Paz
Lake Poopó
BOLIVIA
Sucre
Brasília
Salvador
Belo Horizonte
PACIFIC OCEAN
20°S
Tropic of Capricorn
San Ambrosio Island (CHILE)
San Félix Island (CHILE)
PARAGUAY
Asunción
Campinas
São Paulo
Curitiba
Río de Janeiro
Tropic of Capricorn
CHILE
Pôrto Alegre
Córdoba
Rosario
URUGUAY
ATLANTIC OCEAN
Juan Fernández Islands (CHILE)
Valparaíso
Santiago
Buenos Aires
Montevideo
30°S
ARGENTINA

ATLANTIC OCEAN

⊕ National capital
● Other city

0   250   500 Miles
0   250   500 Kilometers

Projection: Azimuthal Equal-Area

Strait of Magellan
Falkland Islands (U.K.)
Tierra del Fuego
South Georgia Island (U.K.)

20°N
10°N
0° Equator
10°S
20°S
30°S
40°S
50°S

ASIA

SOUTHWEST
ASIA

AFRICA

Europe: Physical

ELEVATION

Feet	Meters
13,120	4,000
6,560	2,000
1,640	500
656	200
(Sea level) 0	0 (Sea level)
Below sea level	Below sea level

Ice cap

300 Miles
300 Kilometers
0 150
0 150

Projection: Azimuthal Equal Area

URAL MOUNTAINS

NORTHERN EUROPEAN PLAIN

ALPS

Caspian Sea

CAUCASUS MTS.
Mt. Elbrus 18,510 ft (5,642 m)

Black Sea

CRIMEAN PENINSULA

Sea of Azov

KOLA PENINSULA

Barents Sea

White Sea

Lake Onega
Lake Ladoga

Rybinsk Reservoir

BALTIC PLAINS

KJOLEN MOUNTAINS

ARCTIC OCEAN

North Cape

Gulf of Bothnia

Lake Vänern
Lake Vättern

Gulf of Finland

Baltic Sea

Kattegat
Skagerrak

Norwegian Sea

Faeroe Islands

Iceland

Shetland Islands
Orkney Islands
Hebrides
British Isles
Irish Sea

North Sea

PENNINES

English Channel

Thames River
Seine River
Loire River

Bay of Biscay

Cape Finisterre

IBERIAN PENINSULA

Douro River
Tagus River
Guadiana River
Guadalquivir River
Ebro River

Strait of Gibraltar

PYRENEES

Garonne River

Rhine River
Rhône River
Lake Geneva
Mont Blanc 15,781 ft (4,810 m)

Po River
APENNINES
Tiber River

Corsica
Sardinia
Balearic Islands

Mediterranean Sea

Tyrrhenian Sea
Sicily
Malta

ATLANTIC OCEAN

Danube River
CARPATHIAN
TRANSYLVANIAN ALPS
DINARIC ALPS
BALKAN PENINSULA
Adriatic Sea
Aegean Sea
Sea of Marmara
Crete
Rhodes

Dnipro River
Dniester River
Nistru River
Don River
Volga River
Kama River
Ural River
Pechora River
Northern Dvina River
Daugava R.
Dvina River
Oder River
Elbe River
Vistula River

Europe: Political

ASIA

URAL MOUNTAINS

RUSSIA

Nizhniy Novgorod

Moscow

Caspian Sea

SOUTHWEST ASIA

Barents Sea

North Cape

White Sea

St. Petersburg

ARCTIC OCEAN

FINLAND

Helsinki

Gulf of Bothnia

Gulf of Finland

Tallinn
ESTONIA

LATVIA
Riga

LITHUANIA
Vilnius

RUSSIA

Minsk

BELARUS

Kiev

UKRAINE

MOLDOVA
Chisinau

Black Sea

SWEDEN

Stockholm

Göteborg

Baltic Sea

POLAND
Warsaw

Krakow

ROMANIA
Bucharest

Sofia
BULGARIA

Aegean Sea

Rhodes

Crete

NORWAY

Oslo

Bergen

DENMARK
Copenhagen

Hamburg

Berlin

Dresden

GERMANY

Cologne
Bonn

CZECH REPUBLIC
Prague

SLOVAKIA
Bratislava

Vienna
AUSTRIA

Budapest
HUNGARY

Zagreb
CROATIA

SLOVENIA
Ljubljana

BOSNIA AND HERZEGOVINA
Sarajevo

Belgrade
SERBIA

MONTENEGRO
Podgorica

KOSOVO
Pristina

Skopje
MACEDONIA

Tirana
ALBANIA

GREECE
Athens

North Sea

THE NETHERLANDS
Amsterdam

Brussels
BELGIUM

LUXEMBOURG
Luxembourg

Paris

Munich

LIECHTENSTEIN
Vaduz

SWITZERLAND
Bern

Lake Geneva

Milan

Lyon

FRANCE

Marseille

A L P S

ITALY
Rome
VATICAN CITY

SAN MARINO
San Marino

MONACO
Monaco

Naples

Corsica
(FRANCE)

Sardinia
(ITALY)

Sicily

MALTA
Valletta

Adriatic Sea

Mediterranean Sea

SCOTLAND
Edinburgh

Liverpool

ENGLAND
London

WALES

UNITED KINGDOM

NORTHERN IRELAND
Belfast

IRELAND
Dublin

British Isles

Shetland Islands

Faeroe Islands
(DENMARK)

ICELAND
Reykjavik

Arctic Circle

Channel Islands
(U.K.)

English Channel

Bay of Biscay

PYRENEES

ANDORRA
Andorra la Vella

Barcelona

Balearic Islands
(SPAIN)

SPAIN
Madrid

Valencia

Seville

Gibraltar
(U.K.)

Strait of Gibraltar

PORTUGAL
Lisbon

ATLANTIC OCEAN

AFRICA

National capital
Other city

300 Miles
150
0
300 Kilometers
150
0

Projection: Azimuthal Equal-Area

ATLAS

Asia: Physical

ELEVATION

Feet	Meters
13,120	4,000
6,560	2,000
1,640	500
656	200
(Sea level) 0	0 (Sea level)
Below sea level	Below sea level

Ice cap

750 Miles
500   750 Kilometers
250   500   750

0   250   500   750

Projection: Two-Point Equidistant

AUSTRALIA

PACIFIC OCEAN

Maoke Mountains
New Guinea
Arafura Sea
Molucca Sea
Banda Sea
Celebes Sea
Celebes
Borneo
Java Sea
Java
Bangka
Sumatra
Mentawai Islands
Philippines
Mindanao
Luzon
Luzon Strait
Taiwan
South China Sea
Hainan
Ryukyu Islands
Okinawa
East China Sea
Yellow Sea
Kyushu
Shikoku
Honshu
Korea Strait
Japan Sea (East Sea)
Sea of Okhotsk
Hokkaido
Sakhalin Island
Kuril Islands
Kamchatka Peninsula
Bering Sea
Aleutian Islands
Wrangel Island
New Siberian Islands
North Land
North Pole
Franz Josef Land
Novaya Zemlya
Barents Sea
Kara Sea
Laptev Sea

Tropic of Cancer
Equator

CENTRAL RANGE
KOLYMA MTS.
CHERSKIY RANGE
VERKHOYANSKY RANGE
STANOVOY MOUNTAINS
YABLONOVY RANGE
GREATER KHINGAN RANGE
Aldan River
Amur River
Shilka River
Lena River
Central Siberian Plateau
Tunguska River
Angara River
Lower Tunguska River
Yenisey River
Lake Baikal
SAYAN MOUNTAINS
ALTAY MOUNTAINS
MONGOLIAN PLATEAU
GOBI
QIN LING
NORTH CHINA PLAIN
BOHAI HILLS
Huang He (Yellow River)
Yellow River
Xi River
Hong River
Gulf of Tonkin
Chang Jiang (Yangtze) River
INDOCHINA PENINSULA
Mekong River
Chao Phraya River
Gulf of Thailand
MALAY PENINSULA
Andaman Sea
Nicobar Islands
Andaman Islands
Bay of Bengal
Sri Lanka
Maldives
Lakshadweep Islands
Arabian Sea
INDIAN OCEAN
Socotra Island
Gulf of Aden
Red Sea
AFRICA
RUB' AL-KHALI
AN-NAFUD
SYRIAN DESERT
SINAI PENINSULA
Cyprus
ANATOLIAN PLATEAU
Mount Ararat 16,945 ft (5,165 m)
Mediterranean Sea
Black Sea
Bosporus
EUROPE
CAUCASUS MTS.
ZAGROS MTS.
Persian Gulf
Gulf of Oman
Tigris River
Euphrates River
GREAT SALT DESERT
Caspian Sea
USTYURT PLATEAU
Aral Sea
KARA KUM
KYZYL KUM
TURAN LOWLAND
Amu Darya
Syr Darya
HINDU KUSH
TIAN SHAN
KAZAKH UPLANDS
Balqash Lake
TAKLIMAKAN DESERT
TARIM BASIN
KUNLUN MOUNTAINS
PLATEAU OF TIBET
Mount Everest 29,035 ft (8,850 m)
HIMALAYAS
Sutlej River
Indus River
THAR DESERT
INDO-GANGETIC PLAIN
Ganges River
Brahmaputra River
Nu River
Irrawaddy River
DECCAN PLATEAU
Godavari River
EASTERN GHATS
WESTERN GHATS
Ishim River
Irtysh River
Ob River
Ural River
WEST SIBERIAN PLAIN
S I B E R I A
URAL MOUNTAINS
TAIMYR PENINSULA

N

Asia: Political

National capitals
Other cities

| | 250 | 500 | 750 Miles |
| 0 | 250 | 500 | 750 Kilometers |

Projection: Two-Point Equidistant

EUROPE

RUSSIA

Moscow

Yekaterinburg

Chelyabinsk

Omsk

Novosibirsk

Astana

KAZAKHSTAN

Aral Sea

Lake Balkhash

Almaty

UZBEKISTAN

Tashkent

KYRGYZSTAN

Bishkek

TAJIKISTAN

Dushanbe

TURKMENISTAN

Ashgabat

Caspian Sea

AZERBAIJAN

Baku

GEORGIA

Tbilisi

ARMENIA

Yerevan

Black Sea

Istanbul

Ankara

TURKEY

Izmir

CYPRUS

Nicosia

LEBANON

Beirut

ISRAEL

Tel Aviv

Jerusalem

Damascus

SYRIA

Amman

JORDAN

Mosul

Baghdad

IRAQ

Basra

Mediterranean Sea

AFRICA

Red Sea

Jidda

Mecca

Sanaa

YEMEN

Gulf of Aden

Socotra (YEMEN)

SAUDI ARABIA

Riyadh

KUWAIT

Kuwait City

BAHRAIN

Manama

QATAR

Doha

UNITED ARAB EMIRATES

Abu Dhabi

OMAN

Masqat (Muscat)

Persian Gulf

IRAN

Tehran

Shiraz

AFGHANISTAN

Kabul

Arabian Sea

PAKISTAN

Islamabad

Lahore

Karachi

URAL MOUNTAINS

Yakutsk

MONGOLIA

Ulaanbaatar

Irkutsk

Lake Baykal

CHINA

Beijing

Fushun

Harbin

Chengdu

Chongqing

Wuhan

Nanjing

Shanghai

Qingdao

Yellow Sea

Dalian

Guangzhou

Macao

Hong Kong

Hainan (CHINA)

RUSSIA

Vladivostok

Sakhalin Island

Sea of Okhotsk

Kuril Islands (RUSSIA)

Sapporo

JAPAN

Tokyo

Yokohama

Osaka

Kyoto

Hiroshima

Nagasaki

NORTH KOREA

Pyongyang

SOUTH KOREA

Seoul

Pusan

East China Sea

TAIWAN

Taipei

Aleutian Islands

Bering Sea

PACIFIC OCEAN

Tropic of Cancer

Ryukyu Islands (JAPAN)

PHILIPPINES

Manila

Luzon Strait

South China Sea

VIETNAM

Hanoi

Ho Chi Minh City

LAOS

Vientiane

THAILAND

Bangkok

CAMBODIA

Phnom Penh

Gulf of Thailand

MYANMAR (BURMA)

Yangon (Rangoon)

Mandalay

BHUTAN

Thimphu

NEPAL

Kathmandu

BANGLADESH

Dhaka

Kolkata (Calcutta)

INDIA

New Delhi

Delhi

Jaipur

Ahmadabad

Mumbai (Bombay)

Bangalore

Chennai (Madras)

Bay of Bengal

Andaman Islands (INDIA)

Nicobar Islands (INDIA)

Andaman Sea

SRI LANKA

Colombo

MALDIVES

Male

Lakshadweep Islands (INDIA)

INDIAN OCEAN

BRUNEI

Bandar Seri Begawan

MALAYSIA

Kuala Lumpur

SINGAPORE

Singapore

Medan

INDONESIA

Jakarta

Bandung

Surabaya

Ujung Pandang

Java Sea

Celebes Sea

TIMOR-LESTE

Dili

Arafura Sea

New Guinea

AUSTRALIA

Equator

Barents Sea

Kara Sea

North Pole

Arctic Circle

Africa: Physical

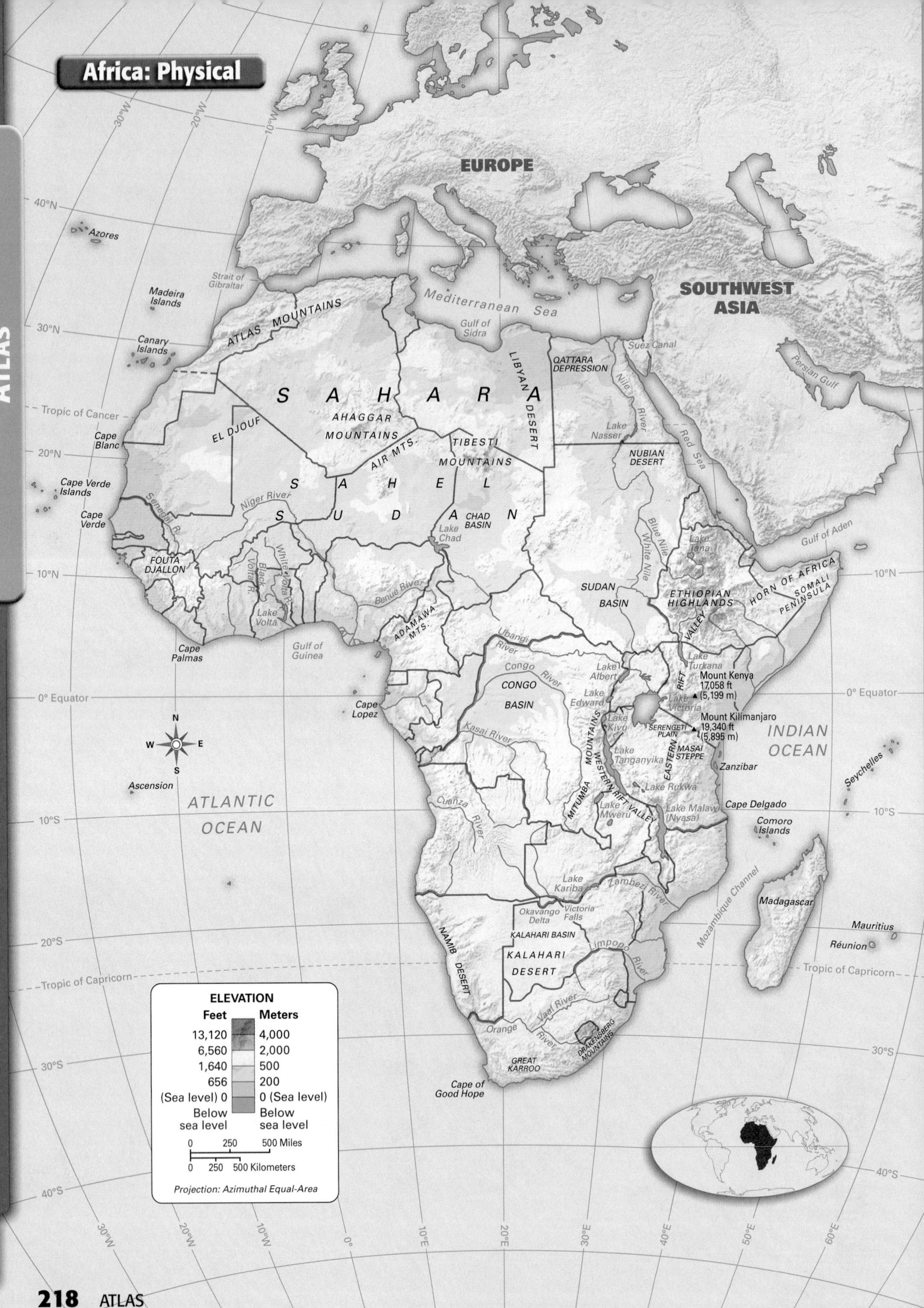

ATLAS

EUROPE

SOUTHWEST ASIA

Mediterranean Sea

Strait of Gibraltar

Gulf of Sidra

Suez Canal

Persian Gulf

ATLAS MOUNTAINS

QATTARA DEPRESSION

Azores

Madeira Islands

Canary Islands

Cape Blanc

40°N

30°N

Tropic of Cancer

20°N

S A H A R A

AHAGGAR MOUNTAINS

AIR MTS.

TIBESTI MOUNTAINS

LIBYAN DESERT

EL DJOUF

NUBIAN DESERT

Nile River

Lake Nasser

Red Sea

Cape Verde Islands

Cape Verde

Senegal R.

Niger River

S A H E L

S U D A N

CHAD BASIN

Lake Chad

10°N

FOUTA DJALLON

White Volta R.

Black Volta R.

Lake Volta

Benue River

Blue Nile

White Nile

Lake Tana

Gulf of Aden

SOMALI PENINSULA

HORN OF AFRICA

ETHIOPIAN HIGHLANDS

SUDAN BASIN

Cape Palmas

Gulf of Guinea

ADAMAWA MTS.

Ubangi River

Congo River

CONGO BASIN

Lake Albert

Lake Edward

RIFT VALLEY

Mount Kenya 17,058 ft (5,199 m)

Lake Turkana

0° Equator

Cape Lopez

Kasai River

Lake Kivu

Lake Victoria

SERENGETI PLAIN

Mount Kilimanjaro 19,340 ft (5,895 m)

MASAI STEPPE

INDIAN OCEAN

Zanzibar

Seychelles

N W E S

Ascension

ATLANTIC OCEAN

MITUMBA MOUNTAINS

Lake Tanganyika

WESTERN RIFT VALLEY

EASTERN RIFT VALLEY

Lake Rukwa

Cape Delgado

10°S

Cuanza River

Lake Mweru

Lake Malawi (Nyasa)

Comoro Islands

Madagascar

Lake Kariba

Zambezi River

Mauritius

Okavango Delta

Victoria Falls

Réunion

Tropic of Capricorn

NAMIB DESERT

KALAHARI BASIN

KALAHARI DESERT

Limpopo River

Mozambique Channel

20°S

Vaal River

Orange River

DRAKENSBERG MOUNTAINS

30°S

GREAT KARROO

Cape of Good Hope

ELEVATION

Feet		Meters
13,120		4,000
6,560		2,000
1,640		500
656		200
(Sea level) 0		0 (Sea level)
Below sea level		Below sea level

0 250 500 Miles

0 250 500 Kilometers

Projection: Azimuthal Equal-Area

40°S

30°W 20°W 10°W 0° 10°E 20°E 30°E 40°E 50°E 60°E

10°N 0° Equator 10°S Tropic of Capricorn (right side)

EUROPE

SOUTHWEST ASIA

Mediterranean Sea

Strait of Gibraltar

Azores (PORTUGAL)

Madeira (PORTUGAL)

Casablanca • Rabat   Algiers   Tunis
MOROCCO   TUNISIA   Tripoli

Canary Islands (SPAIN)

El Aaiún
WESTERN SAHARA (Claimed by Morocco)

ALGERIA   LIBYA   Alexandria
                                          Giza • Cairo
                                          EGYPT

Tropic of Cancer

MAURITANIA   MALI

Nouakchott

CAPE VERDE

Praia

SENEGAL   NIGER   CHAD   Red Sea
Dakar   Khartoum   ERITREA
GAMBIA   Bamako   BURKINA   Asmara
Banjul   FASO   N'Djamena   SUDAN   DJIBOUTI
Bissau   Ouagadougou Lake Chad   Djibouti
GUINEA-   Niamey
BISSAU   GUINEA   BENIN   ETHIOPIA
Conakry   TOGO NIGERIA   Addis Ababa
Freetown CÔTE   Abuja
SIERRA LEONE D'IVOIRE GHANA
Yamoussoukro Lomé Lagos
Monrovia Abidjan Accra Porto-   CENTRAL AFRICAN
LIBERIA   Novo   REPUBLIC
                   CAMEROON Bangui   SOMALIA
          Gulf of   Yaoundé   Mogadishu
          Guinea   Malabo
SÃO TOMÉ AND PRÍNCIPE   UGANDA
EQUATORIAL GUINEA   Kampala   KENYA
São Tomé   Libreville REPUBLIC   Nairobi
           GABON   OF THE   Kisangani
                       CONGO   INDIAN
                                 RWANDA Kigali   OCEAN
           Brazzaville DEMOCRATIC   Bujumbura BURUNDI   Victoria
           Kinshasa   REPUBLIC   SEYCHELLES
CABINDA   OF THE CONGO Lake Victoria
(ANGOLA)   Mombasa
                                      TANZANIA Pemba
                                      Dodoma   Zanzibar
                                      Dar es Salaam
           Luanda   Lake
                                      Tanganyika

ATLANTIC OCEAN

0° Equator

10°S   ANGOLA   Lake Malawi (Nyasa)   COMOROS
                          Lubumbashi   Moroni
St. Helena (U.K.)   ZAMBIA   MALAWI
                          Lusaka   Lilongwe

                                      MOZAMBIQUE
                          Harare   Antananarivo
                          ZIMBABWE   MAURITIUS
                          Bulawayo   MADAGASCAR Port Louis
NAMIBIA   BOTSWANA   Réunion
Windhoek   (FRANCE)
             Gaborone   Pretoria
Tropic of Capricorn   Johannesburg Maputo
                         Bloemfontein Mbabane
                                       SWAZILAND
                         Maseru
                         LESOTHO
             SOUTH AFRICA

Cape Town

N E S W

National capital
Other city

0   250   500 Miles
0   250   500 Kilometers

Projection: Azimuthal Equal-Area

ATLAS

The Pacific: Political

ASIA

NORTH AMERICA

NORTH PACIFIC OCEAN

SOUTH PACIFIC OCEAN

INDIAN OCEAN

Tropic of Cancer

0° Equator

Tropic of Capricorn

International Date Line

National capital
Other city

1,000 Miles
1,000 Kilometers
500
500

Projection: Azimuthal Equal-Area

N
E
S
W

30°N
15°N
15°S
30°S
45°S

120°W
135°W
150°W
165°W
180°
165°E
150°E
135°E
120°E

30°N
15°N
0°
15°S
30°S
45°S

NORTH AMERICA

Hawaii (U.S.)
Hawaiian Islands

Midway Island (U.S.)
Johnston Island (U.S.)
Wake Island (U.S.)

Marquesas Islands (FRANCE)
Tuamotu Archipelago (FRANCE)
Rapa Island (FRANCE)

Easter Island (CHILE)
Pitcairn (U.K.)
Ducie Island
Pitcairn Island

POLYNESIA

Starbuck Island

Kingman Reef (U.S.)
Palmyra Island (U.S.)
Washington Island
Fanning Island

French Polynesia

Society Islands (FRANCE)
Tahiti (FRANCE)
Papeete
Tubuai Islands (FRANCE)

Jarvis I. (U.S.)
Howland I. (U.S.)
Baker I. (U.S.)
McKean I.
Gardner
Phoenix Islands

KIRIBATI

Manihiki Island
Cook Islands (NEW ZEALAND)
Rarotonga Island

Tokelau (N.Z.)
American Samoa
Pago Pago
Niue (N.Z.)

SAMOA
Apia
Wallis & Futuna (FR.)

TONGA
Nuku'alofa

Suva
FIJI

Kermadec Islands (N.Z.)

Chatham Islands (N.Z.)

MARSHALL ISLANDS
Eniwetok I.
Kwajalein Island
Majuro
Palikir
Tarawa
Gilbert Islands

TUVALU
Funafuti

NAURU

MICRONESIA
Truk Is.
FEDERATED STATES OF MICRONESIA

SOLOMON ISLANDS
Honiara
Guadalcanal I.
Bismarck Archipelago

MELANESIA

VANUATU
Port Vila
Espiritu Santo I.
Malekula I.
New Caledonia (FRANCE)
Noumea
Loyalty Islands (FRANCE)

Coral Sea

PAPUA NEW GUINEA
Port Moresby
New Guinea

Norfolk Island (AUSTRALIA)

North Island
Auckland
Wellington
Christchurch
South Island
NEW ZEALAND
Bounty Islands (N.Z.)
Auckland Islands (NEW ZEALAND)

Northern Marianas (U.S.)

Bonin Islands (JAPAN)
Volcano Islands (JAPAN)

Guam (U.S.)
Agana

Koror
PALAU

Philippine Sea

South China Sea

Timor Sea
Arafura Sea

Darwin

AUSTRALIA

Brisbane
Sydney
Canberra
Hobart
Melbourne
Adelaide
Perth

Tasman Sea

Christmas Island (AUSTRALIA)

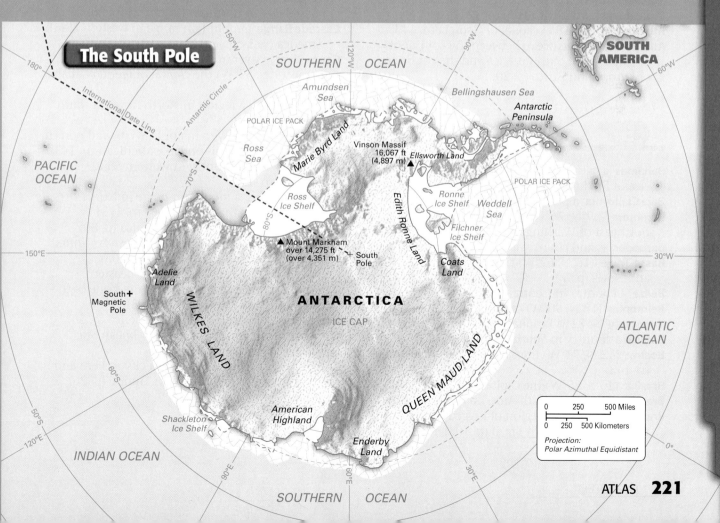

The North Pole

0   200   400 Miles
0   200   400 Kilometers

Projection:
Polar Azimuthal Equidistant

Kara
Sea

Barents
Sea

EUROPE

Norwegian
Sea

Laptev
Sea

Arctic Circle

ASIA

ARCTIC
OCEAN

Greenland
Sea

90°E

120°E

150°E

80°N

70°N

60°N

50°N

180°

International Date Line

North
Pole

POLAR ICE PACK

North
Magnetic
Pole

150°W

120°W

90°W

60°W

30°W

0°

30°E

60°E

Greenland
(DENMARK)

ATLANTIC
OCEAN

Baffin
Bay

Bering Sea

Beaufort
Sea

NORTH
AMERICA

ATLAS

The South Pole

180°

International Date Line

150°W

120°W

90°W

60°W

SOUTHERN   OCEAN

SOUTH
AMERICA

Antarctic Circle

PACIFIC
OCEAN

Amundsen
Sea

Bellingshausen Sea

Antarctic
Peninsula

POLAR ICE PACK

Ross
Sea

Marie Byrd Land

Vinson Massif
16,067 ft
(4,897 m) ▲ Ellsworth Land

POLAR ICE PACK

70°S

Ross
Ice Shelf

Ronne
Ice Shelf

Weddell
Sea

80°S

Edith Ronne Land

Filchner
Ice Shelf

150°E

▲ Mount Markham
over 14,275 ft
(over 4,351 m)

South
Pole

Coats
Land

30°W

South +
Magnetic
Pole

Adelie
Land

ANTARCTICA

ICE CAP

ATLANTIC
OCEAN

60°S

WILKES   LAND

QUEEN MAUD LAND

50°S

120°E

Shackleton
Ice Shelf

American
Highland

Enderby
Land

90°E

60°E

30°E

0°

INDIAN OCEAN

0   250   500 Miles
0   250   500 Kilometers

Projection:
Polar Azimuthal Equidistant

SOUTHERN   OCEAN

ATLAS   **221**

Gazetteer

A

Acapulco (17°N, 100°W) a resort on the Pacific Ocean in southwest Mexico (p. 37)

Alabama (AL) a state in the southern United States; admitted in 1819 (pp. 204–205)

Alaska (AK) a state in northwestern North America; admitted in 1959 (pp. 204–205)

Alberta a province in western Canada (p. 171)

Amazon Basin a huge basin in the heart of South America (p. 212)

Amazon River the major river in South America (p. 212)

Andes Mountains (AN-deez) a long mountain range along the west coast of South America (p. 212)

Appalachian Mountains a mountain system in eastern North America (p. 145)

Argentina a country in South America (p. 101)

Arizona (AZ) a state in the southwestern United States; admitted in 1912 (pp. 204–205)

Arkansas (AR) a state in the south-central United States; admitted in 1836 (pp. 204–205)

Asunción (ah-soon-SYOHN) (25°N, 58°W) the capital of Paraguay (p. 116)

Atacama Desert a desert located in northern Chile near the border with Peru (p. 125)

Atlanta (33°N, 84°W) capital of Georgia (p. 143)

Atlantic Ocean the ocean between the continents of North and South America and the continents of Europe and Africa (p. 206)

B

Bahamas a country and group of islands located east of Florida in the Atlantic Ocean (p. 59)

Baja California a peninsula in Mexico (p. 39)

Baltimore (39°N, 76°W) a large city in Maryland northeast of Washington, D.C. (p. 143)

Barbados island country in the Caribbean (p. 57)

Basse-Terre (16°N, 62°W) the capital of Saint Kitts and Nevis (p. 57)

Belize a country in Central America (p. 57)

Belmopan (17°N, 90°W) capital of Belize (p. 57)

Bogotá (4°N, 72°W) capital of Colombia (p. 81)

Bolivia a country in South America (p. 123)

Boston (42°N, 71°W) the capital of Massachusetts (p. 143)

Brasília (10°S, 55°W) the capital of Brazil (p. 109)

Brazil a country in South America (p. 101)

Brazilian Highlands a region of rugged, old, eroded mountains in eastern Brazil (p. 103)

British Columbia a province in Canada (p. 171)

Buenos Aires (BWAY-nuhs y-reez) (36°S, 60°W) the capital of Argentina (p. 101)

C

Calgary (51°N, 114°W) a large city in the province of Alberta in Canada (p. 170)

California (CA) a state in the western United States; admitted in 1850 (pp. 204–205)

Callao (kah-YAH-oh) (12°S, 77°W) a port city in Peru west of Lima (p. 136)

Canada a country in North America (p. 170)

Canadian Shield a region of ancient rock that covers more than half of Canada (p. 173)

Cancún (21°N, 87°W) a popular resort on Mexico's Caribbean coast (p. 37)

Caracas (11°N, 67°W) the capital of Venezuela (p. 81)

Caribbean Islands a group of islands in the Caribbean Sea (p. 57)

Caribbean Sea an arm of the Atlantic Ocean between North and South America (p. 57)

Cartagena (kahr-tah-HAY-nuh) (10°N, 74°W) a coastal city in northern Colombia (p. 80)

Cascade Range a mountain range in western North America (p. 145)

Cauca River a river in Colombia (p. 83)

Cayenne (4°N, 53°W) the capital of French Guiana (p. 81)

Central America a region in North America south of Mexico (p. 56–57)

Chicago (42°N, 88°W) a major U.S. city and port in northeastern Illinois on Lake Michigan (p. 143)

Chile (CHEE-lay) a country in western South America (p. 123)

Coast Mountains a mountain range in North America along the Pacific coast (p. 173)

Colombia a country in South America (p. 80)

Colorado (CO) a state in the southwestern United States; admitted in 1876 (pp. 204–205)

Connecticut (CT) a state in the northeastern United States; admitted in 1788 and one of the original 13 colonies (pp. 204–205)

Costa Rica a country in Central America (p. 56)

Cuba an island country in the Caribbean Sea south of Florida (p. 57)

Cuzco (KOO-skoh) (14°S, 72°W) a city in Peru and the former capital of the Inca Empire (p. 26)

D

Dallas (33°N, 97°W) a major U.S. city and transportation and financial center in Texas (p. 143)

Delaware (DE) a state in the eastern United States; admitted in 1787 and one of the original 13 colonies (pp. 204–205)

Detroit (42°N, 83°W) a large U.S. city in Michigan (p. 143)

District of Columbia (39°N, 77°W) a federal district between Maryland and Virginia; the capital of the United States (p. 143)

Dominican Republic a country in the Caribbean (p. 57)

E

Ecuador a country in South America (p. 123)

El Salvador a country in Central America (p. 56)

equator the imaginary line of latitude that circles the globe halfway between the North and South Poles (p. 206–207)

F

Florida (FL) a state in the southeastern United States; admitted in 1845 (p. 204–205)

French Guiana (gee-A-nuh) a region of France in northern South America (p. 81)

G

Galápagos Islands a group of islands in the Pacific Ocean that are part of Ecuador (p. 122)

Georgetown (5°N, 59°W) capital of Guyana (p. 81)

Georgia (GA) a state in the southeastern United States; admitted in 1788 and one of the original 13 colonies (pp. 204–205)

Gran Chaco (grahn CHAH-koh) a region of lowlands in South America (p. 103)

Grand Banks (47°N, 52°W) a rich fishing ground near Newfoundland, Canada (p. 173)

Greater Antilles an island group in the Caribbean that includes Cuba, Jamaica, Hispaniola, and Puerto Rico (p. 59)

Great Lakes a group of five large freshwater lakes in North America; they are Lake Superior, Lake Michigan, Lake Huron, Lake Erie, and Lake Ontario (p. 145)

Great Plains a large region of plains and grasslands in central North America (p. 145)

Greenland a large island in North America that was settled by the Vikings (p. 210)

Guadalajara (21°N, 103°W) the second-largest city in Mexico (p. 37)

Guadeloupe a group of islands in the Caribbean that are part of France (p. 57)

Guatemala a country in Central America (p. 56)

Guatemala City (15°N, 91°W) the capital of Guatemala (p. 56)

Guayaquil (gwah-ah-KEEL) (2°S, 80°W) a city in Ecuador (p. 123)

Guiana Highlands (gee-YAH-nah) a large plateau region in northern South America (p. 83)

Guianas (gee-AH-nuhz) a term used to refer to Guyana, Suriname, and French Guiana (p. 81)

Gulf of Mexico a large gulf off the southeastern coast of North America (p. 37)

Guyana (gy-AH-nuh) a country in northern South America (p. 81)

H

Haiti a country in the Caribbean (p. 57)

Havana (23°N, 82°W) the capital of Cuba (p. 57)

Hawaii (HI) state in the Pacific Ocean comprised of the Hawaiian Islands; admitted in 1959 (pp. 204–205)

Hispaniola (ees-pah-nee-O-lah) an island in the Caribbean (p. 59)

Honduras a country in Central America (p. 56)

Houston (30°N, 95°W) a major U.S. port city in Texas (p. 143)

Hudson Bay a large bay in central Canada (p. 173)

I

Idaho (ID) a state in the northwestern United States; admitted in 1890 (pp. 204–205)

Illinois (IL) a state in the north-central United States; admitted in 1819 (pp. 204–205)

Indiana (IN) a state in the north-central United States; admitted in 1816 (pp. 204–205)

Interior Plains a large plains region of North America (p. 145)

Iowa (IA) a state in the north-central United States; admitted in 1846 (pp. 204–205)

J, K

Jamaica an island country in the Caribbean (p. 58)
Kansas (KS) a state in the central United States; admitted in 1861 (pp. 204–205)
Kentucky (KY) a state in the east-central United States; admitted in 1792 (pp. 204–205)

L

Lake Maracaibo (mah-rah-KY-boh) (10°N, 72°W) an oil-rich body of water in Venezuela (p. 83)
Lake Texcoco (tays-KOH-koh) an ancient lake in Mexico; it was the site of Tenochtitlán (p. 21)
La Paz (17°S, 65°W) the capital of Bolivia (p. 123)
Latin America a region in the Western Hemisphere; it includes countries where Spanish, Portuguese, or French culture shaped life (p. 38)
Lesser Antilles a group of small islands in the Caribbean; they stretch from the Virgin Islands in the north to Trinidad in the south (p. 59)
Lima (10°S, 75°W) the capital of Peru (p. 123)
Llanos a plains region in South America (p. 83)
Louisiana (LA) a state in the southeastern United States; admitted in 1812 (pp. 204–205)

M

Machu Picchu (MAH-choo PEEK-choo) (13°S, 73°W) a sacred city and fortress of the Incas (p. 26)
Magdalena River a river in Colombia (p. 83)
Maine (ME) a state in the northeastern United States; admitted in 1820 (pp. 204–205)
Manaus (3°S, 60°W) a major port and industrial city in Brazil's Amazon rain forest (p. 101)
Manitoba a province in central Canada (p. 171)
Martinique a group of islands in the Caribbean that are part of France (p. 57)
Maryland (MD) a state in the eastern United States; admitted in 1788 and one of the original 13 colonies (pp. 204–205)
Massachusetts (MA) a state in the northeastern United States; admitted in 1788 and one of the original 13 colonies (pp. 204–205)
Mato Grosso Plateau a high plateau area in Brazil (p. 103)
Mesoamerica a region in North America; the first permanent farming settlements in the Americas developed in Mesoamerica (p. 14)
Mexican Plateau a high, mostly rugged region covering much of the interior of Mexico (p. 39)
Mexico a country in North America (p. 36–37)

Mexico City (23°N, 104°W) the capital of Mexico (p. 37)
Michigan (MI) a state in the north-central United States; admitted in 1837 (pp. 204–205)
Minnesota (MN) a state in the north-central United States; admitted in 1858 (pp. 204–205)
Mississippi (MS) a state in the southeastern United States; admitted in 1817 (pp. 204–205)
Mississippi River a major river in the United States (p. 145)
Missouri (MO) a state in the central United States; admitted in 1821 (pp. 204–205)
Montana (MT) a state in the northern United States; admitted in 1889 (pp. 204–205)
Monterrey (26°N, 100°W) a large city and industrial center in northern Mexico (p. 37)
Montevideo (mawn-tay-vee-DAY-oh) (35°S, 56°W) the capital of Uruguay (p. 101)
Montreal (46°N, 74°W) a major Canadian city in Quebec; founded by the French in 1642 (p. 171)
Mount Saint Helens (46°N, 122°W) a volcano in Washington state that erupted in 1980 (p. 146)

N

Nassau (25°N, 77°W) the capital of the Bahamas (p. 57)
Nebraska (NE) a state in the central United States; admitted in 1867 (pp. 204–205)
Nevada (NV) a state in the western United States; admitted in 1864 (pp. 204–205)
New Brunswick a province in Canada (p. 171)
Newfoundland and Labrador an island province in eastern Canada (p. 171)
New Hampshire (NH) a state in the northeastern United States; admitted in 1788 and one of the original 13 colonies (pp. 204–205)
New Jersey (NJ) a state in the northeastern United States; admitted in 1787 and one of the original 13 colonies (pp. 204–205)
New Mexico (NM) a state in the southwestern United States; admitted in 1912 (pp. 204–205)
New Orleans (30°N, 90°W) a major U.S. port city located in southeastern Louisiana (p. 162)
New York (NY) a state in the northeastern United States; admitted in 1788 and one of the original 13 colonies (pp. 204–205)
New York City (41°N, 74°W) the largest city in the United States (p. 143)
Niagara Falls waterfall on the border of the United States and Canada (p. 172)
Nicaragua a country in Central America (p. 56)
North America a continent including Canada, the United States, Mexico, Central America, and the Caribbean islands (p. 210)

North Carolina (NC) a state in the southeastern United States; admitted in 1789 and one of the original 13 colonies (pp. 204–205)

North Dakota (ND) a state in the north-central United States; admitted in 1889 (pp. 204–205)

Northern Hemisphere the northern half of the globe, between the equator and the North Pole (p. H7)

Northwest Territories a territory in Canada (p. 170)

Nova Scotia (noh-vuh SKOH-shuh) a province in eastern Canada (p. 170)

Nunavut (NOO-nah-VOOT) a territory in northern Canada created as a homeland for Canada's Inuit people (p. 170)

Ohio (OH) a state in the north-central United States; admitted in 1803 (pp. 204–205)

Oklahoma (OK) a state in the south-central United States; admitted in 1890; admitted in 1907 (pp. 204–205)

Ontario a province in east-central Canada (p. 170)

Oregon (OR) a state in the northwestern United States; admitted in 1859 (pp. 204–205)

Orinoco River (OHR-ee-NOH-koh) a major river in Venezuela (p. 83)

Ottawa (45°N, 76°W) capital of Canada (p. 171)

P

Pacific Ocean the world's largest ocean; located between Asia and the Americas (p. 206)

Palenque (pay-LENG-kay) (18°N, 92°W) an ancient Maya city in southern Mexico (p. 15)

Pampas a fertile plains region in southern South America located mainly in Argentina (p. 103)

Panama a country in Central America (p. 57)

Panama Canal (26°N, 80°W) a canal built by the United States in the early 1900s across the Isthmus of Panama (p. 68)

Panama City (8°N, 81°W) capital of Panama (p. 57)

Paraguay a country in South America (p. 116)

Paraguay River a river in South America (p. 103)

Paramaribo (6°N, 55°W) the capital of Suriname (p. 81)

Paraná River a river in South America (p. 103)

Patagonia a region of dry plains and plateaus east of the Andes in southern Argentina (p. 103)

Pennsylvania (PA) a state in the eastern United States; admitted in 1787 and one of the original 13 colonies (pp. 204–205)

Peru a country in western South America (p. 123)

Philadelphia (40°N, 75°W) a major U.S. city located in southeastern Pennsylvania; it was the capital of the United States from 1790 to 1800 (p. 143)

Pittsburgh (40°N, 80°W) a major U.S. city in Pennsylvania (p. 205)

Popocatépetl (poh-poh-cah-TE-pet-uhl) (19°N, 99°W) a volcano near Mexico City (p. 39)

Port-au-Prince (pohr-toh-PRINS) (19°N, 72°W) the capital of Haiti (p. 57)

Port of Spain (11°N, 61°W) the capital of Trinidad and Tobago (p. 57)

Prince Edward Island (46°N, 64°W) a small province in eastern Canada (p. 171)

Puerto Rico an island east of Cuba and southeast of Florida; it is a U.S. territory (p. 57)

Q, R

Quebec a province in eastern Canada (p. 171)

Quito (2°S, 78°W) the capital of Ecuador (p. 123)

Rhode Island (RI) a state in the northeastern United States; admitted in 1790 and one of the original 13 colonies (pp. 204–205)

Río Bravo the Mexican name for the river known as the Rio Grande in the United States; it forms the border between Mexico and Texas (p. 37)

Rio de Janeiro (23°N, 43°W) the second-largest city in Brazil; it is a major port city and Brazil's former capital (p. 101)

Rio de la Plata (REE-oh day lah PLAH-tah) a body of water in South America (p.103)

Rocky Mountains a major mountain range in western North America (p. 145)

S

St. Kitts and Nevis country in the Caribbean (p. 57)

St. Lawrence River a river in North America that flows from the Great Lakes to the Atlantic Ocean (p. 173)

St. Lawrence Seaway a shipping waterway in North America built in the 1950s to connect the Great Lakes with the Atlantic Ocean (p. 205)

San Francisco (37°N, 122°W) a major U.S. port city in Northern California (p. 143)

San Jose (10°N, 84°W) capital of Costa Rica (p. 56)

San Salvador (14°N, 89°W) the capital of El Salvador (p. 56)

Santiago (33°S, 71°W) the capital of Chile (p. 123)

Santo Domingo (19°N, 71°W) the capital of the Dominican Republic (p. 57)

São Paulo (24°S, 47°W) the largest city in Brazil and South America (p. 101)

Saskatchewan a province in Canada (p. 171)

Seattle (48°N, 122°W) a major U.S. port and city in Washington state (p. 143)

Sierra Madre (SYER-rah MAH-dray) the chief mountain range in Mexico (p. 39)

Sierra Nevada a large mountain range mainly in California (p. 145)

South America a continent in the Western and Southern hemispheres (p. 212)

South Carolina (SC) a state in the southeastern United States; admitted in 1788 and one of the original 13 colonies (pp. 204–205)

South Dakota (SD) a state in the north-central United States; admitted in 1889 (pp. 204–205)

Southern Hemisphere the southern half of the globe, between the equator and the South Pole (p. H7)

Spain a country in Southern Europe; it colonized much of the Americas (p. 215)

Strait of Magellan a waterway through the southern tip of South America (p. 125)

Sucre (SOO-kray) (19°S, 65°W) the capital of Bolivia (p. 123)

Suriname (soohr-uh-NAHM) a country in northern South America (p. 81)

Tegucigalpa (15°N, 87°W) the capital of Honduras (p. 56)

Tennessee (TN) a state in the south-central United States; admitted in 1796 (pp. 204–205)

Tenochtitlán (tay-nawch-teet-LAHN) the capital of the Aztec Empire (p. 21)

Texas (TX) a state and former independent republic in the south-central United States; admitted in 1845 (pp. 204–205)

Tierra del Fuego a group of islands in southern South America (p. 125)

Toronto (44°N, 79°W) Canada's largest city (p. 171)

Trinidad and Tobago a country in the Caribbean just north of Venezuela (p. 57)

United States of America a country in North America located between Canada and Mexico (p. 204–205)

Uruguay a country in South America (p. 101)

Utah (UT) a state in the western United States; admitted in 1896 (pp. 204–205)

Valley of Mexico a large plateau region in central Mexico (p. 39)

Valparaiso (bahl-pah-rah-EE-soh) (33°S, 72°W) a city and major port in Chile (p. 123)

Vancouver (49°N, 123°W) a city in western Canada just north of the U.S. border (p. 170)

Venezuela a country in South America (p. 81)

Vermont (VT) a state in the northeastern United States; admitted in 1791 (pp. 204–205)

Virginia (VA) a state in the eastern United States; admitted in 1788 and one of the original 13 colonies (pp. 204–205)

Virgin Islands a group of small islands in the Caribbean (p. 57)

Washington (WA) a state in the northwestern United States; admitted in 1889 (pp. 204–205)

Washington, D.C. (39°N, 77°W) the capital of the United States (p. 143)

West Indies a group of more than 1,200 islands in the Caribbean Sea (p. 70)

West Virginia (WV) a state in the east-central United States; admitted in 1863 (pp. 204–205)

Western Hemisphere the half of the globe between 180° and the prime meridian that includes North and South America and the Pacific and Atlantic oceans (p. H7)

Windsor (42°N, 83°W) a city in Canada near the U.S. border (p. 171)

Wisconsin (WI) a state in the north-central United States; admitted in 1848 (pp. 204–205)

Wyoming (WY) a state in the northwestern United States; admitted in 1890 (pp. 204–205)

Yucatán Peninsula (yoo-kah-TAHN) a large peninsula that separates the Caribbean Sea from the Gulf of Mexico (p. 39)

Yukon Territory a territory in Canada (p. 170)

English and Spanish Glossary

MARK	AS IN	RESPELLING	EXAMPLE
a	alphabet	a	*AL-fuh-bet
ā	Asia	ay	AY-zhuh
ä	cart, top	ah	KAHRT, TAHP
e	let, ten	e	LET, TEN
ē	even, leaf	ee	EE-vuhn, LEEF
i	it, tip, British	i	IT, TIP, BRIT-ish
ī	site, buy, Ohio	y	SYT, BY, oh-HY-oh
	iris	eye	EYE-ris
k	card	k	KAHRD
kw	quest	kw	KWEST
ō	over, rainbow	oh	OH-vuhr, RAYN-boh
u̇	book, wood	ooh	BOOHK, WOOHD
ȯ	all, orchid	aw	AWL, AWR-kid
ȯi	foil, coin	oy	FOYL, KOYN
au̇	out	ow	OWT
ə	cup, butter	uh	KUHP, BUHT-uhr
ü	rule, food	oo	ROOL, FOOD
yü	few	yoo	FYOO
zh	vision	zh	VIZH-uhn

*A syllable printed in small capital letters receives heavier emphasis than the other syllable(s) in a word.

Phonetic Respelling and Pronunciation Guide

Many of the key terms in this textbook have been respelled to help you pronounce them. The letter combinations used in the respelling throughout the narrative are explained in this phonetic respelling and pronunciation guide. The guide is adapted from Merriam-Webster's Collegiate Dictionary, Eleventh Edition; Merriam-Webster's Geographical Dictionary; and Merriam-Webster's Biographical Dictionary.

A

altiplano a broad, high plateau that lies between the ridges of the Andes (p. 125)
 altiplano meseta amplia y elevada que se extiende entre las cadenas montañosas de los Andes (pág. 125)

archipelago (ahr-kuh-PE-luh-goh) a large group of islands (p. 59)
 archipiélago grupo grande de islas (pág. 59)

B

bilingual a term used to describe people who speak two languages (p. 156)
 bilingüe término utilizado para describir a las personas que hablan dos idiomas (pág. 156)

C

cash crop a crop that farmers grow mainly to sell for a profit (p. 49)
 cultivo comercial cultivo que los agricultores producen principalmente para vender y obtener ganancias (pág. 49)

causeway a raised road across water or wet ground (p. 20)
 carretera elevada camino construido sobre agua o terreno pantanoso (pág. 20)

civil war a conflict between two or more groups within a country (p. 66)
 guerra civil conflicto entre dos o más grupos dentro de un país (pág. 66)

cloud forest a moist, high-elevation tropical forest where low clouds are common (p. 60)
 bosque nuboso bosque tropical de gran elevación y humedad donde los bancos de nubes son muy comunes (pág. 60)

colony a territory inhabited and controlled by people from a foreign land (p. 152)
colonia territorio habitado y controlado por personas de otro país (pág. 152)

commonwealth a self-governing territory associated with another country (p. 73)
mancomunidad o estado libre asociado territorio autogobernado asociado con otro país (pág. 73)

conquistadors (kahn-KEES-tuh-dohrs) Spanish soldiers in the Americas who explored new lands, searched for gold and silver, and tried to spread Christianity (p. 24)
conquistadores soldados españoles en América que exploraron nuevas tierras, buscaron oro y plata e intentaron difundir el cristianismo (pág. 24)

continental divide an area of high ground that divides the flow of rivers towards opposite ends of a continent (p. 146)
línea divisoria de aguas zona de terreno elevado que divide el flujo de los ríos en dos direcciones, hacia los extremos opuestos de un continente (pág. 146)

cooperative an organization owned by its members and operated for their mutual benefit (p. 74)
cooperativa organización cuyos miembros son los propietarios y que es operada para beneficio de todos (pág. 74)

cordillera (kawr-duhl-YER-uh) a mountain system made up of roughly parallel ranges (p. 82)
cordillera sistema de cadenas montañosas aproximadamente paralelas entre sí (pág. 82)

coup (KOO) a sudden overthrow of a government by a small group of people (p. 137)
golpe de estado derrocamiento repentino de un gobierno por parte de un grupo reducido de personas (pág. 137)

Creole an American-born descendant of Europeans (p. 132)
criollo persona de ascendencia europea y nacida en América (pág. 132)

deforestation the clearing of trees (p. 105)
deforestación tala de árboles (p. 105)

dialect a regional variety of a language (p. 72)
dialecto variedad regional de un idioma (pág. 72)

ecotourism the practice of using an area's natural environment to attract tourists (p. 66)
ecoturismo uso de regiones naturales para atraer turistas (pág. 66)

El Niño an ocean and weather pattern that affects the Pacific coast of the Americas; about every two to seven years, it warms normally cool ocean water and causes extreme ocean and weather events (p. 127)
El Niño patrón oceánico y del tiempo que afecta a la costa del Pacífico de las Américas; aproximadamente cada dos a siete años, calienta las aguas normalmente frías del océano, y provoca sucesos oceánicos y climatológicos extremos (pág. 127)

empire a land with different territories and peoples under a single ruler (p. 43)
imperio zona que reúne varios territorios y pueblos bajo un solo gobernante (pág. 43)

estuary a partially enclosed body of water where freshwater mixes with salty seawater (p. 103)
estuario masa de agua parcialmente rodeada de tierra en la que el agua de mar se combina con agua dulce (pág. 103)

favela (fah-VE-lah) a huge slum in Brazil (p. 109)
favela enorme barriada en Brasil (pág. 109)

G

gaucho (GOW-choh) an Argentine cowboy (p. 113)
gaucho vaquero argentino (pág. 113)

guerrilla a member of an irregular military force (p. 89)
guerrillero miembro de una fuerza militar irregular (pág. 89)

hacienda (hah-see-en-duh) a huge expanse of farm or ranch land in the Americas (p. 44)
hacienda granja o rancho de gran tamaño en las Américas (pág. 44)

inflation a rise in prices that occurs when currency loses its buying power (p. 48)
inflación aumento de los precios que ocurre cuando la moneda de un país pierde poder adquisitivo (pág. 48)

informal economy a part of the economy that is based on odd jobs that people perform without government regulation through taxes (p. 115)
economía informal parte de la economía basada en trabajos pequeños que se realizan sin el pago de impuestos regulados por el gobierno (pág. 115)

isthmus a narrow strip of land that connects two larger land areas (p. 58)
istmo franja estrecha de tierra que une dos zonas más grandes (pág. 58)

landlocked completely surrounded by land with no direct access to the ocean (p. 116)
sin salida al mar completamente rodeado de tierra, sin acceso directo al océano (pág. 116)

llanero (yah-NAY-roh) Venezuelan cowboy (p. 92)
llanero vaquero venezolano (pág. 92)

maize corn (p. 14)
maíz cereal también conocido como elote o choclo (pág. 14)

maquiladora (mah-kee-lah-DORH-ah) a U.S. or other foreign-owned factory in Mexico (p. 51)
maquiladora fábrica estadounidense o de otro país establecida en México (pág. 51)

maritime on or near the sea (p. 183)
marítimo en o cerca del mar (pág. 183)

masonry stonework (p. 27)
mampostería obra de piedra (pág. 27)

megacity a giant urban area that includes surrounding cities and suburbs (p. 108)
megaciudad zona urbana enorme que incluye los suburbios y ciudades de alrededor (pág. 108)

megalopolis a string of large cities that have grown together (p. 161)
megalópolis serie de ciudades grandes que han crecido hasta unirse (pág. 161)

Mercosur an organization that promotes trade and economic cooperation among the southern and eastern countries of South America (p. 114)
Mercosur organización que promueve el comercio y la cooperación económica entre los países del sur y el este de América del Sur (pág. 114)

mestizo (me-STEE-zoh) a person of mixed European and Indian ancestry (p. 44)
mestizo persona de origen europeo e indígena (pág. 44)

mission a church outpost (p. 44)
misión asentamiento de la Iglesia (pág. 44)

newsprint cheap paper used mainly for newspapers (p. 175)
papel de prensa papel económico utilizado principalmente para imprimir periódicos (pág. 175)

observatory a building from which people study the sky (p. 18)
observatorio edificio desde el cual las personas estudian el cielo (pág. 18)

peninsula a piece of land surrounded on three sides by water (p. 38)
península pedazo de tierra rodeado de agua por tres lados (pág. 38)

pioneer an early settler; in the United States, people who settled the interior and western areas of the country were known as pioneers (p. 154)
pionero poblador; en Estados Unidos, las personas que se establecieron en el interior y el oeste del país se llamaron pioneros (pág. 154)

plantation a large farm that grows mainly one crop (p. 153)
plantación granja muy grande en la que se produce principalmente un solo tipo de cultivo (pág. 153)

province an administrative division of a country (p. 178)
provincia división administrativa de un país (pág. 178)

pulp softened wood fibers; used to make paper (p. 175)
pulpa fibras ablandadas de madera; usadas para hacer papel (pág. 175)

Quechua (ke-chuh-wuh) the official Inca language (p. 26)
quechua idioma oficial de los incas (pág. 26)

referendum a recall vote (p. 94)
referéndum voto para quitar a alguien de su cargo (pág. 94)

refugee someone who flees to another country, usually for political or economic reasons (p. 73)
refugiado persona que escapa a otro país, generalmente por razones económicas o políticas (pág. 73)

regionalism the strong connection that people feel toward the region in which they live (p. 183)
regionalismo gran conexión que las personas sienten con la región en la que viven (pág. 183)

slash-and-burn agriculture the practice of burning forest in order to clear land for planting (p. 49)
agricultura de tala y quema práctica de quemar los bosques para despejar el terreno y sembrar en él (pág. 49)

smog a mixture of smoke, chemicals, and fog (p. 50)
smog mezcla de humo, sustancias químicas y niebla (pág. 50)

soil exhaustion the process of soil becoming infertile because it has lost nutrients needed by plants (p. 105)
agotamiento del suelo proceso por el cual el suelo se vuelve estéril porque ha perdido los nutrientes que necesitan las plantas (pág. 105)

strait a narrow passageway that connects two large bodies of water (p. 125)
estrecho paso angosto que une dos grandes masas de agua (pág. 125)

strike a work stoppage by a group of workers until their demands are met (p. 94)
huelga interrupción del trabajo por parte de un grupo de trabajadores hasta que se cumplan sus demandas (pág. 94)

terrorism violent attacks that cause fear (p. 166)
terrorismo ataques violentos que provocan miedo (pág. 166)

tributary a smaller stream or river that flows into a larger stream or river (p. 145)
tributario río o corriente más pequeña que fluye hacia un río o una corriente más grande (pág. 145)

viceroy governor (p. 131)
virrey gobernador (pág. 131)

ENGLISH AND SPANISH GLOSSARY

Index

INDEX

INDEX

INDEX

Credits and Acknowledgments

For permission to reproduce copyrighted material, grateful acknowledgment is made to the following sources:

Atheneum Books for Young Readers, an imprint of Simon & Schuster Children's Publishing Division: From *Bearstone* by Will Hobbs. Copyright ©1989 by Will Hobbs. All rights reserved.

Sources used by The World Almanac® for charts and graphs:

Geographical Extremes: The Americas: *The World Almanac and Book of Facts, 2005; The World Factbook, 2005;* U.S. Bureau of the Census; The Americas: *The World Factbook, 2005;* U.S. Bureau of the Census, International Database; United Nations Statistical Yearbook; World's Largest Cities: United Nations Population Division National Censuses; Urban Populations in the Americas: United Nations Population Division; Major Food Exports of the Americas: Food and Agriculture Organization of the United Nations; Languages of the Caribbean: Joshua Project; World's Top Oil Exporters: Energy Information Administration of the U.S. Department of Energy; Argentina's Largest Cities: National Institute of Statistics and Censuses, Argentina, 2001 Census; Languages in Pacific South America: Ethnologue: Languages of the World, 15th Edition; Population of Major U.S. Cities: U.S. Census Bureau; Canadian Ethnic Groups: The World Factbook, 2005

Illustrations and Photo Credits

Cover: (l), Ray Boudreau, (r), Chris Rennie/Robert Harding/Getty Images.

Front Matter: ii, Victoria Smith/HMH; iv, Sally Brown/Index Stock Imagery, Inc.; v, Juan Silva/The Image Bank/Getty Images; vi, James Cheadle/Alamy; vii, Index Stock Imagery, Inc.; viii, Corbis; H16 (t), Earth Satellite Corporation/Photo Researchers, Inc.; H16 (tc), Frans Lemmens/Getty Images; H16 (c), London Aerial Photo Library/Corbis; H16 (bc), Harvey Schwartz/Index Stock Imagery/Fotosearch; H16 (b), Tom Nebbia/Corbis.

Introduction: A, Royalty-Free/Corbis; B (bc), David W. Hamilton/The Image Bank/Getty Images; B (cl), Ryan/Beyer/Photographer's Choice/Getty Images; B (bkgd), Planetary Visions; 1 (c), John Wang/PhotoDisc Red/Getty Images; 3 (c), Gavin Hellier/Robert Harding; 11 (b), Russell Gordon/Das Fotoarchiv/Photolibrary.

Chapter 1: 12 (br), Justin Kerr, K4806/Kerr Associates; 13 (tr), 2010 A&E Television Networks, LLC. All rights reserved; 13 (br), Kevin Schafer/Corbis; 13 (bl), Trustees of the British Museum/Art Resource, NY; 15 (br), Erich Lessing/Art Resource, NY; 15 (bl), Justin Kerr, k4809/Kerr Associates; 17 (c), Scala/Art Resource, NY; 18 (tr), Trustees of the British Museum/Art Resource, NY; 18 (tl), Charles & Josette Lenars/Corbis; 21 (tr), Mexican National Museum, Mexico City/DDB Stock Photography; 23 (tl), Image Trustees of the British Museum/Art Resource, NY; 25 (b), Frederic Soreau/Photolibrary; 26 (tl), New York Historical Society, New York, USA/Bridgeman Art Library; 27 (tr), The Granger Collection, New York; 28 (tr), Museo del Banco Central de Ecuador/DDB Stock Photograph; 28 (tc), Stuart Franklin/Magnum Photos; 28 (tl), American Museum of Natural History, New York/Bridgeman Art Library; 29 (c), De Agostini/SuperStock; 29 (t), Bildarchiv Preussischer Kulturbesitz/Art Resource, NY; 33 (b), Museo del Banco Central de Ecuador/DDB Stock Photograph; 33 (t), Erich Lessing/Art Resource, NY; 35 MC1-MC2, imagebroker/Alamy.

Chapter 2: 36, Rommel/Masterfile; 37 (tr), 2010 A&E Television Networks, LLC. All rights reserved; 37 (bl), Age Fotostock/SuperStock; 37 (br), Danny Lehman/CORBIS; 39, Charles & Josette Lenars/CORBIS; 40-41, Sally Brown/Index Stock Imagery, Inc.; 42, Kevin Schafer/CORBIS; 43 (br), Werner Forman/Art Resource, NY; 43 (bl), Fred Lengnick/Imagestate; 44, Schalkwijk/Art Resource, NY; 46, Liba Taylor/CORBIS; 49, NASA; 50 (tl), Michael E. Long/National Geographic/Getty Images; 50 (c), Danita Delimont/Alamy; 51 (cr), Macduff Everton/CORBIS; 51 (tc), Age Fotostock/SuperStock; 53 (tr), Age Fotostock/SuperStock; 53 (tc), Schalkwijk/Art Resource, NY; 53 (tl), Charles & Josette Lenars/CORBIS; 55 MC1-MC2, PCL/Alamy.

Chapter 3: 56, Tom Uhlman/Alamy; 57 (tr), 2010 A&E Television Networks, LLC. All rights reserved; 57 (br), Taxi/Getty Images; 57 (bl), Mark Eveleigh/Alamy; 59, Peter Treanor/Pictures Colour Library Ltd.; 60 (tr), Robert Escobar/epa/Corbis; 61, CORBIS; 63 (tl), David Alan Harvey/Magnum Photos; 63 (cr), Bettmann/CORBIS; 66, Look GMBH/eStock Photo; 72, Robert Fried/Alamy; 73, Dave Bartruff/DanitaDelimont.com; 74 (cr), Hans Deryk/AP/Wide World Photos; 74 (b), AFP/NewsCom; 75, Picture Finders/Pictures Colour Library Ltd.; 77 (r), Dave Bartruff/DanitaDelimont.com; 77 (l), Peter Treanor/Pictures Colour Library Ltd.

Chapter 4: 80, Krzysztof Dydynski/Lonely Planet Images; 81 (br), Olivier Grunewald/Photolibrary; 81 (bl), Kevin Schafer/kevinschafer.com; 83 (cr), MedioImages/SuperStock; 83 (cl), Robert Caputo/Aurora; 84 (bl), Ed Darack/D. Donne Bryant Photography; 84 (bc), Juan Silva/The Image Bank/Getty Images; 84 (r), James Marshall/CORBIS; 86, Bridgeman Art Library; 87, Jane Sweeney/Lonely Planet Images; 88, Stone/Getty Images; 89 (tr), Krzysztof Dydynski/Lonely Planet Images; 89 (tl), Alex Segre/Alamy; 91 (tl), Jorge Silva/Reuters/NewsCom; 92, Chico Sanchez/EPA/Landov; 93, John Van Hasselt/CORBIS; 94, Pablo Corral V/CORBIS; 95, Luxner.com; 97 (r), Jorge Silva/Reuters/NewsCom; 97 (c), Bridgeman Art Library; 97 (l), James Marshall/Corbis.

Chapter 5: 100, Dario Lopez-Mills/AP/Wide World Photos; 101 (bl), Steve Vidler/eStock Photo; 101

(br), Robert Frerck/Getty Images; 103 (tr), George Hunter/Pictures Colour Library Ltd.; 103 (cr), Kit Houghton/CORBIS; 107, Renzo Gostoli/AP/Wide World Photos; 108 (cl), SIME s.a.s/eStock Photo; 109 (tl), Andrew Kemp/Alamy; 110, Science Photo Library/ Photo Researchers, Inc.; 113 (br), Bettmann/CORBIS; 113 (t), HIP/ Art Resource, NY; 115, Prisma/ SuperStock; 116 (br), Wayne Walton/Lonely Planet Images; 116 (cr), Julio Etchart/Photolibrary; 118, Andrea Booher/Stone/Getty Images; 119 (c), SIME s.a.s/eStock Photo; 119 (r), Julio Etchart/Photolibrary.

Chapter 6: 122, Francesc Muntada/ CORBIS; 123 (tr), 2010 A&E Television Networks, LLC. All rights reserved; 123 (br), MIVA Stock/SuperStock; 123 (bl), Peter Horree/Alamy; 125, Graham Neden; Ecoscene/CORBIS; 127, CNES, Distribution Spot Image/ Science Photo Library; 131 (t), Lew Bobertson/Getty Images; 133 (tc), James Cheadle/Alamy; 135, Robert Fried/Alamy; 136, Photodisc/ Fotosearch Stock Photography; 137 (tl), Peter M. Wilson/Alamy; 137

(tr), Ron Giling/Photolibrary; 138, Randa Bishop/DanitaDelimont. com; 139 (tl), Graham Neden; Ecoscene/CORBIS; 139 (tr), Peter M. Wilson/Alamy; 139 (tc), James Cheadle/Alamy.

Chapter 7: 142, Photo/PictureQuest; 143 (tr), 2010 A&E Television Networks, LLC. All rights reserved; 143 (bl), Ron Watts/CORBIS; 143 (br), Tom Grill/Photographer's Choice/Getty Images; 145, Altrendo/Getty Images; 146, NASA/Photo Researchers, Inc.; 147 (cr), Alan Schein/CORBIS; 147 (br), Dallas and John Heaton/ Stock Connection/IPN; 151 (tl), Eric Gay/AP/Wide World Photos; 151 (tr), NASA/CORBIS; 153 (b), Metropolitan Museum of Art, New York/ Bridgeman Art Library; 155, *The Signing of the Constitution of the United States in 1787*, 1940. Christy, Howard Chandler (1873-1952) Hall of Representatives, Washington D.C., USA/www.bridge-man.co.uk; 157, Jeff Greenberg/ Alamy; 159, Sam Dudgeon/HMH; 161, Alan Schein Photography/ CORBIS; 163 (tl), Royalty Free/ CORBIS; 163 (cl), Thinkstock/Getty

Images; 164, Tony Waltham/Getty Images; 165, Emmanuel Dunand/ AFP/Getty Images; 167 (bl), Alan Schein Photography/CORBIS; 167 (tl), Altrendo/Getty Images; 169 MC1-MC2, Ted Spiegel/Corbis.

Chapter 8: 170 (br), David Reede/ First Light/Getty Images; 171 (tr), 2010 A&E Television Networks, LLC. All rights reserved; 171 (bl), Steve Vidler/eStock Photo; 171 (br), All Canada Photos/ SuperStock; 173, Joseph Sohm; Visions of America/CORBIS; 174, Simon Harris/eStock Photo; 175, CNES, 1988 Distribution Spot Image/Photo Researchers, Inc.; 176 (br), AKG-Images; 176 (bl), Steve Vidler/eStock Photo; 177 (br), Photocanada Digital Inc.; 177 (bl), Photocanada Digital Inc.; 178, PhotoDisc Green, Inc./HMH; 180, SuperStock RF/SuperStock; 181, Albert Normandin/Masterfile; 186 (tr), Index Stock Imagery, Inc.; 186 (t), First Light/Alamy; 187, Joseph Sohm/Visions of America; 189 (tc), Steve Vidler/eStock Photo; 189 (tl), Simon Harris/eStock Photo.

Staff Credits

The people who contributed to *Holt McDougal: The Americas* are listed below. They represent editorial, design, production, emedia, and permissions.

Melanie Baccus, Angela Beckmann, Julie Beckman-Key, Genick Blaise, Ed Blake, Jennifer Campbell, Henry Clark, Grant Davidson, Nina Degollado, Rose Degollado, Christine Devall, Michelle Dike, Lydia Doty, Chase Edmond, Susan Franques, Stephanie Friedman, Bob Fullilove, Matthew Gierhart, Bill Gillis, Ann Gorbett, Janet Harrington, Betsy Harris, Wendy Hodge, Tim Hovde, Cathy Jenevein, Carrie Jones, Kadonna Knape, David Knowles, Aylin Koker, Laura Lasley, Sarah Lee, Sean McCormick, Joe Melomo, Richard Metzger, Andrew Miles, Joeleen Ornt, Debra O'Shields, Jarred Prejean, Paul Provence, Shelly Ramos, Curtis Riker, Michelle Rimsa, Michael Rinella, Jennifer Rockwood, Carole Rollins, Beth Sample, Annette Saunders, Jenny Schaeffer, Kay Selke, Chris Smith, Jeremy Strykul, Jeannie Taylor, Terri Taylor, Joni Wackwitz, Mary Wages, Diana Holman Walker, Nadyne Wood, Robin Zaback